T0259553

Advances in
COMPUTERS
VOLUME 84

Advances in
COMPUTERS

Dependable and Secure Systems Engineering

EDITED BY

ALI HURSON AND SAHRA SEDIGH*

Department of Computer Science
*Department of Electrical and Computer Engineering
Missouri University of Science and Technology
Rolla, Missouri, USA

VOLUME 84

AMSTERDAM • BOSTON • HEIDELBERG • LONDON • NEW YORK • OXFORD
PARIS • SAN DIEGO • SAN FRANCISCO • SINGAPORE • SYDNEY • TOKYO
Academic Press is an imprint of Elsevier

ACADEMIC
PRESS

Academic Press is an imprint of Elsevier

525 B Street, Suite 1900, San Diego, CA 92101-4495, USA
225 Wyman Street, Waltham, MA 02451, USA
32 Jamestown Road, London, NW1 7BY, UK
Linacre House, Jordan Hill, Oxford OX2 8DP, UK
Radarweg 29, PO Box 211, 1000 AE Amsterdam, The Netherlands

First edition 2012

Library of Congress Cataloging-in-Publication Data
A catalog record for this book is available from the Library of Congress

British Library Cataloguing-in-Publication Data
A catalogue record for this book is available from the British Library

ISBN: 978-0-12-396525-7

ISSN: 0065-2458

For information on all Academic Press publications
visit our web site at store.elsevier.com

Printed and bound by CPI Group (UK) Ltd, Croydon, CR0 4YY

Transferred to digital print 2012

Working together to grow
libraries in developing countries

www.elsevier.com | www.bookaid.org | www.sabre.org

ELSEVIER   BOOK AID
            International   Sabre Foundation

Contents

Combining Performance and Availability Analysis in Practice

Kishor Trivedi, Ermeson Andrade, and Fumio Machida

Modeling, Analysis, and Testing of System Vulnerabilities

Fevzi Belli, Mutlu Beyazit, Aditya P. Mathur, and Nimal Nissanke

System Dependability: Characterization and Benchmarking

Yves Crouzet and Karama Kanoun

Pragmatic Directions in Engineering Secure Dependable Systems

M. Farrukh Khan and Raymond A. Paul

Preface

Advances in Computers is the oldest series to chronicle the rapid evolution of computing. The series has been in continual publication since 1960. Several volumes, each typically comprising four to eight chapters describing new developments in the theory and applications of computing, are published each year. The theme of this 84th volume is "Engineering Dependable Systems," and the contents provide comprehensive coverage of diverse aspects of dependable computing, while illustrating the use of computing in improving the dependability of critical systems in various application domains.

Computing is permeating the everyday life of much of the world's population at an ever-increasing rate. The scope of systems and applications that now exhibit significant reliance on cyberinfrastructure is unprecedented, as is the extent of coupling between physical components and the computing hardware and software by which they are governed. Domains as diverse as electric power, medicine, and education are now heavily reliant on computing and communication. The distributed nature of computer-based control is a double-edged sword; it adds redundancy, yet makes the system more complex—the net effect on dependability depends both on the individual components used and the interplay implemented among them. Similarly, communication and networking make it possible to incorporate more information in decision support for physical systems, which should improve the "quality" of computer-based control; however, the connectivity created can also facilitate the propagation of failures, compromising dependability.

In this volume, we adopt the definition and taxonomy of "dependability" presented in the seminal paper by Avižienis, Laprie, Randell, and Landwehr—an integrating concept that subsumes reliability, availability, and other attributes that lead to justifiable trust in the operation of a service or system [1]. In the 7 years that have passed since the publication of the paper, the relevance of the definition and taxonomy has only increased. The aim of our volume is to inform the reader of the state of the art and science of dependable systems. The chapters that comprise this volume were solicited from renowned authorities in the field, each of whom brings to bear a unique perspective on the topic.

In the first chapter, "Combining Performance and Availability Analysis in Practice," Trivedi, Andrade, and Machida articulate approaches to analytic modeling of such attributes and present practical examples where these models have been applied to computing and communication systems. The specific focus of the chapter is on integrating the analysis of performance and availability, achieving a means of quantifying the loss of dependability in terms of degraded performance—rather than the more typical binary view of a system as "failed" or "functional."

Identifying and understanding threats to the dependability of a system are the focus of the second chapter, "Modeling, Analysis, and Testing of System Vulnerabilities," by Belli, Beyazit, and Mathur. This chapter presents a holistic view of dependability that encompasses both desirable attributes that make a system dependable and undesirable attributes that compromise its dependability. The chapter also articulates a framework where model-based testing can be used throughout the system life cycle—that is, from the design stage through implementation and maintenance—to analyze vulnerabilities in entities that range from requirements to complete deployments of a system.

The third chapter, "System Dependability: Characterization and Benchmarking," extends the discussion of reliability measures to the broader scope of characterizing dependability. The focus of this chapter by Crouzet and Kanoun is on modeling- and measurement-based benchmarks for dependability. Relevant concepts and techniques are presented in the context of systems that utilize commercial-off-the-shelf (COTS) components. Documentation for COTS components is typically focused on the interfaces—a justifiable choice in light of the importance of interoperability in component-based systems. However, intellectual property concerns (among other reasons) lead to a dearth of documentation about the internal operation of COTS components. This shortcoming significantly complicates the assessment of dependability. The fourth chapter details measures and techniques that overcome this challenge and illustrates the proposed approach using two case studies.

"Pragmatic Directions in Engineering Secure Dependable Systems," by Khan and Paul, is the fourth and final chapter of this volume. This chapter aims to provide several techniques that can be considered axiomatic in achieving dependability for future complex systems across a broad range of application domains. The authors enumerate challenges to dependability and propose solutions for addressing these challenges, with focus on three overlapping areas: dependable hardware/software systems, secure dependable systems, and dependable cloud computing. This chapter, among others, touches upon security, which is complementary to dependability as a measure of system assurance, and encompasses a number of the same system attributes—foremost among them availability.

We hope that you find these articles of interest and useful in your teaching, research, and other professional activities. We welcome feedback on the volume and suggestions for topics for future volumes.

Ali R. Hurson
Sahra Sedigh
Missouri University of Science and Technology
Rolla, MO, USA

REFERENCE

[1] A. Avižienis, J.-C. Laprie, B. Randell, C. Landwehr, Basic concepts and taxonomy of dependable and secure computing, IEEE Trans. Dependable Secure Comput. 1 (1) (Jan.-March 2004), pp. 11–33.

Combining Performance and Availability Analysis in Practice

KISHOR TRIVEDI

Department of Electrical and Computer Engineering, Duke University, Durham, North Carolina, USA

ERMESON ANDRADE

Department of Electrical and Computer Engineering, Duke University, Durham, North Carolina, USA
Informatics Center, Federal University of Pernambuco (UFPE), Recife, Pernambuco, Brazil

FUMIO MACHIDA

Department of Electrical and Computer Engineering, Duke University, Durham, North Carolina, USA
Service Platforms Research Laboratories, NEC Corporation, Kawasaki, Japan

Abstract

Composite performance and availability analysis of computer systems has gained considerable attention in recent years. Pure performance analysis of a system tends to be optimistic since it ignores the failure–repair behavior of the system. On the other hand, pure availability analysis tends to be too conservative since the behavior of the system is captured by only two states (functioning or failed). To analyze the degradation of a system's performance in consideration with availability metrics, combined measures of performance and availability are essential. This chapter introduces the basics of analytic models for the combined performance and availability analysis of computer systems together with some practical examples.

ADVANCES IN COMPUTERS, VOL. 84
ISSN: 0065-2458/DOI: 10.1016/B978-0-12-396525-7.00001-0

1

1. Introduction

The need for combining performance and availability analysis of computer systems is increasing, since most computer systems can continue their operations even in the presence of faults. However, software/hardware designers are still using performance and availability measures separately to evaluate the quality of the systems. Such separated analysis is not sufficient to properly understand and predict the behavior of these systems because the performance is affected by the failures and recoveries of the system components. Thus, the use of evaluation methods which combine performance and availability analysis is essential [1–7].

In recent decades, several approaches have been developed for considering the combined evaluation of performance, availability, and reliability [8–14]. Beaudry [15] is the first author to develop the measures which provide trade-offs between reliability and performance of degradable systems. Thereafter, the term performability, where the concept of performance and reliability is unified, was introduced by Meyer [16]. He developed a general modeling framework that covers performability measures.

Quantitative evaluation of systems' performance and reliability/availability can be broadly classified into measurement and model-based approaches. In the measurement approach, the collected data accurately show the phenomena observed in the system, but the evaluation tends to be expensive. Some experiments are not always feasible because they are either time-consuming or need expensive procedures (like fault injections). By contrast, in the model-based approach, the evaluation of systems can be carried out without the actual execution on the real system. The model provides an abstraction of the system which does not always predict the performance and availability accurately. However, if the models are properly validated, the model-based approach might present a better cost-effective approach over the measurements. Both the approaches can be used together depending on the criticality of the system and/or availability of resources. Often, measurements are made at the subsystem level, and these are rolled up to the system level by means of models [17,18]. In this chapter, we discuss the model-based approach.

Different modeling techniques can be used for combining performance and availability analysis. Among of them, the exact composite approach [3] has been widely used because of its accuracy. However, this approach faces largeness and stiffness problems. Largeness occurs because of a cross-product of states of performance model and availability model. To deal with the largeness problem, two basic techniques can be applied: largeness tolerance and largeness avoidance [4]. Stiffness arises when the rates related to performance models are much faster than the rates of availability models. Aggregation techniques [19] and stiffness-tolerance [20] are effective methods in dealing with the stiffness problem. Hierarchical modeling approach [12] is another potential largeness and stiffness avoidance technique. This approach divides the system model into several small submodels. The submodels can be of different types, such as non-state-space models and state-space models. The solution of the hierarchical model is computed by passing outputs of lower-level submodels as inputs to the higher level submodels. In case of cyclic dependence among submodels, fixed-point iterative can be applied [8,21].

This chapter aims to present an overview of main techniques used in model construction and solution of composite performance and availability analysis, such as exact composite approach and hierarchical modeling approaches. We also describe techniques used for pure availability analysis and pure performance analysis. Practical examples where such techniques were successfully applied are detailed.

The chapter is organized as follows: Section 2 introduces basics of analytic models for evaluating performance and availability of systems and also describes modeling techniques for combining performance and availability analysis. Section 3 describes a set of practical examples for combining availability and performance analysis. Section 4 concludes the chapter.

2. Approaches to Modeling

In pure performance modeling, probabilistic nature of user demands (workload) as well as internal state behavior needs to be represented under the assumption that the system/components do not fail [4]. Several stochastic models can be used for performance analysis, such as series–parallel directed acyclic graphs [4], product form queuing networks [22], Markov chains [23], semi-Markov process (SMP) [1],

Markov regenerative process [24], generalized stochastic Petri nets (GSPNs) [25], stochastic reward nets (SRNs) [4], hierarchical [12] and fixed-point iterative [26], and the combination of these. Metrics such as throughput, blocking probability, mean response time, response time distribution, and utilization can be computed based on these models.

According to ITU-T Recommendation E.800 [27], "availability is the ability of an item to be in a state to perform a required function at a given instant of time or at any instant of time within a given time interval, assuming that the external resources, if required, are provided". On February 1991, the Patriot missile defense system failed to intercept an incoming missile. This incident resulted in the death of 28 US Army reservists [28]. Thus, high availability of mission-critical systems is extremely important, since failures can be catastrophic. For business critical systems and critical infrastructures, high availability is also important to minimize the cost of downtime.

Analytic models have been widely used to predict the system availability. These models can provide important insights about the availability considering different scenarios before the system is released for use. The availability aspects of the system are usually described by non-state-space models (reliability block diagram (RBD), fault tree (FT), and reliability graph), state-space models such as Markov chains, SMP, Markov regenerative process, stochastic Petri nets (SPNs) of various ilk, and hierarchical and fixed-point iterative models. Downtime, steady-state availability, instantaneous availability, and interval availability are frequently used as measures. Assuming exponential failure and repair time distributions with respective rates λ and μ, the availability at time t and the interval availability can be computed by the following expressions [23]:

$$A(t) = \frac{\mu}{\lambda + \mu} + \frac{\mu}{\lambda + \mu} e^{-(\lambda+\mu)t}$$

$$A_I(t) = \frac{\int_0^t A(x)\mathrm{d}x}{t} = \frac{\mu}{\lambda + \mu} + \frac{\lambda}{(\lambda + \mu)^2 t}\left(1 - e^{-(\lambda+\mu)t}\right)$$

Taking a limit to infinity of the instantaneous availability, the steady-state availability A_{ss} can be computed as below

$$A_{ss} = \lim_{t\to\infty} A(t) = \frac{\mu}{\lambda + \mu}$$

The steady-state unavailability U_{ss} and downtime (in minutes per year) are obtained from A_{ss} by the following expressions

$$U_{ss} = (1 - A_{ss})$$

$$\text{Downtime} = (1 - A_{ss}) \times 8760 \times 60$$

Composite performance and availability analysis is required especially in the evaluation of degradable systems. In degradable systems, when some system components fail, the system can undergo a graceful degradation of performance and still be able to continue operation at a reduced level of performance. In other words, the system can have more than two working states (i.e., functioning, partially functioning, and down). One of the most used analytic model types for combining performance and availability analysis is Markov reward model in which each state of Markov chain is assigned a reward rate according to the performance delivered in the state. In the following subsections, we introduce the basics of analytic modeling for performance and availability evaluation based on two types of models: non-state-space models and state-space models.

2.1 Non-State-Space Models

Availability models can be constructed using non-state-space models such as reliability block diagram (RBD), reliability graph (Relgraph), and FT with and without repeated events. Non-state-space models are easy to use and have a relatively quick solution because they can be solved without generating the underlying state space [29]. For a rapid solution, these models assume that system components are independent of each other. System availability, system unavailability, system reliability, and system mean time to failure can be computed using these models. The three commonly used solution techniques for non-state-space model are factoring [23], sum of disjoint products [23], and binary decision diagram [30]. Large non-state-space model can be solved by deriving upper and lower bounds as described in Ref. [31].

RBD is a non-state-space model type that enables analysis of reliability and availability of complex systems using block diagrams. In a block diagram model, components are combined into blocks in series, parallel, or *k-out-of-n*. A series structure represents a direct dependency between the components where the entire system fails if one of its components fails. A parallel structure is used to show redundancy and means that the whole system can work properly as long as at least one component is working properly. A *k-out-of-n* structure represents that the whole subsystem can work properly as long as *k* or more components are working properly out of *n* components. Series and parallel structures are special cases of *k-out-of-n* structures [4]. A series structure is an *n-out-of-n* and a parallel structure is a *1-out-of-n* structure. Figure 1 shows an RBD representing a storage system availability model with one server, one hub, and *n* storages devices. The system is working properly if at least one of each device (server, hub, and storage) is working properly.

FT can be used for quantitative analysis of system reliability/availability as well as qualitative analysis. FT depicts a combination of events and conditions that can lead to an undesired event such as system failure. Basic FT consists of events and logical event connectors such as OR gates, AND gates, and *k-out-of-n* gates. The events can be combined in several ways using logical gates according to the system configuration. FT can have repeated events in situations in which the same failure event propagates along different paths. Figure 2 presents an FT model for the storage system with one server (S), one hub (H), and *n* storage devices (SD). In contrast to the RBD model, the FT takes a "negative" view in that it describes the condition under which the system fails. Since FTs allow repeated events, they are more powerful than series–parallel RBDs. For a comparison of modeling power of these model types, see Ref. [32].

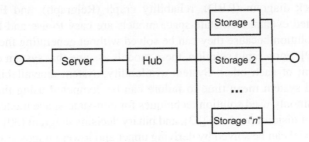

FIG. 1. RBD for a storage system.

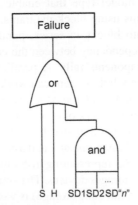

FIG. 2. FT for a storage system.

2.2   State-Space Models

Non-state-space models such as RBD and FT cannot easily handle detailed failure/repair behavior such as imperfect coverage, correlated failures, repair dependencies, etc. On the other hand, state-space models are capable of capturing such detailed behavior. As a well-known state-space model type, continuous-time Markov chains (CTMCs) are widely used in performance and availability studies. Homogenous CTMCs are represented by states and transitions between the states whose sojourn time follows exponential distribution. If we relax the assumption of exponential distribution, then it might become an SMP [1], a Markov regenerative process [24], or a non-homogeneous Markov chain [33]. Labels on the transitions for homogenous CTMC are time-independent rates. Figure 3 presents a simple example of CTMC model for a two-component parallel redundant system with the same repair rate μ. The failure rate of both components is μ. When both components have failed, the system is considered as failed. There is a single shared repair person.

Solving for the steady-state probabilities, we have:

$$\pi_2 = \frac{\mu}{2\lambda}\pi_1$$

$$\pi_1 = \frac{\mu}{\lambda}\pi_0$$

Since

$$\pi_0 + \pi_1 + \pi_2 = 1$$

Thus

$$\pi_0 + \frac{\mu}{\lambda}\pi_0 + \left(\frac{\mu}{\lambda}\right)\left(\frac{\mu}{2\lambda}\right)\pi_0 = 1$$

Then, the steady-state unavailability of the parallel redundant system with a shared repair is expressed as below:

$$\pi_0 = \frac{1}{1 + \frac{\mu}{\lambda} + \frac{\mu^2}{2\lambda^2}}$$

As an approach for combining performance and availability analysis, this chapter focuses on Markov reward models. MRMs are one of the most commonly used techniques for combining performance and availability analysis of degradable systems. Formally, an MRM consists of a CTMC $\{Z(t), t \geq 0\}$ with state space Ω. Let $P_i(t)$ be the unconditional probability of the CTMC being in state i at time t, then the row vector $P(t)$ represents the *transient state probability vector*. Given

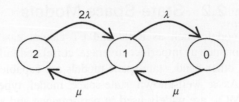

FIG. 3. An example of CTMC.

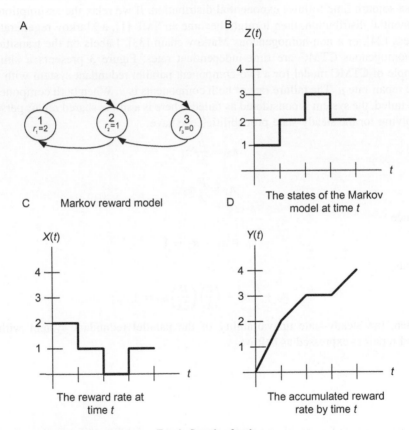

FIG. 4. Sample of paths.

$L(t) = \int_0^t P(u)\mathrm{d}u$, $L_i(t)$ is the expected total time spent by the CTMC in state i during the interval $[0,t)$. The MRMs are obtained by assigning a reward rate r_i to each state i of the CTMC (See Fig. 4A). Let $X(t)=r_{Z(t)}$ denote the reward rate at time t and $Y(t)$

represent the accumulated reward in the interval $[0,t)$. Then, the Markov reward model and the possible sample paths of $X(t)$, $Y(t)$, and $Z(t)$ are detailed in Fig. 4.

The expected instantaneous reward rate $E[X(t)]$, the expected accumulated reward $E[Y(t)]$, and the steady-state expected reward rate $E[X(\infty)]$ can be computed as follows [23]:

$$E[X(t)] = \sum_{i \in \Omega} r_i P_i(t),$$

$$E[Y(t)] = \sum_{i \in \Omega} r_i \int_0^t P_i(\tau) = \sum_{i \in \Omega} r_i L_i(t),$$

and

$$E[X] = E[X(\infty)] = \sum_{i \in \Omega} r_i \pi_i.$$

where π_i is the limiting state probability, that is, $\pi_i = \lim_{t \to \infty} P_i(t)$.

The expected accumulated reward until absorption and the distribution $X(t)$ can be computed by the following expressions:

$$E[Y(\infty)] = \sum_{i \in \Omega} r_i \int_0^\infty P_i(\tau) d\tau = \sum_{i \in B} r_i z_i,$$

and

$$P[X(t) \leq x] = \sum_{r_i \leq x, \ i \in \Omega} P_i(t).$$

One major drawback of MRM (or CTMC) is the largeness of their state space, since Markov chain for complex systems can easily reach hundreds, thousands, or millions of states. SPNs can be used for the specification and automatic generation of the underlying Markov chain in order to tolerate the state explosion problem through a more concise and smaller model as a starting point. CTMC underlying the SPN can then be generated, stored, and solved using efficient and numerically stable algorithms [22,23,34]. SPNs are composed of places, transitions (timed and immediate), arcs, and tokens. Figure 5 presents a simple SPN that shows the failure/recovery behavior of a system. The server starts in Up state, indicated by a token in place P_{up}. The transition T_{fail} fires when the server goes down, and then the token in P_{up} is removed and a token is deposited in P_{down}. T_{recv} fires when the server has recovered, then the token in P_{down} is removed and a token is deposited in P_{up}.

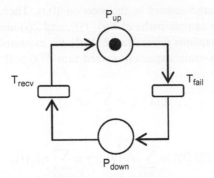

FIG. 5. SPN example.

Many extensions of SPNs have been proposed for allowing more concise and powerful description of Petri net models, such as GSPN. GSPN is a generalization of SPN by allowing both immediate transitions and timed transitions. To facilitate the automatic generation of MRMs, reward rates are also defined in term of GSPN. Thus, GSPNs are extended by introducing reward and guard functions to obtain the SRNs. For a comparison of GSPN and SRN, the reader should refer to Refs. [35,36]. Some of the most prominent functionalities of SRNs are

- *Priorities.* This extension is used when more than one transition is enabled at the same time, where the transition with higher priority is the only one allowed to fire. Although inhibitor arcs can be used to achieve the same purpose, priorities make the model simpler.
- *Guards.* This feature extends the concept of priorities and inhibitor arcs, providing a powerful means to simplify the graphical representation and to make SRNs easier to understand, since it allows the designers to use the entire state-space of the model by adding an enabling expression to a transition.
- *Marking-dependent arc multiplicity.* This feature provides a way to model situations where the number of tokens removed (or deposited) from (to) a place can depend upon the system state.
- *Marking-dependent firing rates.* This functionality allows the firing rate of a transition to depend on the current marking of the model.
- *Rewards.* This feature allows the assignment of reward rates to the marking of the SRN model. It can be used to obtain not only system performance/availability measures, but also combined measures of performance and availability.

Petri net-based models have been successfully applied to several types of systems [37–42] and allow the modeling of parallel, concurrent, asynchronous, and non-deterministic behaviors. Many tools for modeling and analysis of Petri nets are available like TimeNet [43], GreatSPN [44], SHARPE [45], and SPNP [46]. For review of other Petri net extensions, see Ref. [47].

Although CTMCs provide a useful approach to construct models of systems that include structural variations and performance levels, the models can be very large and complex, and the model construction becomes error-prone. A two-level hierarchical model utilizing MRMs can alleviate these problems in the combined performance and availability analysis. In this hierarchical approach, a sequence of lower performance models is solved, one for each state of the availability model. The obtained performance measures become reward rates to be assigned to states of the upper level MRM availability model. Upper level MRM is then solved to compute the overall performance measure. Although approximation is involved in this process, the errors caused by the approximation are generally acceptable in practice. CTMC/MRM for real complex systems tend to be composed of huge number of states. Hence, formalisms for a concise description of the models as well as the automatic conversion into a CTMC/MRM are necessary. GSPN and SRN have been widely used for this purpose, since they are isomorphic to CTMCs and MRMs, respectively. In the Petri net-based models, SRN models are more powerful and more manageable than GSPN models [35,36].

3. Practical Examples

We next review several studies on pure availability and pure performance analysis as well as composite performance and availability analysis. For some examples, we detail the SHARPE input files. SHARPE (Symbolic Hierarchical Automated Reliability/Performance Evaluator) [45] is a software package which allows the specification and analysis of stochastic models. It supports the following model types: Markov chains (acyclic, irreducible, and phase type), semi-Markov chains (acyclic and irreducible), Markov regenerative processes, RBDs, FTs, reliability graphs, single-chain product form queuing networks, multiple-chain product form queuing networks, GSPN, SRN, and series–parallel acyclic graphs.

3.1 Pure Reliability/Availability and Pure Performance Analysis

In this subsection, we describe techniques used in the construction and solution of pure availability models and pure performance models.

3.1.1   Two-Board System

Many techniques have been proposed to capture the multistate system availability. In Ref. [48], we used three analytic model types (CTMC, SRN, and FT) and compared the results among them. To show the comparative study, we adopted an example of two-board system as shown in Fig. 6. The system consists of two boards (B_1 and B_2), each of which has a processor (P_1 or P_2) and a memory (M_1 or M_2). The state of each board is (1) both P and M are down, (2) P is working properly but M is down, (3) M is working properly but P is down, or (4) both P and M are functional. We assumed that the time to failure of the processor and the memory is exponentially distributed with rates λ_p and λ_m, respectively. Common cause failure in which both the processor and the memory on the same board fail is also taken into account by assuming exponential distribution with rate λ_{mp}.

Figure 8 presents the CTMC reliability model of the two-board system. The states of the CTMC are represented by a binary vector showing the states of P_1, M_1, P_2, and M_2. Note that 1 represents up state of the device and 0 represents its down state. Figures 7 and 9 depict the SHARPE input file for the CTMC. First of all, any character after "*"(asterisk) is considered to be a comment and is ignored for SHARPE execution. On line 1, *format 8* means the number of digits after the decimal point to be printed in results. On lines 4 through 8, the variables used as parameters are given values. The failure rates of the processor and the memory (λ_p and λ_m) are set to 1/1000 and 1/2000 failures per hour, respectively. The mean time to common cause failure, $1/\lambda_{mp}$, is 1/3000h. When a group of parameters is given values, then the block must start with a keyword *bind* and finishes with the keyword *end*.

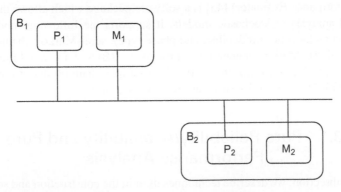

FIG. 6. Two-board system example.

1	format 8	26	1011 1001	lambda_p
2		27	1011 0011	lambda_p
3		28	1011 1000	lambda_mp
4	bind	29	0111 0110	lambda_m
5	lambda_mp 1/3000	30	0111 0101	lambda_p
6	lambda_p 1/1000	31	0111 0011	lambda_m
7	lambda_m 1/2000	32	0111 0100	lambda_mp
8	end	33	1100 1000	lambda_m
9		34	1100 0100	lambda_p
10	markov PM	35	1100 0000	lambda_mp
11	1111 1110 lambda_m	36	1010 1000	lambda_p
12	1111 1101 lambda_p	37	1010 0010	lambda_p
13	1111 1011 lambda_m	38	0110 0100	lambda_p
14	1111 0111 lambda_p	39	0110 0010	lambda_m
15	1111 0011 lambda_mp	40	1001 1000	lambda_m
16	1111 1100 lambda_mp	41	1001 0001	lambda_p
17	1110 1100 lambda_p	42	0101 0100	lambda_m
18	1110 1010 larnbda_m	43	0101 0001	lambda_m
19	1110 0110 lambda_p	44	0011 0010	lambda_m
20	1110 0010 lambda_mp	45	0011 0001	lambda_p
21	1101 1100 lambda_m	46	0011 0000	lambda_mp
22	1101 1001 lambda_m	47	1000 0000	lambda_p
23	1101 0101 lambda_p	48	0100 0000	lambda_m
24	1101 0001 lambda_mp	49	0010 0000	lambda_p
25	1011 1010 lambda_m	50	0001 0000	lambda_m

FIG. 7. SHARPE input for the CTMC example.

The model specification begins with a model type and a name (see line 10). In this case, the model type is *markov* which denotes Markov chain (CTMC) and the name is *PM*. SHARPE allows three kinds of Markov chains: irreducible, acyclic, and PH type. Lines 10 through 50 define the states and state transitions of the Markov chain. From lines 50 through 68, we define the reward configuration, where for each state of the CTMC a reward rate is assigned to it. Note that the keyword *reward* (see line 51 in Fig. 9) denotes that in the next group of lines, SHARPE will assign reward

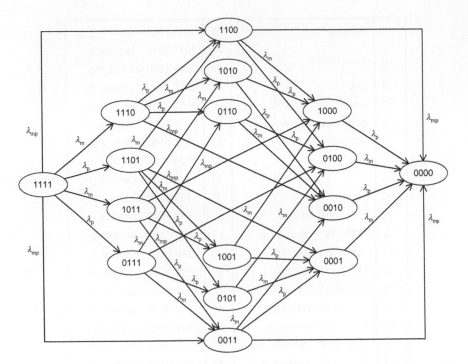

Fɪɢ. 8. CTMC for a two-board system.

rates to the model states. For the two-board system, we adopted the CTMC model to compute the expected reward rate at time *t* for the case that at least one processor and both of the memories are operational. For that, we assigned the reward rate 1 to the UP states ((1,1,1,1) (1,1,0,1), and (0,1,1,1)) and 0 to the other states (down states). From lines 70 through 86, the initial state probabilities are specified. Initial state probabilities denote the likelihood of a sequence starting in a certain state. On lines 88 through 91, we define a function (*func*) to compute the expected reward rate at $t=100$ and $t=200$. It is important to highlight that the keyword *exrt* is a built-in function which gives the expected reward rate at time *t*. It takes as arguments a variable *t* and a Markov model name. The keyword *expr* says to evaluate an expression. Finally, line 93 contains the keyword *end* which means the end of the input file. The outputs for this example are shown in Fig. 10.

The SRN model for the same two-board system is shown in Fig. 11. Figure 11A describes the failure behavior of the processor P_1 and the memory M_1, while Fig. 11B depicts the failure behavior of the processor P_2 and the memory M_2. Tokens in the places M1U and M2U represent that the memories are operational.

50	* Reward configuration:	74	0111 0
51	Reward	75	1100 0
52	1111 1	76	1010 0
53	1110 0	77	0110 0
54	1101 1	78	1001 0
55	1011 0	79	0101 0
56	0111 1	80	0011 0
57	1100 0	81	1000 0
58	1010 0	82	0100 0
59	0110 0	83	0010 0
60	1001 0	84	0001 0
61	0101 0	85	0000 0
62	0011 0	86	end
63	1000 0	87	*Output
64	0100 0	88	func Exp_Reward_Rate_T(t) exrt(t; PM)
65	0010 0	89	loop t,100,200,100
66	0001 0	90	expr Exp_Reward_Rate_T(t)
67	0000 0	91	end
68	end	92	
69	* Initial Probabilities:	93	end
70	1111 1		
71	1110 0		
72	1101 0		
73	1011 0		

FIG. 9. SHARPE input for the CTMC example (continuation).

Otherwise they are down. Likewise, tokens in the places P1U and P2U represent that the processors are operational. Otherwise, they are down. The SHARPE input file for the SRN model is shown in Fig. 13. From lines 4 through 8, the variables are given values. Note that the parameter values are the same as the ones used for the CTMC model. On lines 10 through 16, we define a reward function to compute the probability that at least one processor and both of the memories are operational. That is, the places P1U or P2U must have at least one token and the places M1U and M2U must have exactly two tokens.

t=100.000000

    Exp_Reward_Rate_T(t): 8.41314039e-001

t=200.000000

    Exp_Reward_Rate_T(t): 7.00480977e-001

Fɪɢ. 10. SHARPE output for CTMC example.

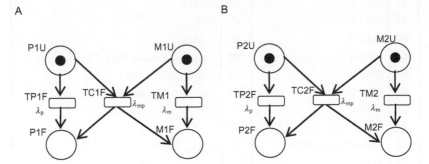

A   B

Fɪɢ. 11. SRN for a two-board system.

t=100.000000

    ExRwRt (t): 8.41314039e-001

t=200.000000

    ExRwRt (t): 7.00480977e-001

Fɪɢ. 12. SHARPE output for SRN example.

1	format 8	35	TP2F ind lambda_p
2		36	end
3		37	* == Immediate Transitions ==
4	bind	38	end
5	lambda_mp 1/3000	39	* == ARC ==
6	lambda_p 1/1000	40	* Input Arcs
7	lambda_m 1/2000	41	P1U TP1F 1
8	end	42	P1U TC1F 1
9		43	M1U TC1F 1
10	func aval()	44	M1U TM1F 1
11	if((#(P1U)+#(P2U)>=1)and(#(M1U)+#(M2U)==2))	45	P2U TP2F 1
12	1	46	M2U TM2F 1
13	else	47	M2U TC2F 1
14	0	48	P2U TC2F 1
15	end	49	end
16	end	50	* Output Arcs
17		51	TP1F P1F 1
18	srn BS	52	TM1F M1F 1
19	* == PLACE ==	53	TC1F M1F 1
20	P6 0	54	TC1F P1F 1
21	P1U 1	55	TP2F P2F 1
22	M1U 1	56	TM2F P6 1
23	P1F 0	57	TC2F P2F 1
24	M1F 0	58	TC2F P6 1
25	P2F 0	59	end
26	P2U 1	60	* Inhibtor Arcs
27	M2U 1	61	end
28	end	62	
29	* == Timed Transitions ==	63	func ExRwRt(t) srn_exrt(t,BS; aval)
30	TP1F ind lambda_p	64	loop t,100,200,100
31	TC1F ind lambda_mp	65	expr ExRwRt(t)
32	TM1F ind lambda_m	66	end
33	TM2F ind lambda_m	67	
34	TC2F ind lambda_mp	68	end

FIG. 13. SHARPE input for the SRN example.

On line 18, we begin the specification of model with a keyword *srn* which means SRNs and a name *BS*. The SRN specification is divided into the following basic blocks: places, timed transitions, immediate transitions, inputs arcs, output arcs, and inhibitor arcs. Lines 20 through 28 specify the places. Each line contains the name of a place and the number of token in the place. Lines 30 through 36 comprise the timed transitions. Each line contains the name of a timed transition followed by the keyword *ind* and the value/variable assigned to it. Lines 41 through 49 define the input arcs. Each line consists of a place name followed by a transition name and the multiplicity of the arc. Lines 51 through 59 specify the output arcs. Each line consists of a transition name followed by a place name and the multiplicity of the arc. Note that the SRN models do not have immediate transitions and inhibitor arcs. On lines 63 through 66, we define a function to compute the reward rate at time $t=100$ and $t=200$. The keyword *srn_exrt* is a built-in function which computes the expected reward rate at time t. It takes as arguments a variable t, an SRN model name, and a reward function, as multiple reward functions can be defined for the SRN. The outputs for the specified model are presented in Fig. 12. One should note that the results from the SRN models are identical to those from the CTMC model.

Finally, the multistate FT model considering that at least one processor and both of the memories are operational is depicted in Fig. 14. The SHARPE input file for the FT model is shown in Fig. 15. On line 4, we begin the specification of the FT

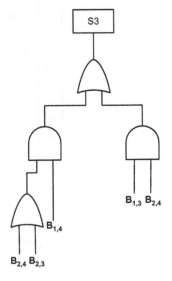

FIG. 14. FT for a two-board system.

1	****t=100	17	*****t=200
2	format 8	18	
3		19	mstree BS200
4	mstree BS100	20	basic B1:4 prob(0.6930)
5	basic B1:4 prob(0.8325)	21	basic B1:3 prob(0.1588)
6	basic B1:3 prob(0.0891)	22	basic B2:4 prob(0.6930)
7	basic B2:4 prob(0.8325)	23	basic B2:3 prob(0.1588)
8	basic B2:3 prob(0.0891)	24	or gor321 B2:3 B2:4
9	or gor321 B2:3 B2:4	25	and gand311 B1:4 gor321
10	and gand311 B1:4 gor321	25	and gand312 B1:3 B2:4
11	and gand312 B1:3 B2:4	27	or top:1 gand311 gand312
12	or top:1 gand311 gand312	28	end
13	end	29	echo System Probability
14	echo System Probability	30	expr sysprob(BS200, top:1)
15	expr sysprob(BS100, top:1)	31	
16		32	end

FIG. 15. SHARPE input for the multistate FT example.

with a keyword *mstree* which means multistate FT and a name *BS100*. On lines 5 through 8, we define the events. An event begins with the keyword *basic*. For example, line 5 defines the event *B1:4* and assigns to it a transient probability of being in the component state $\pi_{B_{1,4}}(t)$, where $B_{1,4}$ denotes the board B_1 is in state 4. Each board is considered as a component with four states as stated above. The probability is obtained by solving the Markov chain in Fig. 16. The states of the CTMC are represented by a binary vector showing the states of P (processor) and M (memory), where 1 denotes up and 0 denotes down for each device. One should note that the probability is computed at $t=100$ but can be assigned with a variable value of t as a parameter. From lines 9 to 12, the structure of the multistate FT is defined. For instance, on line 9, the gate *or* is defined followed by the name *gor321* and its inputs *B2:3* and *B2:4*. On line 15, the system (failure) probability is computed. Note that for the second part of the specification (from lines 17 through 30), we consider $t=200$h. The results are depicted in Fig. 17. The solutions of the three models (CTMC, SRN, and FT) yield same results within numerical accuracy [48]. Note that the 4-state CTMC of a single board can also be in the input file and its state probabilities at time t can be directly passed onto the multistate FT, making a much better use of the capability of SHARPE.

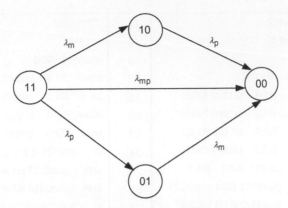

Fig. 16. CTMC model for a single board.

```
System Probability
        sysprob(ex100, top:1) :   8.41407750e-001

System Probability
        sysprob(ex200, top:1) :   7.00345800e-001
```

Fig. 17. SHARPE output for the multistate FT example.

3.1.2 *VAXcluster System*

Availability evaluation of a VAXcluster system using RBD is shown in Ref. [29]. This system consists of two or more VAX processors, a star coupler, one or more storage controllers (HSCs), and a set of disks (see Fig. 18). The RBD of a VAXcluster configuration is presented in Fig. 19 with N_p processors, N_h HSCs, and N_d disks. The system is working properly if at least one component of each set of devices is working properly. Since RBDs are easy to construct and solve, it is necessary to assume failure independence between system components and independent repair for components in order to solve the RBD (without generating the underlying state space). A detailed model using SRN can be found in Ref. [49], and a hierarchical model can be found in Ref. [41].

Figure 20 depicts the SHARPE input file for the VAXcluster system. On line 4, we begin the specification of the model with a keyword *block* which means RBD

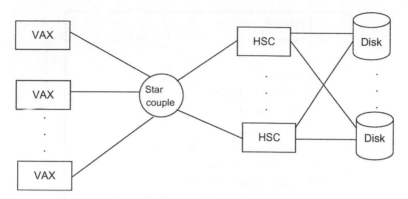

Fɪɢ. 18. VAXcluster system.

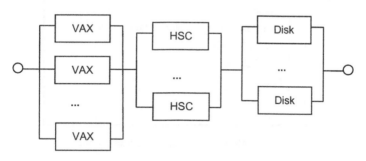

Fɪɢ. 19. Reliability block diagram for VAXcluster system.

and a name *Vax*. From lines 4 through 7, we define the blocks. Each line contains the keyword *comp*, the name of the component type, and a built-in function *exp*. For example, on line 5, the failure rate of each component of type B is 1/2000h. We could have used other built-in distributions such as Weibull. Lines 8 through 11 define the RBD structure. Each line consists of one of the keywords *series* or *parallel*, the name of the structure, and either the components or other structure being combined. Line 8 combines three components of type A in parallel. The name of this structure is *parallel2*. From lines 15 through 18, we compute the reliability of VAXcluster system for various values of t. Note that a loop is used to print the result, where t ranges from 100 to 1000 by using an increment of 100. Figure 21 shows the results. The system reliability decreases as t increases. We could also compute steady-state or instantaneous availability.

```
1   format 8
2   factor on
3
4   block Vax
5   comp B exp(1/2000)
6   comp A exp(1/3000)
7   comp C exp(1/1000)
8   parallel parallel2 A A A
9   parallel parallel3 B B
10  parallel parallel5 C C C C
11  series serie0 parallel2 parallel3 parallel5
12  End
13
14  *output
15  func Reliability(t) 1-tvalue(t;Vax)
16  loop t,100,1000,100
17  expr Reliability(t)
18  End
19
20  End
```

FIG. 20. SHARPE input for the VAXcluster system.

3.1.3 Telecommunication Switching System

Figure 22 presents the performance model of a telecommunication switching system by CTMC [50]. This system is composed of n trunks with an infinite caller population. We assumed call holding times are exponentially distributed with rate μ_h, and the call arrival process is Poison with rate λ_a. This model can be represented as $M/M/n/n$ queuing system. The blocking probability of new calls due to the lack of available trunks is computed by solving the CTMC. The blocking probability is given by π_n which is the probability that the CTMC is in state n in the steady state. As mentioned before, pure performance model does not consider the performance degradation caused by failures of system components.

Figure 23 shows the SHARPE input file for the telecommunication switching system. From lines 4 through 7, we assign values to the input parameters. The parameters are set to $\lambda_a = 5\,\mathrm{s}^{-1}$ and $\mu_h = 0.3\,\mathrm{s}^{-1}$. Lines 8 through 17 specify the

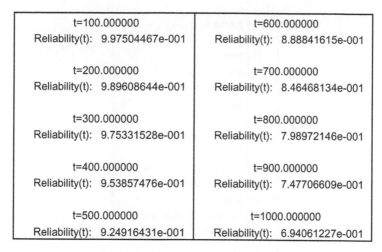

t=100.000000	t=600.000000
Reliability(t): 9.97504467e-001	Reliability(t): 8.88841615e-001
t=200.000000	t=700.000000
Reliability(t): 9.89608644e-001	Reliability(t): 8.46468134e-001
t=300.000000	t=800.000000
Reliability(t): 9.75331528e-001	Reliability(t): 7.98972146e-001
t=400.000000	t=900.000000
Reliability(t): 9.53857476e-001	Reliability(t): 7.47706609e-001
t=500.000000	t=1000.000000
Reliability(t): 9.24916431e-001	Reliability(t): 6.94061227e-001

FIG. 21. SHARPE output for RBD example.

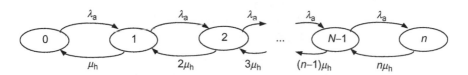

FIG. 22. Performance model of telecommunication switching system.

Markov reward model. Note that the Markov model is specified using a loop. This functionality is extremely powerful, since it allows creating complex models easily. As the blocking probability is given by π_n, the state n is assigned a reward rate 1 (see line 15). By default, the other states are assigned reward rate 0. On lines 19 through 21, the blocking probability is computed with the number of trunks varying from 1 to 10. The outputs are shown in Fig. 24. The outputs can be easily plotted by SHARPE as well.

3.2   Composite Performance and Availability Analysis

In the next subsections, we describe some examples of composite performance and availability analysis.

```
 1 | format 8
 2 |
 3 | bind
 4 | mu_h  0.03
 5 | lambda_a  0.5
 6 | End
 7 |
 8 | markov TeleSys(n)
 9 | loop i,0,n
10 |    $(i) $(i+1) lambda_a
11 |    $(i+1) $(i) (i+1)*mu_h
12 | End
13 | * Reward configuration:
14 | Reward
15 | $(n) 1
16 | End
17 | End
18 |
19 | loop n,1,10,1
20 | expr exrss(TeleSys; n)
21 | End
30 |
```

FIG. 23. SHARPE input for the performance model.

3.2.1 Multiprocessor Systems

In Ref. [3], we discussed the use of MRM for combining performance and availability analysis of fault tolerant systems. Figure 25 presents the availability model of a multiprocessor system. This system is composed of n processors with covered and not covered failures. In covered failure case (whose probability is represented by c), the system must be reconfigured after the failure with a small delay (mean $1/\delta$). On the other hand, not covered failure (the probability of this case is $1-c$) denotes that the system must be rebooted with rate β after the failure. We assumed the system is down during the reconfiguration states $(x_n, x_{n-1}, \ldots, x_2)$ and reboot states $(y_n, y_{n-1}, \ldots, y_2)$. In this example, we were interested in computing unavailability and the normalized throughput loss (NTL), which are both instances of steady-state expected reward rate $E[X]$.

n=1.000000

    exrss(TeleSys; n): 1.06458481e-001

n=2.000000

    exrss(TeleSys; n): 1.49638871e-001

n=3.000000

    exrss(TeleSys; n): 1.86234905e-001

n=4.000000

    exrss(TeleSys; n): 2.16355227e-001

n=5.000000

    exrss(TeleSys; n): 2.40131418e-001

n=6.000000

    exrss(TeleSys; n): 2.57723209e-001

n=7.000000

    exrss(TeleSys; n): 2.69324797e-001

n=8.000000

    exrss(TeleSys; n): 2.75172317e-001

n=9.000000

    exrss(TeleSys; n): 2.75552423e-001

n=10.000000

    exrss(TeleSys; n): 2.70812187e-001

FIG. 24. SHARPE output for the performance model.

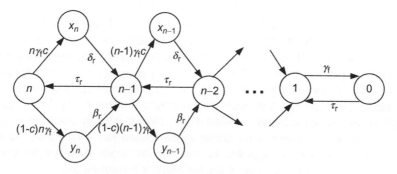

FIG. 25. Markov chain of a multiprocessor system.

Solving for the steady-state probabilities, we have [23]:

$$\pi_{n-i} = \frac{n!}{(n-i)!}\left(\gamma/\tau\right)^i \pi_n,$$

$$\pi_{x_{n-i}} = \frac{n!}{(n-i)!}\frac{\gamma(n-i)^c}{\delta}\left(\gamma/\tau\right)^i \pi_n,$$

$$\pi_{y_{n-i}} = \frac{n!}{(n-i)!} \frac{\gamma(n-i)(1-c)}{\beta} (\gamma/\tau)^i \pi_n,$$

$$i = 0, 1, 2, \ldots, n-2,$$

where

$$\pi_n = \left[\begin{array}{l} \displaystyle\sum_{i=0}^{n} (\gamma/\tau)^i \frac{n!}{(n-i)!} \\[2ex] + \displaystyle\sum_{i=0}^{n-2} (\gamma/\tau)^i \frac{\gamma(n-i)cn!}{\delta(n-i)!} \\[2ex] + \displaystyle\sum_{i=0}^{n-2} (\gamma/\tau)^i \frac{\gamma(n-i)(1-c)n!}{\beta(n-i)!} \end{array} \right]^{-1}.$$

The unavailability of the system was computed by assigning a reward rate 1 to all down states $(x_n, x_{n-1}, \ldots, y_n, y_{n-1}$, and $0)$ and 0 to all the up states $(n, n-1, \ldots, 1)$. Thus,

$$U_s = \sum_{i \in S_{rb}} \pi_i + \sum_{i \in S_{rp}} \pi_i + \sum_{i \in S_e} \pi_i$$

where $S_{rb} = \{y_{n-1} | i = 0, 1, \ldots n-2\}$, $S_{rb} = \{x_{n-1} | i = 0, 1, \ldots n-2\}$, and $S_e = \{0\}$.

Figure 27 depicts SHARPE file to compute steady-state unavailability for the multiprocessor system. Lines 4 through 11 assign the values to the input parameters. The number of processors, n, is 4. The failure rate γ_f of a processor is 1/6000 failures per hours. The mean times to reboot, $1/\beta_r$, and reconfiguration, $1/\delta_r$, are set to be 5 min and 10 s, respectively. The mean time to repair a processor is 1 h. From lines 13 through 44, we define the Markov reward model. Note that the up states are assigned reward rate 0 and the down states are assigned reward rate 1 (see lines 32 thorough 44). From lines 47 through 49, we compute the steady-state system unavailability. Figure 26 presents the output for the Markov reward model.

To obtain the NTL representing the fraction of the jobs rejected, the up states were assigned with reward rate of a task being rejected caused by the fullness of the

SS System Unavailability
SU: 4.53626015e-006

Fig. 26. SHARPE output for multiprocessor system.

1	format 8	27	y2 1 beta_r
2		28	1 2 tau_r
3		29	1 0 gamma_f
4	bind	30	0 1 tau_r
5	tau_r 1	31	* Reward configuration defined:
6	gamma_f 1/6000	32	Reward
7	beta_r 12	33	x4 1
8	delta_r 360	34	y4 1
9	c 0.95	35	4 0
10	n 4	36	3 0
11	end	37	x3 1
12		38	y3 1
13	markov multProc	39	2 0
14	x4 3 delta_r	40	x2 1
15	y4 3 beta_r	41	y2 1
16	4 x4 n*gamma_f*c	42	1 0
17	4 y4 n*gamma_f*(1-c)	43	0 1
18	3 4 tau_r	44	end
19	3 x3 (n-1)*gamma_f*c	45	end
20	3 y3(n-1)*gamma_f*(1-c)	46	
21	x3 2 delta_r	47	var SU exrss(multProc)
22	y3 2 beta_r	48	echo SS System Unavailability
23	2 x2 (n-2)*gamma_f*c	49	expr SU
24	2 y2 (n-2)*gamma_f*(1-c)	50	
25	2 3 tau_r	51	end
26	x2 1 delta_r	52	

FIG. 27. SHARPE input to compute the unavailability of the multiprocessor system.

buffers. Since arriving jobs are always rejected when the system is unavailable, the down states are assigned with reward rate 1. The computation of job loss probability due to full buffers can be carried out using a queuing model [23] or can be based on measurements. For this example, we assumed an $M/M/i/b$ queuing model (see Fig. 28).

The Markov chain for an $M/M/i/b$ queuing model is shown in Fig. 29. The state indices denote the number of jobs in the system. We assume that jobs arriving to the system form a Poisson process with rate λ and that the service requirements of jobs are independent, identically distributed according to an exponential distribution with mean $1/\mu$. We also assume that there is a limited number b of buffers available for

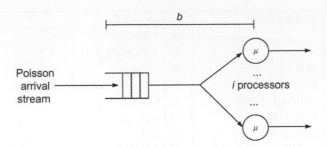

FIG. 28. Queuing system for the multiprocessor system.

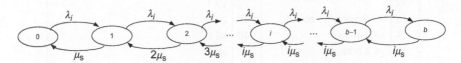

FIG. 29. Performance model for the multiprocessor system.

queuing the jobs. Tasks arriving when all the buffers are full are rejected. As explained earlier, to compute the NTL, we assign reward rates of a task being rejected to all the up state of the availability model by solving a sequence of lower-level performance models. Besides, we assign a reward rate 1 to all the down states. The task will be rejected whenever b tasks are in the system. Therefore, the NTL is given by the probability $q_b(i)$ that the CTMC (see Fig. 29) is in state b [5]:

$$
q_b(i) = \begin{cases} \dfrac{\rho^b}{i^{b-i}i!}\left[\displaystyle\sum_{j=0}^{i-1}\frac{\rho^j}{j!}+\sum_{j=i}^{b}\frac{\rho^j}{i^{j-i}i!}\right]^{-1}, & b \geq i \\[4mm] \dfrac{\rho^b}{b!}\left[\displaystyle\sum_{j=0}^{b}\frac{\rho^j}{j!}\right]^{-1}, & b < i \end{cases}
$$

where $\rho=\lambda/\mu$.

Figures 30 and 31 present the SHARPE input file to compute the NTL. Lines 4 through 13 define the input parameters. The parameter values for the high-level availability model are the same as the ones presented before to compute the steady-state unavailability. For the performance models, we assumed the jobs arrive at $\lambda_j=200$ jobs per second. Each job has a service rate of $\mu_s=100$ jobs per second. The number of buffer is $b=3$. Thus,

1	format 8	35	markov perfMultProc3
2		36	0 1 lambda_j
3		37	1 2 lambda_j
4	bind	38	1 0 mu_s
5	lambda_j 200	39	2 3 lambda_j
6	tau_r 1	40	2 1 2*mu_s
7	gamma_f 1/6000	41	3 4 lambda_j
8	beta_r 12	42	3 2 3*mu_s
9	mu_s 100	43	4 5lambda_j
10	delta_r 360	44	4 3 3*mu_s
11	c 0.95	45	5 6 lambda_j
12	n 4	46	5 4 3*mu_s
13	end	47	6 5 3*mu_s
14		48	end
15	markov perfMultProc4	49	end
16	0 1 lambda_j	50	
17	1 2 lambda_j	51	func R3()\
18	1 0 mu_s	52	prob(perfMultProc3, 6)
19	2 3 lambda_j	53	
20	2 1 2*mu_s	54	
21	3 4 lambda_j	55	markov perfMultProc2
22	3 2 3*mu_s	56	0 1 lambda_j
23	4 5 lambda_j	57	1 0 mu_s
24	4 3 4*mu_s	58	1 2 lambda_j
25	5 6 lambda_j	59	2 1 2*mu_s
26	5 4 4*mu_s	60	2 3 lambda_j
27	6 7 lambda_j	61	3 2 2*mu_s
28	6 5 4*mu_s	62	3 4 lambda_j
29	7 6 4*mu_s	63	4 3 2*mu_s
30	end	64	4 5 lambda_j
31	end	65	5 4 2*mu_s
32		66	end
33	func R4()\	67	end
34	prob(perfMultProc4, 7)	68	

FIG. 30. SHARPE input for the multiprocessor system.

69	func R2()\	98	2 x2 (n-2)*gamma_f*c
70	prob(perfMultProc2, 5)	99	2 y2 (n-2)*gamma_f*(1-c)
71		100	2 3 tau_r
72	markov perfMultProc1	101	x2 1 delta_r
73	0 1 lambda_j	102	y2 1 beta_r
74	1 2 lambda_j	103	1 2 tau_r
75	1 0 mu_s	104	1 0gamma_f
76	2 3 lambda_j	105	0 1 tau_r
77	2 1 mu_s	106	* Reward configuration defined:
78	3 4 lambda_j	107	Reward
79	3 2 mu_s	108	x4 1
80	4 3 mu_s	109	y4 1
81	end	110	4 R4()
82	end	111	3 R3()
83		112	x3 1
84	func R1()\	113	y3 1
85	prob(perfMultProc1, 4)	114	2 R2()
86		115	x2 1
87		116	y2 1
88	markov multProc	117	1 R1()
89	x4 3 delta_r	118	0 1
90	y4 3 beta_r	119	end
91	4 x4 n*gamma_f*c	120	end
92	4 y4 n*gamma_f*(1-c)	121	
93	3 4 tau_r	122	var NTL exrss(multProc)
94	3 x3 (n-1)*gamma_f*c	123	echo NTL for the Multiprocessor System.
95	3 y3 (n-1)*gamma_f*(1-c)	124	expr NTL
96	x3 2 delta_r	125	
97	y3 2 beta_r	126	end

Fig. 31. SHARPE input for the multiprocessor system (continuation).

$$\text{NTL} = \sum_{i \in S_p} q_b(i) + U_s$$

where $S_p = \{ i | 1 \leq i \geq n \}$.

Lines 15 through 105 define the performance models which are solved for each up state of the availability model. For instance, from lines 15 through 31, we define the performance model when 4 processors are operational. This performance model is solved to compute the job loss probability due to full buffers (function on lines 33 through 34). The function computes the probability that the CTMC is in state b. The result is passed as reward rates to the availability model (see line 110). This procedure is carried out for all the up states. Lines 122 through 124 compute the NTL for the multiprocessor system. Figure 32 shows the output for this model. Note that this model specification can be easily modified to consider different number of processors and different number of buffer using loops in the specification of CTMC as presented before for the telecommunication switching case.

3.2.2 Wireless Communication Network System

In Ref. [2], Ma et al. presented two techniques for combining performance and availability analysis in a wireless communication network system. The two modeling techniques used are an exact composite model and a hierarchical performability model. Figure 33 presents a monolithic CTMC model for a system with channel failure and repair. We assumed there are C idle channels and g guard channels. Note that the guard channels are reserved channels which are used by handoff calls only, since the dropping of a handoff call is more severe than the blocking of a new call. Interarrival times for the new and handoff calls are exponentially distributed with respective rates λ_n and λ_h^i. The departure of call due to termination or due to an ongoing call crossing a cell boundary is exponentially distributed with respective rates λ_d and λ_h^0. The channel failure and repair times are exponentially distributed with rates λ_f and μ_r, respectively. For the sake of simplicity, we assume $\lambda_t=\lambda_n+\lambda_h^i$, $\lambda_0=\lambda_d+\lambda_h^0$, $a=C-g$, $b=C-g+1$, and $q=C-1$.

Since the exact approach (see Fig. 33) generally faces largeness and stiffness problems, we advocate the use of hierarchical approaches. The performability model composed of two-level MRMs for the wireless communication network is shown in Fig. 34. The upper level model depicts the failure and repair behavior of the system (see Fig. 34A). The lower-level models describe the performance aspects of the system (see Fig. 34B and C). For each state i $(C,...,C-g-1)$ on the upper level

---

NTL for the Multiprocessor System.

NTL: 1.10182931e-002

FIG. 32. SHARPE output for the multiprocessor system.

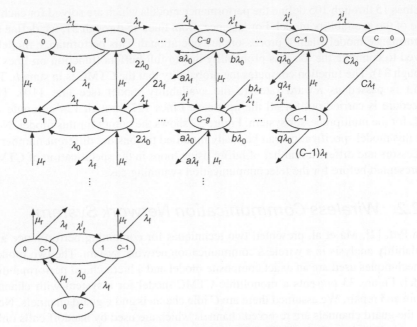

FIG. 33. Monolithic CTMC model for a wireless system with channel failure and repair.

model, the lower-level performance model described in Fig. 34B is solved to compute the dropping probability and blocking probability. These measures are then used as reward rates in the upper level model. Likewise, for each state i $(C-g,\ldots,1)$ on the availability model, the lower-level performance model described in Fig. 34C is solved, and the results are used as reward rates to the availability model. Note that the performance model in Fig. 34B represents the arrival of either new or handoff calls, while the performance model in Fig. 34C represents only handoff call arrival. This approach is an approximation of the exact model by assuming that in each state of the upper level, the lower level reaches steady state. Even though an approximation is involved in this process, the errors caused by the approximation are acceptable. Thus, the use of hierarchical models provides a good alternative for combining performance and availability analysis.

3.2.3 Job Completion Time

Yet another example of combined performance and reliability analysis is computation of the job completion time on a system subject to component failure and repair. The distribution of the job completion time on a computer system considering

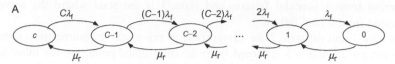

A

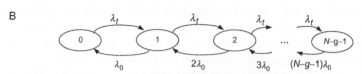

Upper level availability model

B

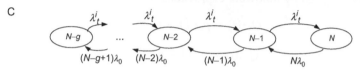

Lower level performance model for arrival of
either new or handoff call

C

Lower level performance model for only
handoff call arrival

FIG. 34. Upper- and lower-level models for a wireless system.

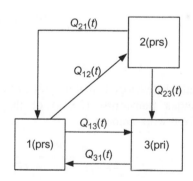

FIG. 35. Three-state CPU model.

CPU failure and repair was originally studied in Ref. [51]. The CPU or the server model used in the study was a three-state SMP, and the job completion time was analyzed in a general manner [29,52]. Figure 35 shows the SMP for the CPU model where state 1 represents the server up state; state 2 is the state where the server is recovering from a nonfatal failure; and state 3 is the state where the server is recovering from a fatal failure.

The state 1 and the state 2 are categorized as pre-emptive resume (prs) states in which the job execution is resumed from the interrupted point. On the other hand, the state 3 is categorized as pre-emptive repeat identical (pri) state in which the job execution is restarted from the beginning. A job that started execution when the server is in state 1 may encounter a nonfatal error that leads to the server state change from 1 to 2. The job execution also faces a fatal error that causes the server state change from 1 to 3. Both of nonfatal error and fatal error are repairable and their times to recovery follow general distribution $G_2(t)$ and $G_3(t)$, respectively. Assuming that failures are exponentially distributed with rate λ and each failure is either nonfatal with probability p_{nf} or fatal with probability $p_f = 1 - p_{nf}$, the SMP kernel distributions are given by following expressions.

$$Q_{12}(t) = p_{nf} \cdot \left(1 - e^{-\lambda t}\right)$$

$$Q_{13}(t) = p_f \cdot \left(1 - e^{-\lambda t}\right)$$

$$Q_{21}(t) = \int_0^t e^{-\lambda p_f \tau} \frac{d}{d\tau} G_2(\tau) d\tau$$

$$Q_{23}(t) = \left(1 - e^{-\lambda p_f \tau}\right) - \int_0^t \lambda \cdot p_f \cdot e^{-\lambda p_f \tau} \frac{d}{d\tau} G_2(\tau) d\tau$$

$$Q_{31}(t) = G_3(t)$$

Using the analysis method developed in Ref. [52] to the SMP model, we can obtain the Laplace–Stieltjes transforms (LSTs) of the job completion time distribution $\tilde{F_1}(s, x)$ for fixed work amount x:

$$\tilde{F_1}(s, x) = \frac{e^{-\tau(s)x}}{1 - \frac{\lambda p_f}{s + \lambda p_f} \cdot \left[1 - e^{-\tau(s)x}\right] \cdot \tilde{G_3}(s)}$$

$$\tau(s) = s + \lambda\left(1 - p_{nf} \cdot \tilde{Q_{21}}(s)\right)$$

where $\tilde{Q_{21}}(s)$ and $\tilde{G_3}(s)$ are the LSTs of $Q_{21}(t)$ and $G_3(t)$.

Then LST can be numerically inverted, or by taking derivatives expected completion time determined.

4. Conclusions

As a result of the proliferation and complexity of computer systems, the use of composite performance and availability analysis has become an important method to analyze degradable systems. Pure performance evaluation of a system tends to be optimistic since it ignores the failure–repair behavior of the system. On the other hand, pure availability analysis tends to be conservative, since performance considerations are not properly taken into account. In order to understand and predict the behavior of these systems, this chapter introduced the main techniques used in model construction and solution of composite performance and availability analysis, such as exact composite approach and hierarchical modeling approaches. We have also shown the basics of analytic models which are useful to compute availability and performance metrics by themselves. To show the applicability of these methods, practical examples have been detailed using the SHARPE software package.

REFERENCES

[1] G. Ciardo, R. Marie, B. Sericola, K.S. Trivedi, Performability analysis using semi-Markov reward processes, IEEE Trans. Comput. 39 (10) (1990) 1251–1264.

[2] Y. Ma, J. Han, K. Trivedi, Composite performance & availability analysis of wireless communication networks, IEEE Trans. Veh. Technol. 50 (5) (2001) 1216–1223.

[3] K.S. Trivedi, J.K. Muppala, S.P. Woolet, B.R. Haverkort, Composite performance and dependability analysis, Perform. Eval. 14 (3–4) (1992) 197–215.

[4] R.A. Sahner, K.S. Trivedi, A. Puliafito, Performance and Reliability Analysis of Computer Systems: An Example-Based Approach Using the SHARPE Software Package, Kluwer Academic Publishers, Dordrecht/Boston/London, 1996.

[5] R.M. Smith, K.S. Trivedi, A.V. Ramesh, Performability analysis: measures, an algorithm, and a case study, IEEE Trans. Comput. 37 (4) (1988) 406–417.

[6] J.K. Muppala, S.P. Woolet, K.S. Trivedi, Real-time systems performance in the presence of failures, IEEE Comput. 24 (1991) 37–47.

[7] Y. Cao, H. Sun, K.S. Trivedi, Performability analysis of TDMA cellular systems, International Conference on the Performance and QoS of Next Generation Networking, P&QNet2000, Nagoya, Japan, 2000.

[8] R. Ghosh, K.S. Trivedi, V.K. Naik, D. Kim, End-to-end performability analysis for infrastructure-as-a-service cloud: An interacting stochastic models approach, Proceedings of the 16th IEEE Pacific Rim International Symposium on Dependable Computing (PRDC), 2010, pp. 125–132.

[9] S. Ramani, K. Goseva-Popstojanova, K.S. Trivedi, A framework for performability modeling of messaging services in distributed systems, Proceedings of the 8th IEEE International Conference on Engineering of Complex Computer Systems (ICECCS 02), Greenbelt, MD, pp.25–34, 2002.

[10] N. Lopez-Benitez, K.S. Trivedi, Multiprocessor performability analysis, IEEE Trans. Reliab. 42 (4) (1993) 579–587.

[11] K.S. Trivedi, X. Ma, S. Dharmaraja, Performability modeling of wireless communication systems, Int. J. Commun. Syst. 16 (6) (2003) 561–577.

[12] M. Lanus, L. Yin, K.S. Trivedi, Hierarchical composition and aggregation of state-based availability and performability models, IEEE Trans. Reliab. 52 (1) (2003) 44–52.

[13] D. Wang, W. Xie, K.S. Trivedi, Performability analysis of clustered systems with rejuvenation under varying workload, Perform. Eval. 64 (3) (2007) 247–265.

[14] B. Haverkort, R. Marie, G. Rubino, K.S. Trivedi, Performability Modeling Tools and Techniques, John Wiley & Sons, Chichester, England, 2001.

[15] M.D. Beaudry, Performance-related reliability measures for computing systems, IEEE Trans. Comput. C-27 (Jun. 1978) 540–547.

[16] J.F. Meyer, On evaluating the performability of degradable computing systems, IEEE Trans. Comput. 29 (8) (Aug. 1980) 720–731.

[17] K.S. Trivedi, D. Wang, D.J. Hunt, A. Rindos, W.E. Smith, B. Vashaw, Availability modeling of SIP protocol on IBM WebSphere, Proceeding Pacific Rim Dependability Conference, 2008, pp. 323–330.

[18] K.S. Trivedi, D. Wang, J. Hunt, Computing the number of calls dropped due to failures, Proceedings of the IEEE International Symposium on Software, Reliability Engineering, 2010, pp. 11–20.

[19] A. Bobbio, K.S. Trivedi, Computing cumulative measures of stiff Markov chains using aggregation, IEEE Trans. Comput. 39 (Oct. 1990) 1291–1298.

[20] M. Malhotra, J.K. Muppala, K.S. Trivedi, Stiffness-tolerant methods for transient analysis of stiff Markov chains, Microelectron Reliab. 34 (11) (1994) 1825–1841.

[21] F. Longo, R. Ghosh, V.K. Naik, K.S. Trivedi, A scalable availability model for Infrastructure-as-a-Service cloud, IEEE/IFIP DSN, 2011.

[22] G. Bolch, S. Greiner, H. Meer, K.S. Trivedi, Queueing Networks and Markov Chains: Modeling and Performance Evaluation with Computer Science Applications, Wiley Interscience, New York, NY, 1998.

[23] K.S. Trivedi, Probability and Statistics with Reliability, Queuing, and Computer Science Applications, second ed., John Wiley and Sons, New York, 2001.

[24] D. Logothesis, K.S. Trivedi, A. Puliato, Markov regenerative models, Proceedings of the International Computer Performance and Dependability Symposium, Erlangen, Germany, 1995, pp. 134–143.

[25] B.R. Haverkort, Approximate performability and dependability analysing using generalized stochastic Petri nets, Perform. Eval. 18 (1993) 61–78.

[26] V. Mainkar, K.S. Trivedi, Fixed point iteration using stochastic reward nets, Proceedings of the 6th International Workshop on Petri Nets and Performance Models (PNPM), Durham, USA, pp. 21–30, 1995.

[27] ITU-T Recommendation E.800. Terms and definitions related to quality of service and network performance including dependability. http://wapiti.telecom-lille1.eu/commun/ens/peda/options/ST/RIO/pub/exposes/exposesrio2008-ttnfa2009/Belhachemi-Arab/files/IUT-T%20E800.pdf. Accessed 18 May 2011.

[28] M. Grottke, K.S. Trivedi, Fighting bugs: remove, retry, replicate and rejuvenate, IEEE Comput. 40 (2) (2007) 107–109.

[29] A. Sathaye, S. Ramani, K.S. Trivedi, Availability models in practice, Proceedings of the International Workshop on Fault-Tolerant Control and Computing (FTCC-1), 2000.

[30] X. Zang, D. Wang, H. Sun, K.S. Trivedi, A BDD-based algorithm for analysis of multistate systems with multistate components, IEEE Trans. Comput. 52 (12) (Dec. 2003) 1608–1618.

[31] D. Wang, K. Trivedi, T. Sharma, A. Ramesh, D. Twigg, L. Nguyen, Y. Liu, A new reliability estimation method for large systems, 2000 The Boeing Company patent application pending.

[32] M. Malhotra, K.S. Trivedi, Power-hierarchy of dependability-model types, IEEE Trans. Reliab. 43 (3) (1994) 34–42.

[33] S.S. Gokhale, M.R. Lyu, K.S. Trivedi, Analysis of software fault removal policies using a non-homogeneous continuous time Markov chain, Softw. Qual. J. 12 (3) (2004) 211–230.

[34] W.J. Stewart, Probability, Markov Chains, Queues, and Simulation, Princeton University Press, USA, 2009.

[35] M. Malhotra, K. Trivedi, Dependability modeling using Petri nets, IEEE Trans. Reliab. 44 (3) (1995) 428–440.

[36] K. Trivedi, G. Ciardo, M. Malhutra, R. Sahncr, Dependability and performability analysis, in: Donatiello Lorenzo, Nelson Randolf (Eds.), Performance Evaluation of Computer and Communication Systems, Springer-Verlag, NY, USA, 1993.

[37] G. Ciardo, J. Muppala, K.S. Trivedi, Analyzing concurrent and fault-tolerant software using stochastic Petri nets, J. Parallel Distrib. Comput. 15 (1992) 255–269.

[38] M. Balakrishnan, K.S. Trivedi, Stochastic Petri nets for the reliability analysis of communication network applications with alternate-routing, Reliab. Eng. Syst. Safety 52 (3) (1996) 243–259 special issue on Reliability and Safety Analysis of Dynamic Process Systems.

[39] J.B. Dugan, K.S. Trivedi, V. Nicola, R. Geist, Extended stochastic Petri nets: applications and analysis, Proceeding Performance '84, North-Holland, Amsterdam, pp. 507–519, 1985.

[40] K.S. Trivedi, Sun Hairong, Stochastic Petri nets and their applications to performance analysis of computer networks, Proceedings of the International Conference on Operational Research, 1998.

[41] O. Ibe, R. Howe, K.S. Trivedi, Approximate availability analysis of VAXCluster systems, IEEE Trans. Reliab. 38 (1) (Apr. 1989) 146–152.

[42] R. Fricks, K.S. Trivedi, Modeling failure dependencies in reliability analysis using stochastic Petri nets, Proceedings of the European Simulation Multi-conference (ESM '97), Istanbul, 1997.

[43] R. German, C. Kelling, A. Zimmermann, G. Hommel, TimeNET—a toolkit for evaluating non-Markovian stochastic Petri nets, Perform. Eval. 24 (1995) 69–87.

[44] G. Chiola, G. Franceschinis, R. Gaeta, M. Ribaudo, GreatSPN 1.7: graphical editor and analyzer for timed and stochastic Petri nets, Perform. Eval. 24 (Nov. 1995) 47–68.

[45] K.S. Trivedi, R. Sahner, SHARPE at the age of twenty two, SIGMETRICS Perform. Eval. Rev. 36 (4) (2009) 52–57.

[46] C. Hirel, B. Tuffin, K.S. Trivedi, SPNP: stochastic Petri nets. Version 6.0, Lect. Notes Comput. Sci. 1786 (2000) 354–357.

[47] A. Bobbio, A. Puliafito, M. Telek, K.S. Trivedi, Recent developments in stochastic Petri nets, J. Circuits Syst. Comp. 8 (1) (Feb. 1998) 119–158.

[48] K.S. Trivedi, D. Kim, X. Yin, Multi-state availability modeling in practice, in: A. Lisnianski, I. Frenkel (Eds.), Recent Advances in System Reliability: Signature, Multi-state Systems and Statistical Inference, Springer, New York, 2011.

[49] J.K. Muppala, A. Sathaye, R. Howe, K.S. Trivedi, Dependability modeling of a heterogeneous VAXcluster system using stochastic reward nets, in: D. Avresky (Ed.), Hardware and Software Fault Tolerance in Parallel Computing Systems, Ellis Horwood Ltd, NJ, USA, 1992, pp. 33–59.

[50] Y. Liu, K.S. Trivedi, Survivability quantification: the analytical modeling approach, International J. Performability Eng. (2006) 29–44.

[51] X. Castillo, D.P. Siewiorek, A performance-reliability model for computing systems, Proceedings of the FTCS-10, Silver Spring, MD, IEEE Computer Society, 1980, pp. 187–192.

[52] P. Chimento, K. Trivedi, The completion time of programs on processors subject to failure and repair, IEEE Trans. Comput. 42 (10) (1993) 1184–1194.

ABOUT THE AUTHOR

Kishor S. Trivedi holds the Hudson Chair in the Department of Electrical and Computer Engineering at Duke University, Durham, NC. He has been on the Duke faculty since 1975. He is the author of a well-known text entitled, *Probability and Statistics with Reliability, Queuing and Computer Science Applications*, published by Prentice-Hall; a thoroughly revised second edition (including its Indian edition) of this book has been published by John Wiley. He has also published two other books entitled, *Performance and Reliability Analysis of Computer Systems*, published by Kluwer Academic Publishers and *Queueing Networks and Markov Chains*, John Wiley. He is a Fellow of the Institute of Electrical and Electronics Engineers. He is a Golden Core Member of IEEE Computer Society. He has published over 450 articles and has supervised 42 Ph.D. dissertations. He is on the editorial boards of *Journal of Risk and Reliability*, *International Journal of Performability Engineering*, and *International Journal of Quality and Safety Engineering*. He is the recipient of IEEE Computer Society Technical Achievement Award for his research on Software Aging and Rejuvenation. His research interests are in reliability, availability, performance, performability, and survivability modeling of computer and communication systems. He works closely with industry in carrying our reliability/availability analysis, providing short courses on reliability, availability, performability modeling, and in the development and dissemination of software packages such as SHARPE and SPNP.

Ermeson C. Andrade graduated in Computer Science from Catholic University of Pernambuco in 2006 and received his M.Sc. degree in Computer Science at Federal University of Pernambuco in 2009. He is currently a Ph.D candidate in Computer Science at Federal University of Pernambuco and visiting scholar of Electrical and Computer Engineering at Duke University. His research interests include performability analysis, component-based modeling, and hard real-time systems.

Fumio Machida is an assistant manager in NEC Service Platforms Research Laboratories. He was a visiting scholar of Electrical and Computer Engineering in Duke University in 2010. His primary research interest is in availability management of large-scale ICT systems such as data centers for cloud computing services. He has experienced real industrial research projects on enterprise system management, server virtualization management, autonomic computing, and dependable computing. He has also contributed industrial standardization activities such as Open Virtualization Format (OVF), Integrated Access Control Policy Management (IAM) in Distributed Management Task Force (DMTF).

Modeling, Analysis, and Testing of System Vulnerabilities

FEVZI BELLI

Department of Electrical Engineering and Information Technology (EIM-E/ADT), University of Paderborn, Paderborn, Germany

MUTLU BEYAZIT

Department of Electrical Engineering and Information Technology (EIM-E/ADT), University of Paderborn, Paderborn, Germany

ADITYA P. MATHUR

Department of Computer Science, Purdue University, West Lafayette, Indiana, USA

NIMAL NISSANKE

Faculty of Business, London South Bank University, London SE1 0AA, United Kingdom

Abstract

Human–machine systems have several *desirable* properties with respect to their friendliness, reliability, safety, security, and other global system attributes. The potential for the lack, or breaches, of any such property constitutes a system vulnerability that may lead to an undesirable behavior from a user's point of view. This undesirable behavior could be triggered by special events in the form of intended, or unintended, attacks emanating in the system's environment. One can view the undesirable system features as the sum of the features that are complementary to the desirable ones that must be taken into account from the

ADVANCES IN COMPUTERS, VOL. 84
ISSN: 0065-2458/DOI: 10.1016/B978-0-12-396525-7.00002-2

39

start of system development to achieve a stable and robust system behavior. This work focuses on the modeling, analysis, and testing of both the desirable and the undesirable system features that form relations between the system, its environment, and its operation. The proposed approach is event based and is demonstrated and analyzed using a case study.

1. Critical Features and Vulnerabilities of Human–Machine Systems

When observing an interactive human–machine system, we differentiate between desirable and undesirable behaviors, or events, depending on the expectations of the user concerning the system behavior. Desirable events, as understood in this chapter, include those related to global critical system properties such as reliability, safety, and security. Any deviation from the expected behavior defines an undesirable state; the fact that the system can be transferred into such a state might be viewed as a *vulnerability* of the system. A vulnerability is often accompanied by *threats*. Therefore, a complementary view of the desirable system behavior is necessary for a holistic modeling, analysis, and testing of the system.

This work uses the term "vulnerability" to refer to any behavior where the violation of the requirements of a system attribute, such as safety or security, may lead to a significant penalty in terms of cost, damage or harm. In the case of *safety*, the threat originates from within the system due to potential failures and its spillover effects causing potentially extensive damage to its environment. In the face of such failures, the environment could be a helpless, passive victim. The goal of the system design in this case is to prevent faults that could potentially lead to such failures or, in worst cases, to mitigate the consequences of run-time failures should they ever occur. In the case of *security*, the system is exposed to external threats originating from the environment, causing losses to the owner of the system. In this case, the environment, typically the user, maybe unauthorized, can be malicious or deliberately aggressive. The goal of system design then is to ensure that it can protect the system itself against such malicious attacks. Although, in this work, the outlined approach is used to test safety aspects, it is applicable to other vulnerability attributes like security, etc.

In the face of such vulnerabilities, testing forms an important part of the system development process in revealing and eliminating faults in the system. In addition, it continues to play an essential role during the maintenance phase. Because of the substantial costs involved in testing, both testability and the choice of tests to be conducted become important design considerations. Because of the conflicting demands of minimizing the extent of tests and maximizing the coverage of faults, it is therefore critically important to follow a systematic approach to identifying the test sets that focus on safety, as well as tests that address specific safety requirements [1,2].

With the above in view, this work proposes an approach where the test design can progress hand in hand with the design process, paying particular attention to safety. It is based on a formal (rule based, graphic, or algebraic) representation of the system and its environment, potentially including the user. User actions and system events in the representation, referred to here as "events" for simplicity, are ordered according to the threats posed by the resulting system states. This ordering is an integral aspect of the finite state representation, making it possible to directly identify the risks associated with each and every functionally desirable, and undesirable, event relative to one another. Tests that target safety requirements are devised by examining possible traces (sequences) of these events exhibiting particular risk patterns. These sequences are represented compactly by regular expressions (REs). The undesirable events in them representing human error and system failures, while the desirable events include, in addition to functional ones, various recovery measures to be undertaken following undesirable events.

Our approach is model based. It enables an incremental refinement of the model and specification, which at the beginning may be rough and rudimentary, or even nonexistent. However, the approach can also be deployed in implementation-oriented analysis and test in a refined format, for example, using the implementation (source code) as a concise description of the system under consideration (SUC), that is, as the ultimate specification and its control flow diagram as a state transition diagram (STD), respectively (see also Refs. [3,4]). To sum up, the approach can be used not only for requirements analysis and validation before implementation, but also for analysis and testing of an existing implementation, detecting input/output faults, erroneous internal states, etc., at low levels of abstraction.

A broader objective of this research is to develop a single framework for dealing with different system vulnerability attributes, carrying risks of different nature and degrees of severity, that is, safety and security, broadly in a similar manner, while capturing their fundamental differences by an appropriate characterization of the risks involved. This work is a formal, detailed and, hopefully, an intuitive introduction to the approach.

An early version of the proposed approach was introduced in Refs. [5,6]. The work in Refs. [7,8] addresses different vulnerability aspects like user-friendliness and safety that have different implications due to potential human error. Furthermore, the work also discusses certain concepts related to test generation based on event sequence graphs (ESGs). This work uses a special form of regular grammars (RGs) [9] to discuss and extend the concepts and outline concrete algorithms, while continuing to rely on ESGs and REs. Furthermore, it also focuses on the testability of event-based systems against vulnerabilities (based on, for example, safety), and it demonstrates test design that targets vulnerability aspects as part of an integrated system development process.

The remainder of this chapter is organized as follows. Section 2 introduces different models of the SUC that are equivalent to each other and to a finite state automaton (FSA). Using the notions introduced in Section 2, Section 3 discusses modeling system functions and vulnerability threats, and model-based testing and analysis. The concept of risk ordering, introduced in Section 4 in relation to attributes such as safety, is another fundamental concept of the approach and is applicable to other vulnerability system attributes as well. In Section 5, a real-life example is given to illustrate the use of risk ordering as the means of: (a) modeling safety aspects and (b) designing tests for verifying these properties. Section 6 summarizes and discusses related work, while Section 7 makes a critical review, considering also the limitations, and concludes the discussion with a summary of achievements and future directions.

2.   Modeling the SUC and Its Environment

This work focuses on event-based modeling for representation of the user and system behavior. In this work, an *event* is an externally observable phenomenon, for example, a user's stimulus or a response of the SUC, punctuating different stages of the system activity. The set of input/output signals (or events) E of a SUC can be partitioned into two subsets E_{env} and E_{sys} such that

$$E = E_{\text{env}} \cup E_{\text{sys}} \quad \text{and} \quad E_{\text{env}} \cap E_{\text{sys}} = \emptyset, \tag{1}$$

where E_{env} is the set of *environmental events* (for example, user inputs) while E_{sys} is the set of *system signals* (for example, responses). The distinction between the sets E_{env} and E_{sys} is important because the events in the latter are controllable from within the system, whereas the events in the former are not subject to such control.

ESGs, *REs*, and special type of *RGs* can be used for event-based modeling. These representations disregard the detailed internal behavior of the system and focus on events and their sequences. Therefore, although they are all equivalent to finite state automata (FSA) in theory, in practice, the models constructed using these representations are generally more abstract when compared to state-based models like FSA or STDs.

Here, we shall use ESGs for graphical visualizations of the concepts, REs for declarative representations (especially, of states which are not explicit in ESG models) and a special form of RGs for the formalization and unification of the concepts. Note that these representations are equivalent to each other in the sense that they all can be used to describe exactly the same subset of formal languages called *regular languages*, that is, $L(ESG)=L(RE)=L(RG)$, where $L(x)$ denotes the language generated by formalism x. We choose to use the formal grammar notation to formalize our concepts due to its expressivity. Still, a special form of RGs is selected to keep the modeling efficient and simple, and to limit our scope to regular models as opposed to stronger models such as context-free (or pushdown) models.

2.1   Models of the SUC

An *ESG* is a quadruple $D=(E, A, S, F)$ where

- E is a finite set of *nodes* (*events*),
- A is a finite set of *directed arcs* which are ordered pairs of elements of E, that is, $A \subseteq E \times E = \{(a,b) | a,b \in E\}$,
- $S \subseteq E$ is a distinguished set of *start* (*initial or entry*) *nodes*, and
- $F \subseteq E$ is a distinguished set of *finish* (*final or exit*) *nodes*.

Furthermore, given an ESG with nonempty set of start and set of finish events, an event $e \in E$ is called *useful* if e is reachable from a start event and a finish event is reachable from e. Also, the language defined by ESG D, denoted by $L(D)$, is the set of all event sequences which begin at a start node and ends at a finish node.

Basically an ESG is a directed graph whose nodes represent events and arcs represent sequences of these events. In practice, *useful ESGs*, that is, ESGs all of whose events are useful, are generally deployed to model the interactions between a system and its user. Since syntax of an ESG requires unique labeling of events, ESG models differentiate between similar events in different contexts of the systems, for example, by indexing (or renaming) [10] these events to make them unique. Also, in general, two additional *pseudo-events* are included in an ESG to mark start and finish events: "[" has no incoming arcs and is used to mark start events, and "]" has no outgoing arcs and is used to mark finish events. The arcs connected to these nodes are called *pseudo-arcs*.

A simple example of an ESG and a related FSA is shown in Fig. 1. In the figure, c denotes *copy*, x denotes *cut* and p denotes *paste*. p can occur in two different contexts, that is, there are two p events ($p1$ and $p2$) in the ESG: ($p1$) After copy, one can perform multiple paste operations. ($p2$) After cut, one can perform only a single paste.

As implied by Fig. 1, being alternative representations, ESGs and FSA can be converted from one form to the other in an "equivalent" manner, the main differences manifesting in the internal details of the FSA.

ESGs are also comparable with the Myhill graphs [11] that are used as computation schemes [12], or as *syntax diagrams*, for example, as used in Refs. [13,14] to define the syntax of Pascal; see also *event sequence* concept as introduced in Ref. [15]. The difference between the Myhill graphs and ESGs is that the symbols, which label the nodes of an ESG, are interpreted here not merely as symbols and meta-symbols of a language, but as operations of an event set.

When compared to ESGs, REs are more of a declarative nature. Inspired by FSA, this work uses REs for describing the patterns of interactivity between the system and its environment, and for identifying system states if required.

A *RE R* over alphabet (of events) E is inductively defined as follows (letting $L(R)$ be the language defined by RE R):

- *Base case*: Let ϕ be the empty language, ε be the empty string and a be any symbol in the alphabet, then
  - The constants ϕ and ε are REs denoting the languages $L(\phi) = \phi$ and $L(\varepsilon) = \{\varepsilon\}$, respectively.
  - a is an RE denoting the language $L(a) = \{a\}$.

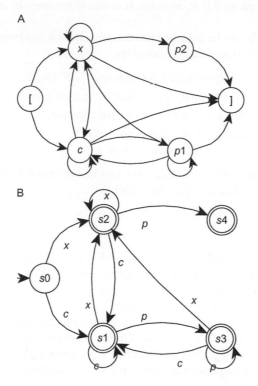

FIG. 1. Relationship between event sequence graphs and finite state automata. (A) An event sequence graph. (B) A finite state automaton.

- *Inductive case*: If R and P are two REs, denoting the languages $L(R)$ and $L(P)$ respectively, then
  - $R+P$, the *union* of R and P, is an RE denoting the language $L(R+P)=L(R)\cup L(P)$.
  - $R \cdot P$, the *concatenation* of R and P, is an RE denoting the language $L(R \cdot P)=L(R) \cdot L(P)$.
  - R^*, the *closure* of R, is an RE denoting the language $L(R^*)=L(R)^*$ and $R^+=R \cdot R^*$.
  - (R), is an RE denoting the language $L((R))=L(R)$.

Furthermore, given an RE R, an event is useful if it occurs in at least one of the strings in $L(R)$.

Intuitively, an RE can be assumed to be a sequence of symbols $a, b, c,\ldots$ of an alphabet that can be connected by operations

- sequence ("." (usually omitted), for example, "ab" means "b follows a"),
- selection ("+," for example, "$a+b$" means "a or b"), and
- iteration ("*," *Kleene's Star Operation*, for example,
  - "a^*" means "zero or more occurrences of a";
  - "a^+" means "at least one occurrence of a").

REs are equivalent to ESGs, since they can be converted to an FSA (and vice versa), and each FSA has an equivalent ESG.

For example, RE

$$R = \left(ab(a + c)^+\right)^*$$

indicates that a is followed by b, leading to ab, which is followed by at least one occurrence of either a or c. The entire sequence can be repeated an arbitrary number of times. Examples of the generated sequences are: *aba, abc, abaaba, abaabc* but also ε for 0 (zero) occurrence in the sequence.

The patterns of interactivity between any system and its environment can also be described in terms of (*formal*) *grammars*. Grammars in our consideration are limited to RGs in a special form, called tail-bijective k-sequence right RGs (integer $k \geq 1$), based on fixed length sequences of events in E of an ESG model and subset of states of its equivalent FSA.

A *tail-bijective k-sequence right regular grammar* ($tbRG_k$) ($k \geq 1$) is a quadruple $G = (E, N, P, S)$ where:

- E is a set of strings (*event sequences*) of fixed length $k \geq 1$,
- N is a finite set of *nonterminal symbols* or *nonterminals*,
- P is a finite set of *production rules* or *productions* of the form

$$Q \rightarrow \varepsilon \quad \text{or} \quad Q \rightarrow r R_r,$$

where $\rightarrow$ is called the *production symbol*, left side of the production is called the *head* of the production and right side is called the *body* or *tail*,

- $S \in N$ is a distinguished nonterminal *start symbol*,
- r is a sequence of k events, that is, $r = r(1)\ldots r(k) \in E, Q \in N$ and $R_r \in N \backslash \{S\}$,
- the function $nt(r) = R_r$ is a bijection from E to $N \backslash \{S\}$.

- if $(Q \to r\ R_r) = (R_q \to r\ R_r)$ then $q(2)...q(k) = r(1)...r(k\text{-}1)$, where $R_q \in N\backslash\{S\}$, and

- ε is the empty string.

Furthermore, a *derivation step* is of the form $xQy \Rightarrow_G xRy$ with $x,y \in (E \cup N)^*$ and $Q \to R \in P$. A *derivation* is a sequence of derivation steps and is denoted by $\Rightarrow_G^*$ (we shall use $\Rightarrow$ and $\Rightarrow^*$ instead of $\Rightarrow_G$ and $\Rightarrow_G^*$ where there is no confusion). The language defined by grammar G, denoted by $L(G)$, is the set of strings $L(G) = \{w \in E^* | S \Rightarrow^* w\}$. Hence, an event sequence of length k is *useful*, if it occurs in at least one of the strings in $L(G)$, and a nonterminal is *useful* if it is used in the derivation of a string in $L(G)$. Also, tbRG$_k$ G is *useful*, if all of its event sequences of length k are useful.

To put it simply, tbRG$_k$ models make it easier to represent the interactions between not only the single events but also the sequences of events of fixed length. Furthermore, in modeling the system, a tbRG$_k$ lies midway between an equivalent ESG and an equivalent FSA, since nonterminals of the grammar can be used additionally to represent states and productions of a tbRG$_1$ represents the sequences of events like the arcs of an ESG. Additionally, a tbRG$_1$ also distinguishes events in different contexts by indexing or renaming.

Figure 2 shows the tbRG$_1$ equivalent of the ESG and the FSA in Fig. 1.

There are plenty of different models with various degrees of expressive power and different semantics, other than the formalisms discussed above. For example:

- Finite state machines [16,17] and timed input/output automata [18] are extended versions of FSA and include explicit system outputs (timed input/output automata also include time parameter). These formalisms have been used, for example, for modeling role-based [19] and timed role-based [20] access control policies and to generate test cases.

1. $S \to c\ nt(c)$	9. $nt(x) \to p2\ nt(p2)$
2. $S \to x\ nt(x)$	10. $nt(x) \to \varepsilon$
3. $nt(c) \to c\ nt(c)$	11. $nt(p1) \to c\ nt(c)$
4. $nt(c) \to x\ nt(x)$	12. $nt(p1) \to x\ nt(x)$
5. $nt(c) \to p1\ nt(p1)$	13. $nt(p1) \to p1\ nt(p1)$
6. $nt(c) \to \varepsilon$	14. $nt(p1) \to \varepsilon$
7. $nt(x) \to c\ nt(c)$	15. $nt(p2) \to \varepsilon$
8. $nt(x) \to x\ nt(x)$	

FIG. 2. tbRG$_1$ equivalent to the model in Fig. 1.

- Pushdown automata [21] can also be considered as FSA with additional stack components to store some elements during the computation. Thus, they have more expressive power than FSA. These models are also used for modeling and testing of specific software functions [22,23].
- Statecharts [24] are an extended form of finite state machines designed to capture hierarchy and concurrency. There are a variety of statecharts with varying execution semantics [25].
- Process algebras such as communicating sequential processes [26,27] and calculus of communicating systems [28] are developed to model, study, and test the systems of concurrent, communicating components.
- Petri nets [29] are formal models that can be considered as an extension of FSA where the notions of "transitions" and "states" are made explicitly disjoint and are used, for instance, to model the behavior of concurrent systems, including synchronization of processes.
- Unified modeling language (UML) [30,31] enables the designer to describe a system at different levels of abstraction by means of a set of diagrams. In order to specify a system more easily, UML is composed of less precisely defined visual formalisms (UML diagrams) which do not have exact semantics [32]. UML diagrams are inspired by basic notions such as automata, statecharts, Petri nets, etc.

In the rest of the discussion, for the sake of simplicity, the concepts will be mainly defined and outlined in detail for $tbRG_1s$ by making use of the copy/cut and paste example in Fig. 2. For intuitive understanding, we will sometimes also include the corresponding ESGs or REs in some parts of the discussion. Note that the concepts outlined in this work can also be adapted to other types of models, such as the ones discussed above.

2.2   Conversions

As already mentioned, the set of languages described by ESGs, REs, and $tbRG_1s$ are equivalent to the set of regular languages. Thus, well-known algorithms in the literature, especially in automata theory and formal languages, can be used to convert a given ESG to the corresponding RE, and vice versa [33]. In order to extract the RE from a given ESG, one may follow the steps given below:

- Convert ESG to a deterministic FSA (by interpreting the ESG as a Moore Machine [17] and FSA as a Mealy Machine [16]).
- Convert the FSA to RE by using the algorithms in the literature [21].

In addition, for the opposite chain of transformations, the following steps can be used:

- Convert RE to an equivalent nondeterministic FSA F.
- Convert F to a deterministic FSA F′ (and minimize, if required).
- Convert F′ to DG (similar to Mealy–Moore conversion).

Nevertheless, one should be careful in these conversions because they might require the use of indexing in order to guarantee the uniqueness of ESG events and to preserve the equivalency to FSA. Furthermore, FSA accepting the empty language or the empty string may also need some special treatment.

Since we are interested in grammar-based discussion/extension of ESG concepts, we outline below an algorithm for ESG to tbRG$_1$ conversion.

Algorithm 1 ESG to tbRG$_1$ Conversion

Input: $D = (V, A, I, F)$ – an ESG
Output: $G = (E, N, P, S)$ – the corresponding tbRG$_1$
$E = \emptyset$, $N = \{S\}$, $P = \emptyset$

for each $e \in V$ **do**
    $E = E \cup \{e\}$ // Add terminals
    $N = N \cup \{R_e\}$ // Add nonterminals
endfor
for each $e \in I$ **do**
    $P = P \cup \{S \rightarrow e\,R_e\}$ // Add production rules for start nodes
endfor
for each $e \in F$ **do**
    $P = P \cup \{R_e \rightarrow \varepsilon\}$ // Add production rules for finish nodes
endfor
for each $(a, b) \in A$ **do**
    $P = P \cup \{R_a \rightarrow b\,R_b\}$ // Add production rules for arcs
endfor

The above algorithm has a running time $O(|V|+|A|+|I|+|F|)$ as it is possible to view it as an implicit mapping $nt(e)=R_e$ which maps a given terminal $x \in E$ to a nonterminal symbol R_e ($nt(\cdot)=R_{(\cdot)}: E \rightarrow N\backslash\{S\}$). Since this mapping can be shown to be bijective, and each arc and each node in an ESG are unique, all set union operations can be performed in $O(1)$ time as simple append operations. Furthermore, it is possible to perform tbRG$_1$ to ESG conversion in $O(|E|+|P|)$ steps.

2.3 Complement and Completed System Models

While testing an SUC, one would also like to test whether the system does not allow any behavior outside the one described by its model. To do this, fault model(s) need to be created. Let us begin with an initial definition of complement and completed models.

Complement of a tbRG$_1$ $G=(E, N, P, S)$ is defined as a tbRG$_1$ $\overline{G} = (E, N, \overline{P}, S)$, where $\overline{P}$ contains all productions of the form

- $S \rightarrow a\ R_a \in P$,
- $R_a \rightarrow \varepsilon \in P$ and
- $R_a \rightarrow b\ R_b \notin P$ for $a, b \in E$.

According to this definition of complement, $\overline{G}$ is likely to contain events that are not useful. Furthermore, even the language defined by $\overline{G}$ may turn out to be empty, that is, $L(\overline{G}) = \emptyset$, if none of the events of $\overline{G}$ are useful.

Figure 3 shows the complement of a tbRG$_1$ $(\overline{tbRG_1})$ and the corresponding ESG $(\overline{ESG})$. Note that, since the start and finish events are left unchanged, only the rules 1, 2, 6, 10, 14, and 15 of the original tbRG$_1$ are retained. Furthermore, additional rules are added that correspond to event sequences that are not in the original tbRG$_1$.

In the examples throughout this text, the rules added to the grammars, and the nodes and arcs added to the ESGs are shown in bold (like **H→T**). Furthermore, the rules removed from the grammars are formatted as strikethrough (like ~~H→T~~), and the nodes and arcs removed from the ESGs are shown using dashed curves.

Given a tbRG$_1$ $G=(E, N, P, S)$, *completed* tbRG$_1$ $(CtbRG_1)$ of G is a tbRG$_1$ $CG=(E, N, P_C, S)$, where P_C contains all productions of the form

- $Q \rightarrow R \in P$ (all productions in P) and
- $R_a \rightarrow b\ R_b \notin P$ for $a, b \in E$.

The language defined by CG is given by $L(CG)=(I \cdot E^* \cdot F)$, where I is the set of start events, that is, $I=\{a \in E | S \rightarrow aR_a \in P\}$, and F is the set of finish events, that is, $F=\{a \in E | R_a \rightarrow \varepsilon \in P\}$.

A completed ESG *(CESG)* and a tbRG$_1$ *(CtbRG$_1$)* are shown in Fig. 4. A completed model is the superposition of the model and its complement.

Note that the above definitions of complement and completion are different from those found usually in the formal languages textbooks like Ref. [21] (for example, start and finish events are always the same), which allow the complement or completed languages to include event sequences that may

- be prefix of some of the event sequences in the language defined by the original model, and
- start with a non-start event of the original model.

A

1. $S \to c\ nt(c)$	16. $nt(c) \to p2\ nt(p2)$
2. $S \to x\ nt(x)$	17. $nt(x) \to p1\ nt(p1)$
6. $nt(c) \to \varepsilon$	18. $nt(p1) \to p2\ nt(p2)$
10. $nt(x) \to \varepsilon$	19. $nt(p2) \to c\ nt(c)$
14. $nt(p1) \to \varepsilon$	20. $nt(p2) \to p1\ nt(p1)$
15. $nt(p2) \to \varepsilon$	21. $nt(p2) \to p2\ nt(p2)$
	22. $nt(p2) \to x\ nt(x)$

B

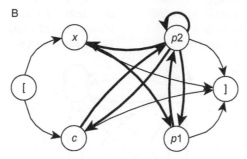

FIG. 3. The complement of the tbRG$_1$ in Fig. 2. (A) The resulting tbRG$_1$. (B) The resulting ESG.

Our intention is to avoid these in practice for the sake of efficiency. However, our current definition of the complement is also problematic since the resulting language may not be useful, as some or all events may lack usefulness. Therefore, we will use model transformation operators to define partial complements of the model.

2.4 Transformed System Models

In order to extend fault-modeling approach based on complement and completed models and treat faults in a more rigorous manner, let us define certain transformation operators and their combinations.

It is possible to classify transformation operators under three categories: *insertion* (*I*), *omission* (*O*) and *marking* (*M*) operators. In general, insertion operators are used to generate models that have additional functionality when compared to the original model; that is, the original model is a correct (sub) model of the transformed model. In addition, application of an omission operator almost always yields a model that is a correct (sub) version of the original model. Thus, omission operators are used to

A

1. $S \rightarrow c\ nt(c)$	12. $nt(p1) \rightarrow x\ nt(x)$
2. $S \rightarrow x\ nt(x)$	13. $nt(p1) \rightarrow p1\ nt(p1)$
3. $nt(c) \rightarrow c\ nt(c)$	14. $nt(p1) \rightarrow \varepsilon$
4. $nt(c) \rightarrow x\ nt(x)$	15. $nt(p2) \rightarrow \varepsilon$
5. $nt(c) \rightarrow p1\ nt(p1)$	**16. $nt(c) \rightarrow p2\ nt(p2)$**
6. $nt(c) \rightarrow \varepsilon$	**17. $nt(x) \rightarrow p1\ nt(p1)$**
7. $nt(x) \rightarrow c\ nt(c)$	**18. $nt(p1) \rightarrow p2\ nt(p2)$**
8. $nt(x) \rightarrow x\ nt(x)$	**19. $nt(p2) \rightarrow c\ nt(c)$**
9. $nt(x) \rightarrow p2\ nt(p2)$	**20. $nt(p2) \rightarrow p1\ nt(p1)$**
10. $nt(x) \rightarrow \varepsilon$	**21. $nt(p2) \rightarrow p2\ nt(p2)$**
11. $nt(p1) \rightarrow c\ nt(c)$	**22. $nt(p2) \rightarrow x\ nt(x)$**

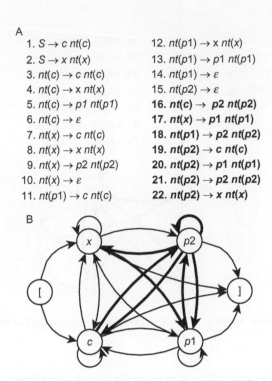

B

FIG. 4. The completion of the tbRG$_1$ in Fig. 2. (A) The resulting tbRG$_1$. (B) The resulting ESG.

omit some specific parts. Marking operators are used to change the type of certain elements in the model.

Considering the elements of a tbRG$_1$ and the fact that we focus on modeling events and their sequences, it makes sense to make use of the following operators that preserve the form of the model and the regularity of the language described by the model:

- Marking: *Mark start (Ms), mark non-start (Mns), mark finish (Mf)* and *mark non-finish (Mnf).*
- Insertion: *Sequence insertion (Is)* and *event insertion (Ie).*
- Omission: *Sequence omission (Os)* and *event omission (Oe).*

2.4.1 Marking Operators

We begin by defining marking operators since these are used by sequence or event manipulation operators to preserve the usefulness of the input $tbRG_1$. Note that some of the markings may not preserve usefulness.

The manipulation operators are defined to mark system events as start, non-start, finish, and non-finish. *Mark start* and *mark finish* operators preserve the usefulness of the input $tbRG_1$, whereas *mark non-start* and *mark non-finish* operators may fail to do so. For the latter two, it is possible to outline usefulness preserving measures. However, we skip these measures because they may involve the direct manipulation of other events in the grammar, for example, while marking an event e as a non-start event, one may have to mark an event other than e as a start event. In the descriptions below, we assume $G=(E, N, P, S)$ is the input $tbRG_1$.

2.4.1.1 Mark Start. The mark start operator relies on insertion of a single production into the grammar.

- Marking an event $e \in E$ as a start event requires the insertion of production $S \rightarrow e\ R_e$, that is, performing $P=P \cup \{S \rightarrow eR_e\}$.
- The language defined by the new grammar is $L(G) \cup \{ex \in E^* | R_e \Rightarrow^* x\ (x \in E^*)\}$, where $L(G)$ is the language defined by the input $tbRG_1$.
- The operation can be performed in $O(|P|)$ steps. However, assuming that production $S \rightarrow e\ R_e$ is not already in the grammar, appending this production takes $O(1)$ time.

2.4.1.2 Mark Finish. The mark finish operator also relies on the insertion of a single production into the grammar.

- Marking an event $e \in E$ as a finish event requires the insertion of production $R_e \rightarrow \varepsilon$, that is, performing $P=P \cup \{R_e \rightarrow \varepsilon\}$.
- The language defined by the new grammar is $L(G) \cup \{xe \in E^* | S \Rightarrow^* xeR_e\ (x \in E^*)\}$, where $L(G)$ is the language defined by the input $tbRG_1$.
- The operation can be performed in $O(|P|)$ steps. However, assuming that production $R_e \rightarrow \varepsilon$ is not already in the grammar, appending this production takes $O(1)$ time.

2.4.1.3 Mark Non-Start. The operator removes a single production from the grammar and it may affect the usefulness of the resulting grammar.

- Marking an event $e \in E$ as a non-start event requires the removal of production $S \rightarrow e\ R_e$, that is, performing $P=P \backslash \{S \rightarrow e\ R_e\}$.

- The language defined by the new grammar is $L(G) \setminus \{ex \in E^* | R_e \Rightarrow^* x \ (x \in E^*)\}$, where $L(G)$ is the language defined by the input tbRG$_1$.
- The operation can be performed in $O(|P|)$ steps.

2.4.1.4 Mark Non-Finish.
The mark non-finish operator also relies on the removal of a single production from the grammar and the resulting grammar may not be useful.

- Marking an event $e \in E$ as a non-finish event requires the removal of production $R_e \to \varepsilon$, that is, performing $P = P \setminus \{R_e \to \varepsilon\}$.
- The language defined by the new grammar is $L(G) \setminus \{xe \in E^* | S \Rightarrow^* xeR_e \ (x \in E^*)\}$, where $L(G)$ is the language defined by the input tbRG$_1$.
- The operation can be performed in $O(|P|)$ steps.

2.4.2 Sequence Manipulation Operators

Sequence manipulation operators are used to insert/omit sequences to/from the model.

2.4.2.1 Sequence Insertion.
Sequence insertion operator introduces a new event sequence to the given model by establishing a connection between two existing events. Due to the form of tbRG$_1$s, it suffices to update the grammar model with a new production rule in order to include the intended sequence. The resulting algorithm is as follows.

Algorithm 2 *Sequence Insertion*

Input: $G = (E, N, P, S)$ – a tbRG$_1$
  (a, b) where $a, b \in E$ – the sequence to be inserted
Output: $G = (E, N, P, S)$ – the updated grammar
  $P = P \cup \{R_a \to b\, R_b\}$ // Add production rule for the sequence (a, b)

Algorithm 2 has $O(1)$ worst case time complexity since sequence insertion assumes that the sequence to be inserted is not already in the model. This check can be performed in $O(|P|)$ time.

In fact, sequence insertion, while connecting two events, adds additional strings into the language defined by the input grammar. The new language is given by $L(G) \cup \{xaby \in E^* | S \Rightarrow^* xaR_a (x \in E^*) \text{ and } R_b \Rightarrow^* y (y \in E^*)\}$, where $L(G)$ is the language defined by the input tbRG$_1$. Note that due to the form of the added rule, the resulting grammar is also a tbRG$_1$. Hence, the operator preserves both the form and the regularity.

Furthermore, given a tbRG$_1$, one can perform $|E|^2 - |P| + (s+f)$ different sequence insertions, where s is the number of productions whose head is S, that is, $S \rightarrow T$, and f is the number of productions whose body is ε, that is, $H \rightarrow \varepsilon$.

Note that a completed tbRG$_1$ is in fact a transformed tbRG$_1$ in which all possible sequence insertions are already performed.

Figure 5 shows the tbRG$_1$ (and its corresponding ESG) resulting from the insertion of sequence $(p2, p1)$ into the tbRG$_1$ in Fig. 2.

2.4.2.2 Sequence Omission.
The sequence omission operator removes an existing connection between two events in the model. Therefore, production rule in the tbRG$_1$ corresponding to this sequence should be removed. In addition, since sequence omission may violate the usefulness of the original

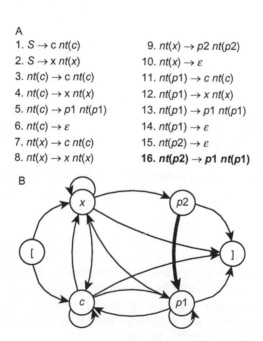

A
1. $S \rightarrow c\ nt(c)$ 9. $nt(x) \rightarrow p2\ nt(p2)$
2. $S \rightarrow x\ nt(x)$ 10. $nt(x) \rightarrow \varepsilon$
3. $nt(c) \rightarrow c\ nt(c)$ 11. $nt(p1) \rightarrow c\ nt(c)$
4. $nt(c) \rightarrow x\ nt(x)$ 12. $nt(p1) \rightarrow x\ nt(x)$
5. $nt(c) \rightarrow p1\ nt(p1)$ 13. $nt(p1) \rightarrow p1\ nt(p1)$
6. $nt(c) \rightarrow \varepsilon$ 14. $nt(p1) \rightarrow \varepsilon$
7. $nt(x) \rightarrow c\ nt(c)$ 15. $nt(p2) \rightarrow \varepsilon$
8. $nt(x) \rightarrow x\ nt(x)$ **16. $nt(p2) \rightarrow p1\ nt(p1)$**

B

FIG. 5. Insertion of sequence $(p2, p1)$ to the tbRG$_1$ in Fig. 2. (A) The resulting tbRG$_1$. (B) The resulting ESG.

tbRG$_1$, additional usefulness preserving operations are performed. Algorithm 3 outlines the effects of a sequence omission on a tbRG$_1$ together with measures to preserve the usefulness of the resulting grammar.

Algorithm 3 Sequence Omission

Input: $G = (E, N, P, S)$ – a tbRG$_1$

   (a, b) where $a, b \in E$ – the sequence to be removed

Output: $G = (E, N, P, S)$ – the updated grammar

   $P = P \setminus \{ R_a \rightarrow b\,R_b \}$ //Remove production rule for the sequence (a, b)

   if $R_a \rightarrow Q \notin P$ for all bodies $Q \neq a\,R_a$ **then**

      $P = P \cup \{ R_a \rightarrow \varepsilon \}$ //Usefulness of a (Part 1: Mark as a finish)

   endif

   if there exists no $S \Rightarrow^* xbR_b$ $(x \in E^*)$ **then**

      $P = P \cup \{ S \rightarrow b\,R_b \}$ //Usefulness of b (Part2: Mark as a start)

   endif

Algorithm 3 runs in $O(|E|+|P|)=O(|P|)$ time because the removal and testing membership of a production rule can both be performed in $O(|P|)$ steps and checking the existence of derivation steps $S \Rightarrow^* xbR_b$ $(x \in E^*)$ can be performed in $O(|E|+|P|)$ time.

After the removal of the rule $R_a \rightarrow b\,R_b$, the grammar may lose usefulness in two ways: (1) Event a may lose usefulness. In this case, derivations starting from S and going through R_a do not terminate, that is, although there exists a derivation of the form $S \Rightarrow^* xaR_a$ $(x \in E^*)$, a derivation of the form $R_a \Rightarrow^* y$ $(y \in E^*)$ does not exist. To preserve the usefulness, a new production rule $R_a \rightarrow \varepsilon$ can be added to the grammar. (2) Event b may also lose usefulness. More precisely, derivations starting from S do not go through R_b, that is, although there exists a derivation of the form $R_b \Rightarrow^* y$ $(y \in E^*)$, a derivation of the form $S \Rightarrow^* xbR_b$ $(x \in E^*)$ does not exist. In this case, to preserve the usefulness, a new production rule of the form $S \rightarrow b\,R_b$ is added.

After the application of a sequence omission operator, the language defined by the resulting grammar becomes $L(G) \setminus \{ w \in L(G) | S \Rightarrow^* xR_a \Rightarrow xbR_b \Rightarrow^* w\ (x \in E^*) \}$, where $L(G)$ is the language defined by the input tbRG$_1$. Of course, in order to preserve usefulness, the new language may also include the sets $\{ xa \in E^* | S \Rightarrow^* xaR_a$ $(x \in E^*) \}$ or $\{ by \in E^* | R_b \Rightarrow^* y\ (y \in E^*) \}$, respectively. In addition, the new language is a regular one, since the obtained grammar is also a tbRG$_1$. Furthermore, the number of different sequence-omitted tbRG$_1$s is given by $|P| - (s+f)$, where s is the number of productions whose head is S and f is the number of productions whose body is ε.

Figure 6 shows the tbRG$_1$ and its corresponding ESG resulting from the omission of sequence $(p1, c)$ from the tbRG$_1$ in Fig. 2.

A
1. $S \rightarrow c\ nt(c)$ 9. $nt(x) \rightarrow p2\ nt(p2)$
2. $S \rightarrow x\ nt(x)$ 10. $nt(x) \rightarrow \varepsilon$
3. $nt(c) \rightarrow c\ nt(c)$ ~~11. $nt(p1) \rightarrow c\ nt(c)$~~
4. $nt(c) \rightarrow x\ nt(x)$ 12. $nt(p1) \rightarrow x\ nt(x)$
5. $nt(c) \rightarrow p1\ nt(p1)$ 13. $nt(p1) \rightarrow p1\ nt(p1)$
6. $nt(c) \rightarrow \varepsilon$ 14. $nt(p1) \rightarrow \varepsilon$
7. $nt(x) \rightarrow c\ nt(c)$ 15. $nt(p2) \rightarrow \varepsilon$
8. $nt(x) \rightarrow x\ nt(x)$

B

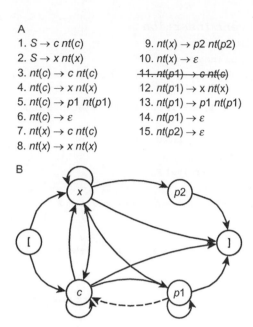

FIG. 6. Omission of sequence $(p1, c)$ from the tbRG$_1$ in Fig. 2. (A) The resulting tbRG$_1$. (B) The resulting ESG.

2.4.3 Event Manipulation Operators

Event manipulation operators are used to insert/omit events to/from the model.

2.4.3.1 Event Insertion.

The event insertion operator adds a new event k to a tbRG$_1$. It is based on sequence insertion because it entails adding a new event to the grammar and connecting it to the others by inserting proper sequences. Naturally, insertion of a new event requires adding a new nonterminal and new production rules for the sequences. Nevertheless, if the usefulness of new event cannot be established, insertion of additional production rules may be required. The steps to update the input tbRG$_1$ with the insertion of a new event are shown in Algorithm 4.

Algorithm 4 Event Insertion

Input: $G = (E, N, P, S)$ – a tbRG$_1$

　　　　e – the event to be inserted

　　　　(e, a_j), where $a_j \in E \cup \{e\}$, $j = 1, \ldots, s$ – the distinct outgoing sequences to be inserted

　　　　(b_k, e), where $b_k \in E$, $k = 1, \ldots, t$ – the distinct ingoing sequences to be inserted

Output: $G = (E, N, P, S)$ – the updated grammar

　$E = E \cup \{e\}$ // Add new event e

　$N = N \cup \{R_e\}$ // Add new nonterminal R_e

　for each (e, a_j) **do**

　　　perform insertion of (e, a_j) on G // See Algorithm 2

　endfor

　for each (b_k, e) **do**

　　　perform insertion of (b_k, e) on G // See Algorithm 2

　endfor

　if $s < 1$ **or** $(s=1$ **and** $a_1 = e)$ **then**

　　　$P = P \cup \{R_e \rightarrow \varepsilon\}$ // Usefulness of e (Part 1: Mark as a finish)

　endif

　if $t < 1$ **then**

　　　$P = P \cup \{S \rightarrow e\,R_e\}$ // Usefulness of e (Part 2: Mark as a start)

　endif

The running time complexity of Algorithm 4 is $O(s+t)$, where s is the number of sequences of the form (e, a_j), called *outgoing sequences*, and t is the number of sequences of the form (b_k, e), called *ingoing sequences*, to be inserted. Note that a looping sequence, that is, (e, e), is considered to be an outgoing sequence and, therefore, $(s+t) \leq 2|E| + 1 = 2(|N|-1)+1$.

Briefly, Algorithm 4 adds new event e to E and the corresponding nonterminal R_e to N. Later, for each sequence to be inserted, a new production is added by the sequence insertion algorithm (Algorithm 2). If the set of outgoing sequences is empty or contains only the looping sequence then $R_e \Rightarrow^* x$ $(x \in E^*)$ does not exist, that is, derivations starting from R_e do not terminate. Thus, the production $R_e \rightarrow \varepsilon$ is added to P. On the other hand, if the set of ingoing sequences is empty, no derivation step of the form $S \Rightarrow^* xeR_e$ $(x \in E^*)$ exists, that is, derivations starting from S do not go through R_e. Therefore, the production $S \rightarrow e\,R_e$ is added to P.

After the event insertion, the language defined by the manipulated grammar includes the words in $\{xaeby \in E^* | S \Rightarrow^* xaR_a$ $(x \in E^*)$ and $R_b \Rightarrow^* y$ $(y \in E^*)\}$, for $a = a_1, \ldots, a_s$ and $b = b_1, \ldots, b_t$, where $L(G)$ is the language defined by the input tbRG$_1$. Naturally, the new language may also include new words ending with event e and/or new words starting with event e to establish usefulness of e. Moreover, insertion operator also preserves regularity, since the resulting grammar is a tbRG$_1$.

The event insertion operator may produce a substantially large number of tbRG$_1$s: Even a single event can be inserted in $2^{2|E|+1}$ different ways.

Figure 7 shows the tbRG$_1$ and its corresponding ESG resulting from the insertion of event d together with $\{(c, d), (x, d), (p1, d)\}$ into the tbRG$_1$ in Fig. 2.

2.4.3.2 *Event Omission.*

The event omission operator removes an existing terminal from a tbRG$_1$. It makes use of sequence omission because, in order to remove an existing event, all the sequences (outgoing and ingoing) related to this event need to be removed. Thus, the proper steps would be to first perform omission of the sequences to remove the corresponding production rules, and then remove the isolated event from the grammar together with the

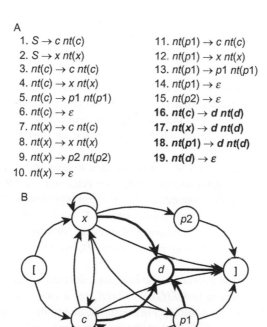

A

1. $S \rightarrow c\ nt(c)$
2. $S \rightarrow x\ nt(x)$
3. $nt(c) \rightarrow c\ nt(c)$
4. $nt(c) \rightarrow x\ nt(x)$
5. $nt(c) \rightarrow p1\ nt(p1)$
6. $nt(c) \rightarrow \varepsilon$
7. $nt(x) \rightarrow c\ nt(c)$
8. $nt(x) \rightarrow x\ nt(x)$
9. $nt(x) \rightarrow p2\ nt(p2)$
10. $nt(x) \rightarrow \varepsilon$
11. $nt(p1) \rightarrow c\ nt(c)$
12. $nt(p1) \rightarrow x\ nt(x)$
13. $nt(p1) \rightarrow p1\ nt(p1)$
14. $nt(p1) \rightarrow \varepsilon$
15. $nt(p2) \rightarrow \varepsilon$
16. $\mathbf{nt(c) \rightarrow d\ nt(d)}$
17. $\mathbf{nt(x) \rightarrow d\ nt(d)}$
18. $\mathbf{nt(p1) \rightarrow d\ nt(d)}$
19. $\mathbf{nt(d) \rightarrow \varepsilon}$

B

FIG. 7. Insertion of event d together with $\{(c, d), (x, d), (p1, d)\}$ to the tbRG$_1$ in Fig. 2. (A) The resulting tbRG$_1$. (B) The resulting ESG.

corresponding nonterminal and the remaining productions. Algorithm 5 accomplishes these tasks.

Algorithm 5 Event Omission

Input: $G = (E, N, P, S)$ - a tbRG$_1$

     e - the event to be omitted

     (e, a_j), where $a_j \in E \cup \{e\}$, $j = 1, \ldots, s$ - the distinct outgoing sequences to be omitted

     (b_k, e), where $b_k \in E$, $k = 1, \ldots, t$ - the distinct ingoing sequences to be omitted

     Output: $G = (E, N, P, S)$ - the updated grammar

       for each (e, a_j) **do**

          perform omission of (e, a_j) on G // See Algorithm 3

       endfor

       for each (b_k, e) **do**

          perform omission of (b_k, e) on G // See Algorithm 3

       endfor

       $P = P \setminus \{S \to e R_e, R_e \to \varepsilon\}$ // Remove productions (Mark as a non-start and non-finish)

       $N = N \setminus \{R_e\}$ // Remove nonterminal symbol R_e

       $E = E \setminus \{e\}$ // Remove event e

Algorithm 5 terminates in $O((s+t) |P| + |E| + |N|)$ steps, where s is the number of sequences of the form (e, a_j), that is, outgoing sequences, and t is the number of sequences of the form (b_k, e), that is, ingoing sequences. Note that a looping sequence is considered to be an outgoing sequence and, thus, $(s+t) \leq 2|E| - 1 = 2(|N| - 1) - 1$.

Algorithm 5 first omits all the sequences related to terminal e, that is, production rules related to event e (and nonterminal R_e) are removed, by subsequent applications of sequence omission operator. After these operations, P contains only two productions related to e. These rules, namely $S \to e R_e$ and $R_e \to \varepsilon$, preserve the usefulness of terminal e. To complete the event omission, it is required to remove productions $S \to e R_e$ and $R_e \to \varepsilon$ from P, nonterminal R_e from N, and terminal e from E.

After an event omission operation, the language defined by the updated grammar does not contain the words in $\{w \in L(G) | S \Rightarrow^* xeR_e \Rightarrow^* w \ (w \in E^*)\}$, where $L(G)$ is the language defined by the input tbRG$_1$. Furthermore, due to the usefulness preserving operations of the sequence omission operator, new words ending with events b_k or starting with events a_j can be included in the resulting language. This language is also regular because the resulting grammar is a tbRG$_1$.

Given a tbRG$_1$, the number of different event omission operations is $|E| = |N| - 1$.

Figure 8 shows the tbRG_1 and its corresponding ESG resulting from the omission of event $p2$ from the tbRG_1 in Fig. 2.

2.4.4   Partial Complement Models via Transformations

As already mentioned, the definition of complement in Section 2.3 is problematic since, given a tbRG_1, its complement is likely to contain non-useful events. It is also possible that the language defined by the complement is empty, that is, $L\left(\overline{tbRG_1}\right) = \emptyset$. Thus, partial complements are used to extend the fault modeling approach to perform more precise and thorough handling of the faults in separate models obtained by the applications of transformation operators and their combinations.

Given a tbRG_1 $G=(E, N, P, S)$, *partial complement of G based on sequence (a, b),* where $a,b \in E$ and $R_a \rightarrow b \; R_b \notin P$ is defined as a tbRG_1 $\overline{G}_{ab} = \left(\overline{E}_{ab}, \overline{N}_{ab}, \overline{P}_{ab}, S\right)$, where

- $\overline{E}_{ab} = \{e \in E \mid R_e \Rightarrow^* xaR_a \; (x \in E^*)\} \cup \{b'\}$, where b' is a new indexed/renamed b event,

A
1. $S \rightarrow c \; nt(c)$
2. $S \rightarrow x \; nt(x)$
3. $nt(c) \rightarrow c \; nt(c)$
4. $nt(c) \rightarrow x \; nt(x)$
5. $nt(c) \rightarrow p1 \; nt(p1)$
6. $nt(c) \rightarrow \varepsilon$
7. $nt(x) \rightarrow c \; nt(c)$
8. $nt(x) \rightarrow x \; nt(x)$

9. ~~$nt(x) \rightarrow p2 \; nt(p2)$~~
10. $nt(x) \rightarrow \varepsilon$
11. $nt(p1) \rightarrow c \; nt(c)$
12. $nt(p1) \rightarrow x \; nt(x)$
13. $nt(p1) \rightarrow p1 \; nt(p1)$
14. $nt(p1) \rightarrow \varepsilon$
15. ~~$nt(p2) \rightarrow \varepsilon$~~

B

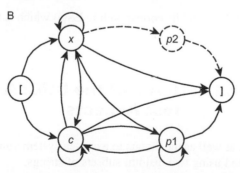

FIG. 8. Omission of event $p2$ from the tbRG_1 in Fig. 2. (A) The resulting tbRG_1. (B) The resulting ESG.

- $\overline{N}_{ab} = \{S\} \cup \{R_e | e \in \overline{E}_{ab}\}$, and
- $\overline{P}_{ab} = \{S \to eR_e \in P | \ e \in \overline{E}_{ab}\} \cup \{R_d \to eR_e \in P | \ d, e \in \overline{E}_{ab}\}$
  $\cup \{R_a \to R_{b'}, R_{b'} \to \varepsilon\}$

Consequently, the language defined by the partial complement is given by $L(\overline{G}_{ab}) = \{xab' | \ S \Rightarrow *xaR_a \ (x \in \overline{E}_{ab}{}^*)\}$. Note that each word in $L(\overline{G}_{ab})$ ends with the same event sequence of length 2. Furthermore, $L(G) \cap L(\overline{G}_{ab}) = \emptyset$.

Algorithm 6 Partial Complement

Input: $G = (E, N, P, S)$ – a tbRG$_1$

    (a, b) – the sequence $(a,b \in E$ and $R_a \to b \, R_b \notin P)$

Output: $G = (E, N, P, S)$ – the updated grammar: the partial complement based on (a, b)

$E = E \cup \{b'\}$, $N = N \cup \{R_{b'}\}$, $P = P \cup \{R_a \to R_{b'}, \, R_{b'} \to \varepsilon\}$

for each $R_e \to \varepsilon \in P$ **do**

    mark event e as non-finish

endfor

for each $e \in E$ such that $R_e \Rightarrow^* xaR_a$ $(x \in E^*)$ does not exist **do**

    omit event e

endfor

$b' = $ a new indexed b event

insert event b' with $\{(a, b')\}$

Algorithm 6 outlines the steps to construct the partial complement of a given tbRG$_1$ based on a sequence. Basically, it runs in $O(|P| + |E| \, (|E| + |P|)) = O(|E||P|)$ time since checking the existence of $R_e \Rightarrow^* xaR_a$ $(x \in E^*)$ can be performed in $O(|E| + |P|)$ steps.

Fig. 9 shows the tbRG$_1$ (and its corresponding ESG) which is the complement of the tbRG$_1$ in Fig. 2 based on $(p2, x)$.

3. Behavioral Patterns of the SUC: Analysis and Test Aspects

System functions, as well as the threats to a chosen system vulnerability attribute, may each be described using two disjoint subsets of strings,

- one belonging to the language $L(M)$ and

A

1. $S \rightarrow c\ nt(c)$	9. $nt(x) \rightarrow p2\ nt(p2)$
2. $S \rightarrow x\ nt(x)$	~~10. $nt(x) \rightarrow \varepsilon$~~
3. $nt(c) \rightarrow c\ nt(c)$	11. $nt(p1) \rightarrow c\ nt(c)$
4. $nt(c) \rightarrow x\ nt(x)$	12. $nt(p1) \rightarrow x\ nt(x)$
5. $nt(c) \rightarrow p1\ nt(p1)$	13. $nt(p1) \rightarrow p1\ nt(p1)$
~~6. $nt(c) \rightarrow \varepsilon$~~	~~14. $nt(p1) \rightarrow \varepsilon$~~
7. $nt(x) \rightarrow c\ nt(c)$	~~15. $nt(p2) \rightarrow \varepsilon$~~
8. $nt(x) \rightarrow c\ nt(c)$	**16. $nt(p2) \rightarrow x2\ nt(x2)$**
	17. $nt(x2) \rightarrow \varepsilon$

B

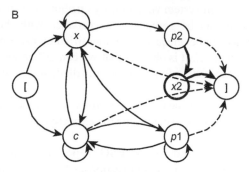

FIG. 9. The partial complement of the $tbRG_1$ in Fig. 2 based on $(p2, x)$. (A) The resulting $tbRG_1$. (B) The resulting ESG.

- another *not* belonging to $L(M)$, respectively,

where M is the system model like a $tbRG_1$ (or an ESG) with event set E.

Legal state transitions are brought about by *desirable* events, leading to symbol sequences belonging to $L(M)$ and specifying system functions. *Illegal* transitions represent the *undesirable* events, leading to faulty symbol sequences not belonging to $L(M)$, signifying breaches to vulnerabilities.

Let us denote the *system functions* as F and *vulnerability threats* as V such that

$$F \subseteq L(M) \quad \text{and} \quad V \subseteq \overline{L(M)}. \tag{2}$$

Note that $L(\overline{M}) \neq \overline{L(M)}$. More precisely, $L(\overline{M}) \subseteq \overline{L(M)}$ (see Section 2.3). Furthermore, some words in $\overline{L(M)}$ are not vulnerability threats because they simply consist of only legal transitions. Therefore, in the following we reformulate the vulnerability threats more precisely using partial complements.

$$V \subseteq \bigcup_{(a\,,\,b)\text{ is illegal}} L(\overline{M}_{ab}) \tag{3}$$

Based on the definition of partial complement, each word in V starts with a start event and ends with undesirable events.

It is important to note that several vulnerability attributes may simultaneously apply to a given application. In this case, F will remain the same in the study of every vulnerability attribute, but V will vary from one vulnerability attribute to another. To avoid mismatching, the relevant threats to each attribute *att* will be identified as V_{att}.

Depending on the chosen system vulnerability attribute, the strings corresponding to vulnerability threats can be grouped in accordance with their length n. This assumes that all threats can be unequivocally identified by patterns of n consecutive symbols, that is, strings, of E. It is obvious that we can utilize the grammar G, or its RE R, to *test* whether the system functions are fulfilled, and/or vulnerability threats occur.

While testing a system by means of *test cases*, one generally has to produce meaningful test *inputs* and then to determine the expected system *outputs* upon these inputs.

Terminals of a tbRG$_1$ (or nodes of an ESG) represent events that interact with the system, leading eventually to system responses that are desirable behaviors in compliance with the user's expectation, as specified by F. Thus, each production of the tbRG$_1$ (or each edge of an ESG) represents a pair of subsequent legal events, which we call a *legal event pair*, or briefly, an *event pair* (*EP*), for example, $nt(x) \rightarrow p2\ nt(p2)$ or $(x,\ p2)$ in Fig. 4. A sequence of n consecutive productions (or edges) represents a sequence of $n+1$ elements that we refer to as an *event sequence* (*ES*) *of length* $n+1$. An ES represents an *event triple* (*ETr*) if $n=3$, *event quadruple* (*EQr*) if $n=4$, etc.

An ES is *complete* if it starts at a start event and ends at a finish event; in this case we have a *complete ES* (*CES*). Figuratively speaking, a CES realizes a *walk* through the model and once arrived at the exit, a desirable behavior is observed. Thus, the set of the CESs specifies the system function F as introduced in Eq. (3); in other words, the CESs are the words of the language defined by the tbRG$_1$ that models the system.

As an analogy to the notion of EP as productions of a tbRG$_1$, we introduce *faulty event pairs* (*FEP*) as the productions of the corresponding $\overline{tbRG}_1$ (or the edges of the corresponding $\overline{ESG}$), for example, $nt(p2) \rightarrow p2\ nt(p2)$ or $(p2, p2)$ in Fig. 4. Further, each EP of the CtbRG$_1$ can be extended to an *illegal*, or, *faulty event triple* (*FETr*) by adding a subsequent FEP to this EP, for example, $(x, p2)$ and $(p2, p2)$ of Fig. 4, resulting in $(x, p2, p2)$. Thus, a FETr consists of three consecutive events while the last two constitute a FEP. Accordingly, a *faulty event quadruple* (*FEQr*) consists of four consecutive events last two of which constitute a FEP, etc. Generally, an *illegal*, or, a *faulty event sequence* (*FES*) of length n consists of $n-1$ events that form a (legal) ES of length $n-1$ and a concluding, subsequent FEP.

Based on the FEPs, we can systematically construct *faulty event sequences* (*FESs*) as elements of V (vulnerability breaches) as follows (see Fig. 3).

- FEPs that start at the entry of the ESG are complete test inputs.
- FEPs that do not start at the entry are not executable. To exercise such FEPs, the corresponding ESs that start at the entry and end at the first symbol of such FEPs will be generated as their prefixes.

Either way, we then have executable *complete faulty* (or *illegal*), *event sequences* (*CFES*) of different lengths. Note that the attribute "complete" within the phrase CFES expresses only the fact that an FEP might have been "completed" by means of an ES as a prefix to make this FEP executable (otherwise it is not complete, that is, not executable). Thus, a CFES will be used as a test sequence, transferring the system into an undesirable or a faulty state (*fault injection*) and, supposedly, invoking a fault detection/correction procedure, provided that an appropriate *exception handling* mechanism has been implemented [34,35].

We can summarize the concepts of EPs, FEPs, ESs, CESs, and CFESs as follows. Given a tbRG$_1$ $G=(E, N, P, S)$:

- A legal EP is of the form ab such that $a,b \in E$ and $S \Rightarrow^* E^* abR \Rightarrow^* w$, where $R \in N$ and $w \in L(G)$. We say that ab *is in* G, if it is a legal EP.
- An illegal EP or FEP is of the form ab such that $a,b \in E$ and there does not exist any derivation $S \Rightarrow^* E^* abR$, where $R \in N$. We say that ab *is not in* G, if it is an FEP.
- A legal ES of length k $(k \geq 1)$ is of the form $e_1 \ldots e_k$ such that $e_1 \ldots e_k \in E$ and $S \Rightarrow^* E^* e_1 \ldots e_k R \Rightarrow^* w$, where $R \in N$ and $w \in L(G)$. We say that $e_1 \ldots e_k$ *is in* G, if it is a legal ES.
- A CES is a word in $L(G)$.
- A CFES is of the form $xab \notin L(G)$ such that ab is a FEP, and $x \in E^*$ and $S \Rightarrow^* xaR_a \Rightarrow^* w$, where $R \in N$ and $w \in L(G)$.

3.1   Coverage Criteria

To systematize the test process and judge the efficiency of the test sequences, and thus to determine when to stop testing, some criteria are needed [36]. Since our methodology includes covering legal and illegal behaviors, we define two sets of coverage criteria for tbRG$_1$s.

3.1.1   Coverage Criteria for Testing of System Functions

First, we define two straightforward event-based coverage criteria, that is, event and event pair coverage. Later, we define k-sequence coverage criterion by generalization of the first two.

Given a tbRG$_1$ $G = (E, N, P, S)$, a set of test sequences $A \subseteq L(G)$ is said to cover an event e in G, if e appears at least in one of the test sequences in A. If the set of test sequences A covers all events in G, then it is said to achieve *event coverage*.

Given a tbRG$_1$ $G = (E, N, P, S)$, a set of test sequences $A \subseteq L(G)$ is said to cover an EP ab in G, if ab appears at least in one of the test sequences in A. If the set of test sequences A covers all EPs in G, then it is said to achieve *event pair coverage*.

Note that achieving EP coverage does not necessarily mean that all events are covered, because there might be some events which cannot be included in any event pairs. However, a set of test sequences that is generated by covering all the productions of a given tbRG$_1$ achieves both event and EP coverage. Thus, EP coverage criterion is weaker than production rule coverage criterion. It is possible to generalize the coverage of ESs of length k ($k \geq 1$) as follows.

Given a tbRG$_1$ $G = (E, N, P, S)$, a set of test sequences $A \subseteq L(G)$ is said to cover an ES of fixed length k (or a k-sequence) ($k \geq 1$) $e_1 \dots e_k$ in G, if $e_1 \dots e_k$ appears in a test sequence in A. If the set of test sequences A covers all ESs of length k ($k \geq 1$) in G, then it is said to achieve *k-sequence coverage*.

Consequently, 1-sequence coverage corresponds to event coverage and 2-sequence coverage is in fact EP coverage. Also, note that k-sequence coverage is not always stronger for increasing value of k, that is, for $k \geq 1$, $k+1$-sequence coverage does not completely subsume k-sequence coverage. This stems from the fact that a test set achieving k-sequence coverage may fail to cover some sequences of smaller length, that is, $<k$. If a sequence of length $<k$ cannot be included in longer sequences, it means that it is, by itself, a word in the language defined by the grammar. Thus, to accomplish a complete subsumption, one should single out such sequences and include them separately.

3.1.2   Coverage Criteria for Testing Vulnerability Threats

The following coverage criteria are defined to assess the adequacy of tests for vulnerability threats.

Given a tbRG$_1$ $G = (E, N, P, S)$, a set of CFESs A is said to cover an FEP ab, if ab appears at least in one of the test sequences in A. If the set of test sequences A covers all possible FEPs, then it is said to achieve *faulty event pair coverage*.

FEPs are generally covered by including them in CFESs, and there are different ways to choose such CFESs. For example, one can cover FEPs using shortest derivations to generate prefix ESs and construct minimized CFESs.

Given a tbRG$_1$ $G = (E, N, P, S)$ and a set of CFESs A achieving FEP coverage, A is said to achieve *shortest complete faulty event sequence coverage*, if for each test sequence $xab \in A$, where $x \in E^*$ and $a,b \in E$, there exists no $y \in E^*$ such that $S \Rightarrow^* yaR_a$ with $|y| < |x|$ and there is no other test sequence in A covering ab.

Shortest CFES coverage guarantees that, for each FEP, a shortest ES starting at a start event is used to complete it to a CFES. However, this is not always desired. It is also possible that one would like to cover all possible k-sequences (leading to the FEP) before exercising the FEP itself. In this case, the following criterion can be used.

Given a tbRG$_1$ $G = (E, N, P, S)$ and a set of CFESs A achieving FEP coverage, let ab be an FEP, b' be the single finish event in the partial complement tbRG$_1$ $\overline{G}_{ab}$ and $A_{ab} = \{xab' |\ xab \in A$, where $x \in E^*\}$. A is said to achieve *k-sequence faulty event pair coverage for FEP ab*, if A_{ab} achieves k-sequence coverage for $\overline{G}_{ab}$. Furthermore, A is said to achieve *k-sequence faulty event pair coverage* if it achieves k-sequence faulty event pair coverage for all FEPs.

The use of k-sequence FEP coverage makes sense, only if one expects a faulty behavior to be visible only after execution of some specific k-sequence in the tbRG$_1$.

3.2 Test Generation

This section outlines algorithms to generate test sequences achieving k-sequence ($k \geq 2$) coverage, shortest CFES coverage and k-sequence ($k \geq 2$) FEP coverage criteria.

3.2.1 Test Generation for Testing System Functions

In order to generate test sequences achieving k-sequence coverage, tbRG$_k$s can be used. Before giving the complete test generation algorithm, we discuss transformation of a given tbRG$_1$ to the corresponding tbRG$_k$.

Algorithm 7 shows the steps to transform a tbRG$_k$ to the corresponding tbRG$_{k+1}$.

Algorithm 7 Sequence Transformation

```
Input: G_k = (E, N, P, S) - a tbRG_k
Output: G_{k+1} = (E_{k+1}, N_{k+1}, P_{k+1}, S) - the corresponding tbRG_{k+1}
  E_{k+1} = ∅, N_{k+1} = {S}, P_{k+1} = ∅
  for each A ∈ P do
    if A = R_q → r R_r where q = q(1)...q(k) and r = r(1)...r(k) then
```

```
        E_{k+1} = E_{k+1} ∪ {qr(k)}
        N_{k+1} = N_{k+1} ∪ {R_{qr(k)}}
    endif
    for each B ∈ P do
        if B = R_r → s R_s where s = s(1)...s(k) then
            if A = R_q → r R_r then
                P_{k+1} = P_{k+1} ∪ {R_{qr(k)} → rs(k) R_{rs(k)}}
            else if A = S → r R_r then
                P_{k+1} = P_{k+1} ∪ {S → rs(k) R_{rs(k)}}
            else if A = R_s → ε then
                P_{k+1} = P_{k+1} ∪ {R_{rs(k)} → ε}
            endif
        endif
    endfor
endfor
```

Algorithm 7 runs in $O(k \ |P|^2)$ worst case time. All set union operations can be performed in $O(1)$ time as append operations, due to the fact that during each respective union operation, a different element is added to the corresponding set. Also, construction of an ES in the new grammar, for example, "$rs(k)$," can be performed in $O(k)$ steps. However, it is still possible to achieve $O(|P|^2)$ running time if the overwriting of the terminal strings of the input tbRG$_k$ is allowed, that is, instead of creating new $(k+1)$-sequences (or terminal strings) by copying and merging the existing k-sequences and 1-sequences in $O(k)$ time, 1-sequences can be appended at the end of the existing k-sequences in $O(1)$ time.

In fact, the transformation of a tbRG$_k$ to the corresponding tbRG$_{k+1}$ can be performed more efficiently if the original tbRG$_k$ is available during transformation. One can use the tbRG$_k$ to extract k-sequences and the tbRG$_1$ (instead of tbRG$_k$) to find out 1-sequences, that is, events, for construction of new $(k+1)$-sequences and the productions in the tbRG$_{k+1}$.

The performance difference can be seen as follows: Let $G_1=(E_1, N_1, P_1, S)$ be the original tbRG$_1$ and $G_k=(E_k, N_k, P_k, S)$ be the corresponding tbRG$_k$, the runtime complexity of Algorithm 7 is $O(k \ |P_k|^2)=O(k \ |P_1|^{2k})$ since $|P_k|= O(|P_1|^k)$. However, if tbRG$_1$ is available and used during the transformation, the runtime complexity can be reduced to $O(k \ |P_k| \ |P_1|)=O(k \ |P_1|^{k+1})$. Furthermore, if the corruption of the input tbRG$_k$ is allowed, the complexity further reduces to $O(|P_1|^{k+1})$. We shall skip the details of the algorithm due to its similarity to Algorithm 7.

Fig. 10 shows the tbRG$_2$ resulting from sequence transformation of the tbRG$_1$ in Fig. 2 using Algorithm 7. Note that "$:$" is used to separate the individual events in the productions of the tbRG$_2$.

1. $S \rightarrow c{:}c\ nt(c{:}c)$	14. $nt(c{:}x) \rightarrow \varepsilon$	27. $nt(x{:}p2) \rightarrow \varepsilon$
2. $S \rightarrow c{:}x\ nt(c{:}x)$	15. $nt(c{:}p1) \rightarrow p1{:}c\ nt(p1{:}c)$	28. $nt(p1{:}c) \rightarrow c{:}c\ nt(c{:}c)$
3. $S \rightarrow c{:}p1\ nt(c{:}p1)$	16. $nt(c{:}p1) \rightarrow p1{:}x\ nt(p1{:}x)$	29. $nt(p1{:}c) \rightarrow c{:}x\ nt(c{:}x)$
4. $S \rightarrow x{:}c\ nt(x{:}c)$	17. $nt(c{:}p1) \rightarrow p1{:}p1\ nt(p1{:}p1)$	30. $nt(p1{:}c) \rightarrow c{:}p1\ nt(c{:}p1)$
5. $S \rightarrow x{:}x\ nt(x{:}x)$	18. $nt(c{:}p1) \rightarrow \varepsilon$	31. $nt(p1{:}c) \rightarrow \varepsilon$
6. $S \rightarrow x{:}p2\ nt(x{:}p2)$	19. $nt(x{:}c) \rightarrow c{:}c\ nt(c{:}c)$	32. $nt(p1{:}x) \rightarrow x{:}c\ nt(x{:}c)$
7. $nt(c{:}c) \rightarrow c{:}c\ nt(c{:}c)$	20. $nt(x{:}c) \rightarrow c{:}x\ nt(c{:}x)$	33. $nt(p1{:}x) \rightarrow x{:}x\ nt(x{:}x)$
8. $nt(c{:}c) \rightarrow c{:}x\ nt(c{:}x)$	21. $nt(x{:}c) \rightarrow c{:}p1\ nt(c{:}p1)$	34. $nt(p1{:}x) \rightarrow x{:}p2\ nt(x{:}p2)$
9. $nt(c{:}c) \rightarrow c{:}p1\ nt(c{:}p1)$	22. $nt(x{:}c) \rightarrow \varepsilon$	35. $nt(p1{:}x) \rightarrow \varepsilon$
10. $nt(c{:}c) \rightarrow \varepsilon$	23. $nt(x{:}x) \rightarrow x{:}c\ nt(x{:}c)$	36. $nt(p1{:}p1) \rightarrow p1{:}c\ nt(p1{:}c)$
11. $nt(c{:}x) \rightarrow x{:}c\ nt(x{:}c)$	24. $nt(x{:}x) \rightarrow x{:}x\ nt(x{:}x)$	37. $nt(p1{:}p1) \rightarrow p1{:}x\ nt(p1{:}x)$
12. $nt(c{:}x) \rightarrow x{:}x\ nt(x{:}x)$	25. $nt(x{:}x) \rightarrow x{:}p2\ nt(x{:}p2)$	38. $nt(p1{:}p1) \rightarrow p1{:}p1\ nt(p1{:}p1)$
13. $nt(c{:}x) \rightarrow x{:}p2\ nt(x{:}p2)$	26. $nt(x{:}x) \rightarrow \varepsilon$	39. $nt(p1{:}p1) \rightarrow \varepsilon$

FIG. 10. The corresponding tbRG$_2$ of the tbRG$_1$ in Fig. 2.

Let G_{k-1} be a tbRG$_{k-1}$ ($k \geq 2$) and G_k be the grammar resulting from the transformation of G_{k-1}. Given Algorithm 7, G_k is a tbRG$_k$, where $\varepsilon \notin L(G_k)$, and for all $w \in L(G_k)$ we have

1. $|w| = l\ k$ for some integer $l \geq 1$, and
2. $w(i)(2) \ldots w(i)(k) = w(i+1)(1) \ldots w(i+1)(k-1)$, where $w = w(1) \ldots w(l)$ and $w(i)$ are (disjoint) consequent ESs of length k.

Given a string s whose length is $\geq k$, Algorithm 8 can be applied to transform s into $T(s)$ for which the above properties hold, and $T(s)$ can be obtained in $O(k + k\,(|s| - k)) = O(|s|\ k)$ time, $|s|$ being length of the input string.

Algorithm 8 T(s) - Transformation of a String

Input: s - a string of length $\geq k$
Output: s' - the transformed string of length $\geq lk$

```
l = length(s)
s' is a string of length k + k*(l-k)
s'(1)...s'(k) = s(1)...s(k)
for i=k+1 to l
    d = (i-k)*k
    s'(d+1)...s'(d+k-1)s'(d+k) = s'(d-k+2)...s'(d)s(i)
endfor
```

Naturally, it is also possible to perform an inverse transformation on a string s, which satisfies above-mentioned properties. To do this, Algorithm 9, $T^{-1}(s)$, can be applied. Algorithm has the worst case time complexity of $O(k + |s|/\ k)$.

Algorithm 9 T⁻¹(s) – *Inverse Transformation of a String*

Input: *s* – a string of length *xk* where integer *x* ≥ 1
Output: *s'* – the transformed strings of length *k*+ *x* - 1
  l = *k* + *length(s)/k* - 1
  s' is a string of length *l*
  s'(1)...s'(k) = *s(1)...s(k)*
  for *i=k+1* **to** *l*
    d = *(i-k)*k*
    s'(i) = *s(d+k)*
  endfor

For example, the word $w = c\,p1\,p1\,p1\,p1\,x$ is in the language described by the $tbRG_2$ in Fig. 10 and it is generated using Rules 3, 17, 37, and 35. When it is transformed using Algorithm 9, $v = c\,p1\,p1\,x$ is obtained. Note that v is in the language described by the $tbRG_1$ in Fig. 2. In this example, w and all the words generated using the $tbRG_2$ in Fig. 10 are also in the language described by the original $tbRG_1$, though, in general, not all the words in the language described by a $tbRG_2$ are also in the language described by its original $tbRG_1$. Therefore, the application of Algorithm 9 is necessary.

In order to generate test sequences achieving k-sequence coverage for a given $tbRG_1$, the following result is needed. Let $G = (E, N, P, S)$ be $tbRG_1$ and A be a set of test sequences. Furthermore, let $G_k = (E_k, N_k, P_k, S)$ be the $tbRG_k$ obtained by repeated $k-1$ applications of Algorithm 7 on G and $T(A)$ be the set which is obtained by the application of Algorithm 8 on A, that is, $T(A) = \{T(s) | s \in A\}$:

1. $k+1$-sequence coverage for grammar G is achievable if and only if $L(G_k)$ contains at least one string of length $\geq 2k$, and
2. A achieves $k+1$-sequence coverage for grammar G if and only if $T(A)$ achieves 2-sequence coverage for grammar G_k.
3. A achieves $k+1$-sequence coverage for grammar G if $T(A)$ achieves production rule coverage for grammar G_k.

Note that (2) above is stronger than (3). It entails coverage of only a subset of production rules depending on the $tbRG_1$, because sometimes coverage of some productions does not lead to the generation of additional EPs. However, since the selection of this specific subset of productions requires additional effort, (2) is also harder to use than (3). For this reason, here, we use (3) to construct an algorithm for generation of test sequences achieving k-sequence coverage.

Algorithm 10 uses Algorithm 7 to transform $tbRG_k$, an external production rule-covering algorithm to generate a set of strings, and Algorithm 9 to perform inverse transformations on these generated strings. Thus, based on the result given above, it generates a set of test sequences that achieves k-sequence coverage for the given $tbRG_1$.

Algorithm 10 Test Generation to Achieve k-sequence Coverage

```
Input: G = (E, N, P, S) - a tbRG₁
       k - an integer ≥ 2
Output: A - a set of strings which achieves k-sequence coverage for G
   A = ∅
   G_{k-1} = G
   for i=2 to k-1
       G_{k-1} = transform G_{k-1} (using G) //See Algorithm 7 (and related discussion)
   endfor
   A' = generate a string set achieving production rule coverage for G_{k-1}
   for each s' ∈ A' such that |s'| ≥ 2k do
       A = A ∪ T⁻¹(s') //See Algorithm 9 for T⁻¹(.)
   endfor
```

The test sequences generated by Algorithm 10 are CESs. It is possible to perform some optimizations by covering each production a minimum number of times while generating a string set achieving production rule coverage. For example, algorithms to solve the Chinese Postman Problem (CPP) over directed graphs, like in Refs. [37–39], can be adapted to $tbRG_k$s (or $tbRG_k$s can be converted to ESGs and CPP can be solved over these ESGs). In this way, each production is covered a minimum number of times resulting in an optimized set of test sequences. However, one should note that optimization algorithms tend to require more resources in terms of both time and space. Thus, algorithms such as those in Refs. [40–42] can also be used to generate relatively short but generally nonoptimized strings from a given grammar, while using less resources.

No matter which type of method is used to cover productions in a grammar, performance of Algorithm 10 quickly declines with increasing k. The running time complexity is given by $O(|P|^{k-1}+C_P(|E|, |N|, |P|, k-1)+C_T(|E|, |N|, |P|, k-1))$, where $O(|P|^{k-1})$ is the runtime complexity of performing $k-1$ consecutive transformations using the original $tbRG_1$ is available, $C_P(|E|, |P|, k-1)$ is the runtime complexity of generating a set of strings achieving production rule coverage for G_{k-1} and $C_T(|E|, |N|, |P|, k-1)$ is the runtime complexity of inverse transforming these strings to obtain test sequences. Generally, $C_P(|E|, |N|, |P|, k-1)$ is the dominant term and it is at least $O(|P|^{k-1})$ because the number of productions in G_{k-1} is $O(|P|^{k-1})$. Since there is no detailed runtime analysis for most of the well-known grammar-based sentence generation algorithms in the literature, we assume that the runtime complexity of Algorithm 10 is $O(|P|^{c(k-1)})$ for some $c \geq 1$. For example, if minimization is performed by solving the CPP, this complexity roughly becomes $O(|E|^{3(k-1)})=O(|P|^{3(k-1)})$ [6].

When Algorithm 10 is executed on the tbRG$_1$ in Fig. 2 with $k=2$, no transformation of the grammar is necessary. One can obtain the following set of test sequences $\{c\,x\,x\,p2, x, c\,p1, c\,c, c\,p1\,x\,c\,p1\,c\,p1\,p1, c, x\}$ which achieves 2-sequence coverage. Furthermore, if $k=3$ is used, the tbRG$_1$ is transformed once to obtain the tbRG$_2$ in Fig. 10 and this tbRG$_2$ is used to generate test sequences. The following is an example of test sequence achieving 3-sequence coverage: $\{c\,c, x\,x, c\,p1\,p1\,c\,p1\,x$ $x\,c\,c\,x, x\,p2, c\,x\,x\,p2, x\,c, c\,p1, c\,p1\,c, x\,c\,p1\,p1\,p1\,x, x\,c\,x\,p2, c\,p1\,p1, c\,x\,c, c\,p1\,c\,c\,c$ $p1\,c\,x, x\,x\,x, c\,p1\,x\,p2, c\,p1\,x\,c, c\,c\}$.

3.2.2 Test Generation for Testing Vulnerability Threats

Given a tbRG$_1$, the generation of CFESs achieving shortest CFES coverage is based on the computation of shortest derivations from the start symbol to each event in the grammar and completing ESs obtained from these derivations with FEPS. Algorithm 11 outlines the steps to generate such CFESs.

Algorithm 11 Test Generation to Achieve Shortest CFES Coverage

Input: $G = (E, N, P, S)$ – a tbRG$_1$
Output: A – a set of strings which achieves shortest CFES coverage for G

  $A = \emptyset$
  for each $a \in E$ **do**
    compute $S \Rightarrow^* x a R_a$ $(w \in E^*)$ such that $|xa|$ is minimum
    for each $b \in E$ such that $R_a \rightarrow b\,R_b \notin P$ **do**
      $A = A \cup \{xab\}$
    endfor
  endfor

The runtime complexity of Algorithm 11 is $O(|E|\,((|E|+|P|)+(|E||P|)))=O(|E|^2|P|)$, because each shortest derivation can be computed in $O(|E|+|P|)$ time using breadth-first search algorithm.

In addition, to generate CFESs achieving k-sequence FEP coverage, one can use partial complement models so that, first, all possible k-sequences are executed, and then the FEPs are exercised. Of course, for each FEP the set of executable k-sequences may be different and it is a subset of all k-sequences in the original tbRG$_1$. Algorithm 12 outlines the steps to generate CFES achieving k-sequence FEP coverage for a given tbRG$_1$.

The following set of test sequences are obtained from the tbRG$_1$ in Fig. 2 using Algorithm 11 and it achieves shortest CFES coverage: $\{x\,p1, c, p2, x\,p2\,x, x\,p2\,c,$ $x\,p2\,p2, x\,p2\,p1, c\,p1\,p2\}$.

Algorithm 12 Test Generation to Achieve k-sequence FEP
Coverage

Input: $G = (E, N, P, S)$ – a tbRG$_1$
 k – an integer ≥ 2
Output: A – a set of strings which achieves k-sequence FEP Coverage for G
 $A = \emptyset$
 for each $a \in E$ **do**
  for each $b \in E$ such that $R_a \rightarrow b\, R_b \notin P$ **do**
   Gc = clone G
   Gc = create partial complement of Gc based on (a,b) // Algorithm 6
   B = generate test sequences achieving k-sequence coverage for Gc
   // Algorithm 10
   b' = the single finish event of Gc (a new indexed version of b in Gc)
   Replace each b' with b in all the strings in B
   $A = A \cup B$
  endfor
 endfor

To calculate the runtime complexity of Algorithm 12, one should note that checking membership of a production can be performed in $O(|P|)$ time, cloning the input tbRG$_1$ takes $O(|E|+|N|+|P|)$ *steps, creation of a partial complement has* $O(|E|\,|P|)$ *time* complexity, generation of test sequence achieving k-sequence coverage can be performed in $O(|P|^{c(k-1)})$ for some $c \geq 1$ (which is determined depending on the algorithm used to cover the productions of the corresponding tbRG$_{k-1}$ of G), and set union operation can be performed in $O(|B|) = O(|P|)$ time. Therefore, Algorithm 12 terminates in $O(|E|^2\,|P|^{c(k-1)})$ steps for some $c \geq 1$ (see the discussion of Algorithm 10).

3.3 Remarks on the Test Process

Having outlined the coverage criteria and test generation algorithms, we can summarize the *test process* as follows:

- Construct a set of test cases composed of CESs that achieve k-sequence coverage $(k \geq 2)$ to represent *desirable* behaviors for testing of system functions.
- Construct a set of test cases composed of CFESs and achieving shortest CFES or k-sequence $(k \geq 2)$ FEP coverage to exercise *undesirable* behaviors for testing of vulnerability threats.
- Execute CESs and CFESs on the SUC.

- Observe the system output that enables a unique decision whether the output leads to a desirable system response or an undesirable (faulty) event occurs.

A major problem is the determination of correct (that is, desirable) and faulty (that is, undesirable) states (*Oracle Problem* [43]). Our approach exploits the fact that CESs do present the meaningful, expected system behavior, and CFESs do represent unexpected system behavior.

In order to perform some length-based optimizations one can use the following strategy.

- Insert a single entry point and a single exit point into a given tbRG$_1$ model of the SUC respectively by using pseudo start and pseudo finish events.
- Using Algorithm 10, generate CESs by covering all the productions of the corresponding tbRG$_k$ a minimal number of times (including the productions related to the inserted pseudo start and finish events).
- Using Algorithm 11, generate CFESs including the pseudo start event in each FCES.

Then, the generated CESs cover all k-sequences ($k \geq 2$) and CFESs achieves shortest CFES coverage keeping the total lengths of the CFESs and CFESs minimal, respectively. (Also see Ref. [10])

The determination and specification of the CESs and CFESs should ideally be carried out during the definition of the user requirements, prior to system implementation. They are then a part of the system specification and test specification. Nevertheless, CESs and CFESs can also be incrementally produced at any later time, even during the testing stage, in order to improve the test process. The generation of the CESs, EPs, CFESs, FEPs, etc., can also be based on ESGs or on REs [33], whichever is more convenient for the system analyst and/or the test engineer.

4. Ordering the Vulnerability Risks, Countermeasures

The vulnerability threats constitute only a part of the specification of system vulnerability. Such threats are often related to the system state. If a representation based on purely ESGs were used, it would be necessary to refer to states indirectly in terms of a subset of the words in $L(M)$, where M is the system model (like a tbRG$_1$ or an ESG with event set E), for example, using REs. However, since our representation is based on tbRG$_1$s, nonterminals of the grammar can be used directly to refer to states. Note that a single nonterminal corresponds to a single state whereas a single state may correspond to multiple nonterminals.

Thus, for a given tbRG$_1$ $M=(E, N, P, S)$, a *vulnerability risk ordering relation* $\sqsubseteq$ is defined on $N \times N$ as follows

$$\sqsubseteq = \{(s_1, s_2) | s_1, s_2 \in N \quad \text{and} \quad rl(s_1) \leq rl(s_2)\} \subseteq N \times N, \tag{4}$$

where $rl(s)$ is the risk level associated with state s. In other words, given two states s_1 and s_2, $s_1 \sqsubseteq s_2$ is true if and only if risk level of s_1 with respect to the chosen system vulnerability is known to be less than or equal to the risk level of s_2 [44]. In this context, *risk level* quantifies the *"degree of the un*acceptability*"* of an event on the grounds of hazardousness, that is, exposure to breaches of safety.

The risk ordering relation $\sqsubseteq$ is intended as a guide to decision making upon the detection of a threat, whether internal or external, and on how to react to it. The required response to breaches of vulnerability needs to be specified in terms of a *defense matrix D*, which is a partial function from $N \times V_{FEP}$ to N, where V_{FEP} is the set of all FEPs representing vulnerabilities. The defense matrix utilizes the risk ordering relation to revert the system state from its current one to a less, or the least, risky state. In this sense, D is defined as follows:

$$D: N \times V_{FEP} \to N \quad \text{and}$$
$$\forall s_1, s_2, v \text{ such that } (s_1, v) \in \text{domain(D)} \wedge D(s_1, v) = s_2 \Rightarrow s_2 \sqsubseteq s_1 \tag{5}$$

The above definition expresses the requirement that, should it encounter the vulnerability v in the state s_1, the system must be brought down to a state s_2 which is of a lower risk level than s_1. The means by which this is brought about is called an *exception handler*, or a defensive action, which is an appropriate enforced sequence of events. If x is a defense action appropriate for the scenario implicit in Eq. (5). above, then $D(s_1, x)=s_2$. The actual definition of the defense matrix and the appropriate set X of *exception handlers* is the responsibility of a domain expert specializing in the risks to a given vulnerability.

In order to ease the construction of the defense matrix, it is possible to make use of risk graphs that partially associate risk levels of functional and vulnerability states.

Given tbRG$_1$ $M=(E, N, P, S)$, let each partial complement of M based on (a, b) be $\overline{M}_{ab} = (\overline{G}_{ab}, \overline{N}_{ab}, \overline{P}_{ab}, S)$. The risk graph of M is a tuple $(N_h, \sqsubseteq_h)$, where N_h is the set of *holistic states (or nonterminals)* and $\sqsubseteq_h$ is the *holistic risk ordering relation* defined as follows:

$$N_h = N \underset{(a,b) \text{ is illegal}}{\cup} \overline{N}_{ab}$$
$$\sqsubseteq_h = \{(s_1, s_2) | s_1, s_2 \in N_h \quad \text{and} \quad rl(s_1) \leq rl(s_2)\} \subseteq N_h \times N_h. \tag{6}$$

By making use of the risk graph, one can build and use the defense matrix more easily and determine more efficient exception handlers. Of course, while creating the risk graph, the defense matrix and the exception handlers, one should always consider the underlying semantics of the SUC.

Finally, the *model* of an application *defended* against vulnerabilities is defined as

$$M_d = (E, N, P, S, V, \sqsubseteq, D, X), \tag{7}$$

where E, N, P, and S are the elements of the tbRG$_1$, V is the set of vulnerability threats, $\sqsubseteq$ is the risk ordering relation, D is the defense matrix and X is the set of exception handlers.

A specific benefit of risk ordering in our framework is that it allows a more systematic approach to selection of test cases by focusing on (one or more) particular vulnerability attributes.

5. Case Study

This section illustrates the use of the approach outlined in this chapter in the area of safety critical systems, using an example that considers a railway level crossing (Fig. 11).

5.1 SUC

Railway crossings, found across minor roads outside towns, normally consist of a pair of gates and two traffic lights: red and green, and also a railway signaling system to control the train movement in the proximity of the crossing, though the latter is ignored here as a simplification. Note that in this model the human is a part of the system environment, for example, as driver, gate controller, etc. Our holistic approach enables the consideration of the driver's expected, that is, correct, as well as the faulty behavior. Despite its simplicity, the example is sufficiently expressive for our purpose. Note, however, that our discussion is based on an ordinary familiarity of the application and, therefore, our representation may not be quite accurate from a specialist's point of view.

A tbRG$_1$ (and its corresponding ESG) model of such a crossing is shown in Fig. 12. The set of input signals (or events) E are (as mentioned in Section 2) partitioned into the subsets E_{sys} and E_{env} with

- $E_{sys} = \{r, g, c, o\}$ as *system signals* and
- $E_{env} = \{v, t\}$ as *environmental events* as detected by a system that monitors the crossing.

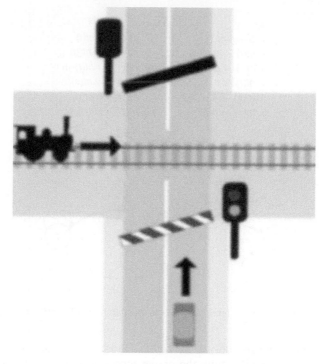

FIG. 11. Simplified railway crossing.

Here r denotes the event of turning traffic signals to red, g the turning of traffic signals to green, c the closing the gate barring vehicle traffic, as well as other road users, from using the crossing, o the opening the gate allowing vehicle traffic through, t a train passing the crossing, and v for a vehicle using the crossing. These events bring about hazardous states posing different risks to road users and rail users alike. The nature of these hazards varies from state to state, some posing greater threats than others. For example, compared to the safest possible state $nt(r)$ (traffic lights being red), the state $nt(o)$ (an opened gate) carries a greater risk since the road users are now free to cross the junction, exposing themselves to danger from a passing-by train. Likewise, the state $nt(t)$ (a train actually crossing the junction) poses a greater risk than the state $nt(c)$ (a closed gate), since the latter includes also cases when there is no train within the crossing.

Figure 12 also indicates the relative risk levels brought about by the occurrence of the respective events. In the diagram, the states posing greater threats to the users of

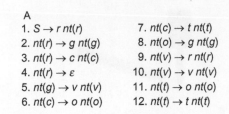

A
1. $S \rightarrow r\, nt(r)$ 7. $nt(c) \rightarrow t\, nt(t)$
2. $nt(r) \rightarrow g\, nt(g)$ 8. $nt(o) \rightarrow g\, nt(g)$
3. $nt(r) \rightarrow c\, nt(c)$ 9. $nt(v) \rightarrow r\, nt(r)$
4. $nt(r) \rightarrow \varepsilon$ 10. $nt(v) \rightarrow v\, nt(v)$
5. $nt(g) \rightarrow v\, nt(v)$ 11. $nt(t) \rightarrow o\, nt(o)$
6. $nt(c) \rightarrow o\, nt(o)$ 12. $nt(t) \rightarrow t\, nt(t)$

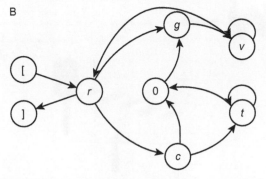

B

Fɪɢ. 12. A tbRG$_1$ model of a railway level crossing. (A) The tbRG$_1$ model. (B) The corresponding ESG.

the system are placed horizontally to the right of those posing relatively lower risks. Note also that, as a simplification, the above representation does not include any means to control the movement of trains. We assume the system to be initialized with a sequence of signals *rc*.

5.2   System Functions and Vulnerability Threats

As implied by the productions of tbRG$_1$ model in Fig. 12, the EPs in this example are

$$rg, rc, gv, co, ct, og, vr, vv, to, tt, \tag{8}$$

where each EP *ab* correspond to a rule of the form $nt(a) \rightarrow b\, nt(b)$ in the tbRG$_1$. Also, the complete event sequences (CESs) in any complete cycle of system operation can be represented by the following RE

$$(rgv^+)^*r + \left((rgv^+)^*rct^*ogv^+\right)^*r = \left((rgv^+)^*(\varepsilon + rct^*ogv^+)\right)^*r. \tag{9}$$

The tbRG$_1$ in Fig. 12 and the RE in Eq. (9) describes the same behaviors. The difference in the two descriptions lies in the fact that REs are of a declarative nature whereas tbRG$_1$s (and ESGs) are of an imperative nature. Thus, sometimes it makes sense to use REs for in-line or brief descriptions.

The FEPs are in this case

$$rr, ro, rv, rt, gr, gg, go, gc, gt, or, oo, oc, ov,$$
$$ot, cr, cg, cc, cv, vg, vo, vc, vt, tr, tg, tc, tv. \tag{10}$$

The above FEPs (Eq. 10) correspond to Rules 13–38 in the CtbRG$_1$ in Fig. 13. In the context of the framework introduced in Section 2, the tbRG$_1$ in Fig. 12 (or the RE

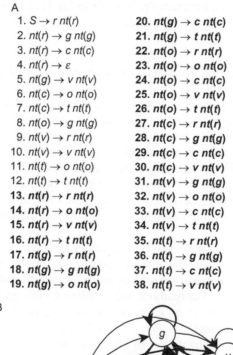

A
1. $S \rightarrow r\, nt(r)$
2. $nt(r) \rightarrow g\, nt(g)$
3. $nt(r) \rightarrow c\, nt(c)$
4. $nt(r) \rightarrow \varepsilon$
5. $nt(g) \rightarrow v\, nt(v)$
6. $nt(c) \rightarrow o\, nt(o)$
7. $nt(c) \rightarrow t\, nt(t)$
8. $nt(o) \rightarrow g\, nt(g)$
9. $nt(v) \rightarrow r\, nt(r)$
10. $nt(v) \rightarrow v\, nt(v)$
11. $nt(t) \rightarrow o\, nt(o)$
12. $nt(t) \rightarrow t\, nt(t)$
13. $\mathbf{nt(r) \rightarrow r\, nt(r)}$
14. $\mathbf{nt(r) \rightarrow o\, nt(o)}$
15. $\mathbf{nt(r) \rightarrow v\, nt(v)}$
16. $\mathbf{nt(r) \rightarrow t\, nt(t)}$
17. $\mathbf{nt(g) \rightarrow r\, nt(r)}$
18. $\mathbf{nt(g) \rightarrow g\, nt(g)}$
19. $\mathbf{nt(g) \rightarrow o\, nt(o)}$
20. $\mathbf{nt(g) \rightarrow c\, nt(c)}$
21. $\mathbf{nt(g) \rightarrow t\, nt(t)}$
22. $\mathbf{nt(o) \rightarrow r\, nt(r)}$
23. $\mathbf{nt(o) \rightarrow o\, nt(o)}$
24. $\mathbf{nt(o) \rightarrow c\, nt(c)}$
25. $\mathbf{nt(o) \rightarrow v\, nt(v)}$
26. $\mathbf{nt(o) \rightarrow t\, nt(t)}$
27. $\mathbf{nt(c) \rightarrow r\, nt(r)}$
28. $\mathbf{nt(c) \rightarrow g\, nt(g)}$
29. $\mathbf{nt(c) \rightarrow c\, nt(c)}$
30. $\mathbf{nt(c) \rightarrow v\, nt(v)}$
31. $\mathbf{nt(v) \rightarrow g\, nt(g)}$
32. $\mathbf{nt(v) \rightarrow o\, nt(o)}$
33. $\mathbf{nt(v) \rightarrow c\, nt(c)}$
34. $\mathbf{nt(v) \rightarrow t\, nt(t)}$
35. $\mathbf{nt(t) \rightarrow r\, nt(r)}$
36. $\mathbf{nt(t) \rightarrow g\, nt(g)}$
37. $\mathbf{nt(t) \rightarrow c\, nt(c)}$
38. $\mathbf{nt(t) \rightarrow v\, nt(v)}$

B

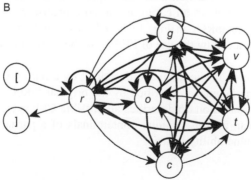

Fig. 13. The completed tbRG$_1$ of the tbRG$_1$ in Fig. 12. (A) The CtbRG$_1$ model. (B) The corresponding ESG.

in Eq. 9) constitutes what we termed as *system function F*, while FEPs in Eq. (10) are the system *vulnerability threats V* posed at the junctures corresponding to any matching subsequences among the ESs that can be generated by the tbRG$_1$ presented in Fig. 12 (or RE represented in Eq. 9), for example,

$$(rgv^+)^*r. \tag{11}$$

Each FEP in Eq. (10) represents the leading pair of signals of an emerging faulty behavioral pattern, with the first event being an acceptable one and the second one an unacceptable one. Should the first event of any of the FEPs, for example, *rv* in Eq. (10), thus happen to match the last event in any of the ESs that can be generated by such a subexpression, for example, $(rgv^+)^*r$ in Eq. (11), then the corresponding pair of the ES and the FEP, for example,

$$(rgv^+)^*rv \tag{12}$$

describes, or signifies the occurrence of, a specific form of a faulty behavioral pattern.

Of course, in our approach, such sequences can easily be generated by creating a partial complement tbRG$_1$ for each FEP as described in Section 2.4.4, and by selecting words from the languages described by these partial complement tbRG$_1$s. Intuitively, this corresponds to the concatenation of the corresponding pairs of ESs and FEPs in the appropriate manner (that is, by dropping either the last signal of the EP or the first signal of the FEP) which results in expressions not belonging to the language described by the original tbRG$_1$ or system model, for example, Eq. (12), and the relevant FEPs denote the illegal transitions in the junctures described.

Note that it is easy to represent all ESs ending with event r (as partially intended in Eq. 11 above) using tbRG$_1$. Since derivations of the form $S \Rightarrow^* xr\, nt(r)$ ($x \in E^*$) generate all such ESs, it makes sense to simply refer to the set of all such sequences using nonterminal $nt(r)$. Furthermore, the required CFESs can be formulated by using partial complements in an easier and a more precise way. For example, the partial complement of tbRG$_1$ in Fig. 12 based on *rv* contains all forms of faulty behavior patterns induced by the use of FEP *rv* as shown by the complement model in Fig. 14.

Naturally, the words in the language described by a partial complement tbRG$_1$ do not belong to the language described by the original tbRG$_1$. More precisely, a partial complement based on *ab* describes all possible CFESs ending with FEP *ab*. Furthermore, one can also use unique nonterminals of a partial complements for representation of vulnerability states.

A
1. $S \to r\, nt(r)$
2. $nt(r) \to g\, nt(g)$
3. $nt(r) \to c\, nt(c)$
4. ~~$nt(r) \to \epsilon$~~
5. $nt(g) \to v\, nt(v)$
6. $nt(c) \to o\, nt(o)$
7. $nt(c) \to t\, nt(t)$

8. $nt(o) \to g\, nt(g)$
9. $nt(v) \to r\, nt(r)$
10. $nt(v) \to v\, nt(v)$
11. $nt(t) \to o\, nt(o)$
12. $nt(t) \to t\, nt(t)$
13. $nt(r) \to v2\, nt(v2)$
14. $nt(v2) \to \epsilon$

B

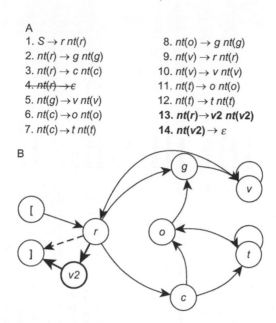

FIG. 14.   The partial complement of the tbRG$_1$ in Fig. 12 based on rv. (A) The partial complement tbRG$_1$. (B) The corresponding ESG.

Table I presents the vulnerabilities relevant to the model given in Fig. 12. In spite of its simplicity, the interpretations of the conjunctions of the appropriate pairs (ES, FEP) demonstrate the effectiveness of the approach in revealing the safety–critical cases. For completeness and the sake of clarity, to represent ESs, we include both nonterminals and REs that lead to these nonterminals in the tbRG$_1$.

5.3   Risk Graph and Defense Mechanism

A graph of the form given in Fig. 15 may be more informative about the relative risk levels. Each node in this *risk graph* is a nonterminal that represents any state belonging to the complete state space which includes the functional states (non-terminals of the tbRG$_1$ model) and the vulnerability states (additional nonterminals of the partial complement tbRG$_1$ models). Each nonterminal can be used to signify a state unambiguously; however, a state may correspond to multiple nonterminals. A directed arc running from a node s_1 to another node s_2 in Fig. 15 suggests that to $s_1 \sqsubseteq s_2$, that is, the risks posed by s_2 is known to be not lower than the risks posed by s_1

TABLE I
LEVEL CROSSING VULNERABILITIES, THE LEVEL OF THE THREATS POSED, AND POSSIBLE DEFENSE ACTIONS

ES (column 1)	FEP (column 2)	Interpretation (column 3)	Comment (column 4)	Defense action (column 5)
$((rgv^+)^* + (rgv^+) rct^* ogv^+))^* r$ $nt(r)$	ro	Gate opens while lights are set to red (No effective state change is possible except immediately after initialization when the gate was closed).	Ignored	—
	rt	A train arrives prematurely.	Danger	rc
	rv	Vehicle traffic passes through red lights.	Danger	a
$(rgv^+) rc$ $nt(c)$	cr	Lights to revert to red, though already red.	Ignored	—
	cv	Vehicle traffic is attempting to cross the closed gate and the red lights.	Danger	a
$(rgv^+)^* rct^+$ $nt(t)$	cg	Lights turn green from red while the gate is closed.	Danger	a
	tr	Lights to revert to red while already in red.	Ignored	—
	tc	Gates to close while already closed.	Ignored	—
	tv	Vehicle traffic crosses as trains pass.	Potential accident	None
$(rgv^+)^* rct^* o$ $nt(o)$	tg	Lights turn green as trains pass.	Danger	—
	or	Lights to revert to red while already in red.	Ignored	—
	oc	Gates to close while already closed.	Ignored	—
	ot	A train arrives after the gate opened.	Danger	rc
	ov	Vehicle traffic crosses as soon as the gate opened but before the lights change to green.	Danger	a
$(rgv^+)^* rct^* og+rg$ $nt(g)$	go	Gates to open though already opened.	Ignored	—
	gc	Gates to close after the lights turn green.	Annoyance	—
$(rgv^+)^* rct ogv^+ + rgv^+$ $nt(v)$	gt	A train arrives soon after the lights turn green.	Danger	rc
	vo	Gates to open though already opened.	Ignored	—
	vc	Gates to close while vehicle traffic moving.	Danger	vr
	vt	A train arrives amidst vehicle traffic.	Potential accident	rc
	vg	Lights to turn green though already green.	Ignored	—

[a] Any defense action is outside the scope of the current model due to lack of features for controlling train movements.

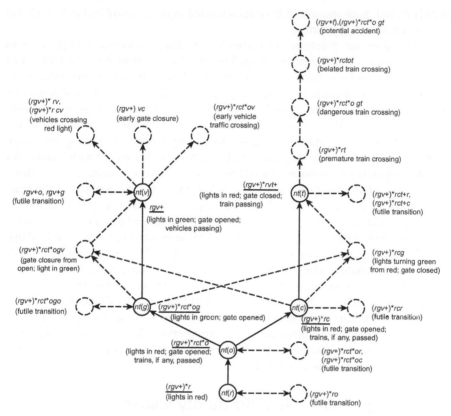

Fig. 15. Risk graph of the crossing the railway crossing, covering both the functional and the vulnerability states.

(the risks posed by s_2 can be at the same level as, or exceed, the risks by s_1). Note also the use of upward running arcs in Fig. 15 is to signify that the state lying above (in the vertical direction) poses a greater risk than the one lying below.

As mentioned above, arcs and nodes drawn in solid lines refer to the normal functional behavior and functional states, while those in dashed lines refer to undesired behavior and vulnerability states. Note that to avoid drawing a spacious graph, some vulnerability states are merged in Fig. 15, that is, each dashed node in the risk graph corresponds to a subset of vulnerability states. Therefore, the dashed states are not named explicitly. Instead, REs are given to identify them. Furthermore, as indicated by Table I, there can be some CFESs that cause no effective change in the state, for example, in issuing a signal to close the gate when it is already closed. Such transitions have been termed as *futile transitions* in Fig. 15 and are not considered any further.

Having identified potential vulnerabilities of safety concerns, it is possible to provide measures that counteract them. This is what is intended by the concept of *defense matrix* and *exception handlers* introduced in Section 4. In this connection, an attempt has been made in Table I to propose the defensive actions that may be taken, although due to the limited scope of our model these actions address only partially the potential vulnerabilities. This is because all defensive actions at the disposal of the current model are limited to closing the gate or turning the traffic lights to red, thus affecting only the vehicle traffic. A richer model with features for modeling signaling mechanisms would have allowed means to address other vulnerabilities, namely, those that can be avoided or mitigated by controlling the train movements. In a complete Table I in these respects, the ESs listed under column 5 would be equivalent to the set of the exception handlers X, while columns 1, 2, and 5 would amount to a definition of the required defense matrix implicitly, provided that the data in these columns satisfies the condition in Eq. (5). Note that column 5 lists the exception handlers, and Columns 1 and 2 give the domain of the defense matrix (function), that is, a nonterminal $nt(a)$ in Column 1 represents set of all possible ESs of the form xa such that $S \Rightarrow^* xa\ nt(a)$ ($x \in E^*$) and an ab in Column 2 is a FEP. Furthermore, the concatenation of Columns 1, 2, and 5 in the appropriate manner (that is, by dropping common signals as appropriate) leads to the nonterminal representing the safe state aimed by the defense matrix as a result of invoking the corresponding exception handler [45].

5.4   Testing Safety Issues

The test process can now be worked out analogously to the test process described in Section 3.3. Thus, we systematically construct the CES and the CFES using the coverage criteria and test generation methods discussed in Sections 3.1 and 3.2, respectively. Then, we combine them to test the system for desirable and undesirable behaviors as discussed in Section 3.3. When the test results are in accordance with the user's expectations, the test succeeds, otherwise the test fails.

As for our example of the railway level crossing, actual testing of the application in real life for safety issues cannot be undertaken; firstly, it places human life at risk, secondly, it is impractical on the grounds of costs and, thirdly, it is unnecessary. Hardly can we run the system with all the test inputs and observe what happens. As an example, the test input Eq. (12) represents the event that the vehicle traffic passes through the red lights, which cannot be realized as a real-life experiment. Furthermore, in order to generate a complete test case, we need a meaningfully reactive controlling system, which is outside the scope of our current model, given the $tbRG_1$ in Fig. 12.

Nevertheless, even this simple approach is useful in that it makes such dangerous behaviors explicit (visible) and highlights the reactions required of the controlling system in response to such inputs. Thus, it is evident that we can use the tbRG$_1$ model in Fig. 12 to simulate all potential test scenarios. All what is required is the proper use of the concepts defined in Sections 2–4 by following the identical steps outlined above.

To avoid unnecessary details, we summarize the results of our analysis to systematically cover all FEPs using the partial complements of the tbRG$_1$ in Fig. 12. It appears that following REs are of particular interest when dealing with system vulnerabilities:

$$\left(rgv^+\right)^*r, \left(rgv^+\right)^*rc, \left(rgv^+\right)^*rct^+, \left(rgv^+\right)^*rct^*o,$$
$$\left(rgv^+\right)^*rct^*og, \left(rgv^+\right)^*rct^*ogv^+, \left(rgv\right)^*rct^*ogv^+r. \tag{13}$$

These REs represent ESs which are possible prefixes, that is, starters, that can be constructed by analyzing the expression Eq. (9). The test inputs can now be constructed as described in the last section, for example, $rgvrv$ which can be generated as an instance of RE $\left(rgv^+\right)^*rv$ Eq. (11), which is extended from the sub RE in Eq. (11) of the RE in Eq. (9).

6. Related Work

FSA-based methods have been used for almost four decades for specification and testing of software and system behavior, for example, for conformance testing Refs. [46,47], as well as for specification and testing of system behavior Refs. [47,48] and more recently by Offutt et al. [49]. Sheady and Siewiorek [50], and White and Almezen [51] introduced an FSA-based method for GUI testing, including a convincing empirical study to validate his approach. Based on Refs. [5–9], our work is intended to extend, refine, and formalize these approaches by taking not only the desired, but also the undesired behaviors of the system into account, for example, testing GUIs not only through exercising them by means of test cases which show that GUI is working properly under regular circumstances, but also exercising all potentially illegal events to verify that the GUI behaves satisfactorily in exceptional cases (it is possible to address other types of errors in a similar manner, particularly those due to poor interface design [52,53]). Thus, we now have a *holistic* view concerning the complete behavior of the system that we want to test. Moreover, having an exact terminology and an appropriate formal framework enabling the use of different types of coverage criteria and test generation methods, we can now precisely scale the test process, justifying the cumulative costs that must be in compliance with the test budget. This strategy is quite different from the combinatorial ones, for example, *pairwise testing*, which requires that for each pair of input parameters of a system, every combination of valid values of these parameters must be covered by at least one test case. This is, in most practical cases, labor intensive [54,55], though the massive amount of practical work performed in Refs. [56,57] shows that it can still be practical.

Another state-oriented approach, based on the traditional SCR (Software Cost Reduction) method, is described by Heitmeyer et al. [58]. This approach uses model checking (which can identify negative and positive scenarios) to generate test cases automatically from formal requirements specifications, using well-known coverage metrics for test case selection. Furthermore, authors use some heuristic methods to cope with the state explosion problem. We also introduce methods for test case selection. Moreover, we enable handling of test coverage aspects for termination of testing in different ways. Using the theoretical knowledge that is well known in conformance testing and has been deemed appropriate in the practice of protocol validation for decades, we suggest the simplification of the approach of Dahbura, Aho et al. to handle the Chinese Postman Problem [37,59] to generate optimized tests, because the complexity of the problem is considerably lower in our case, as summarized in Refs. [10,60]. Furthermore, based on the knowledge of compiler testing, we enable the use of grammar-based test generation methods [40,41] to obtain relaxed sequences, which are commonly used in testing practice. Thus, the results of our work, including the present validation and empirical analysis, enable the use of efficient algorithms of various testing disciplines to generate and select test cases based on a k-sequence, shortest CFES and k-sequence FEP coverage criteria.

As a way to further systematize the test design process, we have also adopted the concept of "risk graphs." Risk graphs, such as the one shown in Fig. 15, are an extension of the concept of *risk graph* originally used in Ref. [44]; this is because the former includes the *complete state space*, that is, the state space of the system including every functionally desirable, as well as undesirable, state, and not just the functional state space augmented with (equipment) failure states used in Ref. [44]. The distinction between desirable and undesirable states, as well as between different degrees of desirability/undesirability, forms the basis of the systematization of the test design process. Failure states in Ref. [44] are a simple solution for modeling equipment failures and, as a result, do not distinguish between different possible failure modes. The given work, therefore, rectifies this limitation in Ref. [44]. The complete state space can be partitioned into two subspaces: a *functional state space* and a *vulnerability state space*. The original concept of risk graph in Ref. [44], introduced in a Statechart-based formalism called *Safecharts*, imposes various restrictions on transitions, including the barring of transitions between states with unknown relative risk levels as a matter of prudence. Obviously, this applies only to any transitions considered in the functional state space. States in the functional state space still pose risks but are considered acceptable in the pursuit of the services provided by the system. On the other hand, the risks posed by the states in the vulnerability state space may be unacceptable on several grounds. Foremost among them is the fact that the risks could be far too great to be acceptable on safety grounds, though there could be others which are undesirable on other lesser grounds, for example, because of the annoyance caused to the system users (for example, turning lights to red and green alternatively with no real reason) or the drain on system resources (for example, by futile transitions). An objective of this research is to develop a single framework where risks of different nature, such as those concerned with safety, usability, testability, etc., can all be considered in a broadly uniform manner, while capturing their fundamental differences by an appropriate collection of corresponding system attributes.

Another concept introduced in Ref. [44] is the concept of *banded risk graph*, designed to alleviate the extent of barring of potentially useful transitions between states noncomparable by $\sqsubseteq$ in terms of the risks posed. Obviously, this does not apply to states outside the functional state space because, by the mere intended definition, no functionally useful transitions are conceivable in the vulnerability state space.

The representation used here is introduced in Ref. [9]. It aims to use model manipulation or transformation operators in mutation testing practice, like Refs. [61–63]. The major difference of the approach discussed in this work is that we do not apply transformation operators one by one to create first order mutants, instead we use combinations of them to generate minimal and precise models for representation of undesirable behaviors or vulnerability threats to generate tests. Furthermore, unlike the mutation testing, our purpose is not the evaluation of test sets but the immediate testing of the system.

7. Conclusion, Limitations, and Future Work

To sum up, based on Refs. [5–10], our work is intended to extend, refine, and formalize event and finite state based testing approaches by taking not only the desired, but also the undesired behaviors into account. Thus, we use a *holistic* view concerning the complete behavior of the system, which includes not only functional behavior but also a range of system vulnerabilities addressed by the attributes like safety, security, usability, etc. Incorporation of both the desired and undesired features of the system in the model allows a practical way to realize the "design for testability" in software design—a concept initially introduced in the seventies [64] for hardware. The degree of undesirability is represented in the form of a risk ordering relation—an expression of relative levels of risks posed by hazardous states. This allows targeting the design of tests at specific system attributes.

The key aspects of this work are: (a) the extension of the previous approach by the use of partial complement models which are obtained by well-defined model transformation operators and enable more precise and thorough handling of the faults, (b) the definition of additional coverage criterion that allows the generation of various additional CFESs, and (c) the formalization of the concepts using a notation which is more suitable for extension and by outlining concrete algorithms.

The complete framework can be based on the concept of tbRG$_k$s—a representation which is close to both ESGs and FSA. Since the approach relies on simple event-based modeling, it can be adapted in other software modeling approaches and tools such as Statecharts [65] and UML [66,67]. This may require further research into modification or extension of our algorithms based on formal definitions of the new models. For example, one may need to consider particularly the problems related to state explosion, hierarchy, and concurrency [68,69], as well as the semantics of these new models. We benefit from the fact that our models have very simple semantics and thus a greater degree of analyzability.

However, keeping the models simple is also our greatest limitation, because it limits the discussion to the domain of regular languages or event-based regular systems. Therefore, in some cases, our models can only make an approximation to the actual behavior of the system. Although, in practice, this can be considered as a simplification to reduce the testing costs, the extension of the introduced concept beyond the domain of regular languages is left for possible future research.

Other aspects of our approach that require further attention are the concepts of indexing and contextualization. Currently, there is no formalization of these concepts, because, in many cases, construction of event-based models used here is quite simple even for an individual with limited knowledge of theory of formal languages. However, the construction of minimal tbRG$_k$ models depends on properly distinguishing the contexts so that an event can be duplicated and indexed with respect to its occurrences in different contexts. These indexed events can be included in the tbRG$_k$ model appropriately. For this reason, the precise formalization, and discussing theoretical and practical implications of these concepts are likely to help improve the holistic testing approach of event-based systems.

REFERENCES

[1] N.G. Leveson, Safeware, System Safety and Computers, Boston, MA, 1995.
[2] N. Storey, Safety-Critical Computer Systems, Boston, MA, 1996.
[3] S. Gossens, Enhancing system validation with behavioral types, in: Proceedings of the 7th International Symposium on High Assurance Systems Engineering (HASE 2002), Washington, DC, 2002, pp. 201–208.
[4] R.E. Prather, Regular expressions for program computations, Am. Math. Mon. 104 (2) (1997) 120–130.

[5] F. Belli, N. Nissanke, C.J. Budnik, Finite-state modeling, analysis and testing of system vulnerabilities—approach and case study, 2003 (Technical Report, Angewandte Datentechnik TR 2003/5, Paderborn, Germany).

[6] F. Belli, N. Nissanke, C.J. Budnik, A.P. Mathur, Test Generation Using Event Sequence Graphs, Paderborn, Germany, 2005 (Technical Report, Angewandte Datentechnik TR 2005/6).

[7] F. Belli, K.-E. Grosspietsch, Specification of fault-tolerant system issues by predicate/transition nets and regular expressions—approach and case study, IEEE Trans. Softw. Eng. 17 (6) (1991) 513–526.

[8] B. Eggers, F. Belli, A Theory on Analysis and Construction of Fault-Tolerant Systems, in: Informatik-Fachberichte, vol. 84, Berlin, 1984, pp. 139–149. (in German).

[9] F. Belli, M. Beyazıt, A formal framework for mutation testing, in: Proceedings of the 4th International Conference on Secure Software Integration and Reliability Improvement (SSIRI 2010), 9–11 June, Washington, DC, 2010, pp. 121–130. (Corrected version is available at http://adt.et.upb.de/download/papers/BB2010_SSIRI2010corrected.pdf.)

[10] F. Belli, Finite-state testing and analysis of graphical user interfaces, in: Proceedings of the 12th International Symposium on Software Reliability Engineering (ISSRE 2001), 27–30 November, Washington, DC, 2001, pp. 34–43.

[11] J. Myhill, Finite Automata and the Representation of Events, 1957 (Technical Report, WADD TR 57-624, Ohio. pp. 112–137).

[12] J.I. Ianow, Logic schemes of algorithms, Probl. Cybern. I (1958) 87–144. (in Russian).

[13] K. Jensen, N. Wirth, Pascal, User Manual and Report, Springer-Verlag, Berlin, 1974 (P.B. Hansen, D. Gries, C. Moler, G. Seegmüller, N. Wirth, Eds.).

[14] R.D. Tennent, Specifying Software, Cambridge University Press, Cambridge, 2002.

[15] B. Korel, Automated test data generation for programs with procedures, in: Proceedings of the International Symposium on Software Testing and Analysis (ISSTA 1996), New York, NY, 1996, pp. 209–215.

[16] G.H. Mealy, A method for synthesizing sequential circuits, Bell Syst. Tech. J. 34 (1955) 1045–1079.

[17] E.F. Moore, Gedanken experiments on sequential machines, in: C.E. Shannon, and J . McCarthy (Eds.), Automata Studies, Annals of Mathematical Studies, vol. 34, Princeton University Press, Princeton, NJ, 1956, pp. 129–153.

[18] D.K. Kaynar, N. Lynch, R. Segala, F. Vaandrager, Timed I/O automata: a mathematical framework for modeling and analyzing real-time systems, in: Proceedings of the 24th Real-Time Systems Symposium (RTSS 2003), 3–5 December, Washington, DC, Cancun, Mexico, 2003, pp. 166–177.

[19] A. Masood, R. Bhatti, A. Ghafoor, A.P. Mathur, Scalable and effective test generation for role-based access control systems, IEEE Trans. Softw. Eng. 35 (5) (2009) 654–668.

[20] A. Masood, A. Ghafoor, A.P. Mathur, Conformance testing of temporal role-based access control systems, IEEE Trans. Depend. Secure Comput. 7 (2) (2010) 144–158.

[21] J.E. Hopcroft, R. Motwani, J.D. Ullman, Introduction to Automata Theory, Languages and Computation, third ed., Boston, MA, 2006.

[22] F. Belli, M. Beyazıt, T. Takagi, Z. Furukawa, Mutation testing of "Go-Back" functions based on pushdown automata, in: Proceedings of the 4th International Conference on Software Testing, Verification and Validation (ICST 2011), 21–15 March, Washington, DC, 2011, pp. 249–258.

[23] T. Takagi, Z. Furukawa, The pushdown automaton and its coverage criterion for testing undo/redo functions of software, in: The 9th International Conference Computer and Information Science (ICIS 2010), 18–20 August, Washington, DC, 2010, pp. 770–775.

[24] D. Harel, Statecharts: a visual formalism for complex systems, Sci. Comp. Programm. 8 (3) (1987) 231–274.

[25] M. von der Beeck, A Comparison of Statecharts Variants, in: Formal Techniques of Real-Time and Fault-Tolerant Systems (FTRTFT 1994), Lecture Notes in Computer Science, vol. 863, Berlin, 1994, pp. 128–148.

[26] J. Davies, Specification and Proof in Real-Time CSP, Cambrigde, 1993.

[27] C.A.R. Hoare, Communicating Sequential Processes, Upper Saddle River, NJ, 1985.

[28] R. Milner, Communications and Concurrency, Upper Saddle River, NJ, 1989.

[29] W. Reisig, Petri Nets: An Introduction, Springer-Verlag, Berlin, 1985.

[30] H.E. Eriksson, M. Penker, B. Lyons, D. Fado, UML 2 Toolkit, New York, NY, 2004.

[31] Object Management Group, Unified Modeling Language (UML), http://www.omg.org/spec/UML/.

[32] V. Cortellessa, A. Di Marco, P. Inverardi, Model-Based Software Performance Analysis, Berlin, 2011.

[33] A. Salomaa, I.N. Sneddon, Theory of Automata, Oxford, 1969.

[34] J.B. Goodenough, Exception handling—issues and a proposed notation, Commun. ACM 18 (12) (1975) 683–696.

[35] B. Randell, Reliability issues in computing system design, ACM Comput. Surv. 10 (2) (1978) 123–165.

[36] H. Zhu, P.A. Hall, J.H. May, Software unit test coverage and adequacy, ACM Comput. Surv. 29 (4) (1997) 366–427.

[37] A. Aho, A. Dahbura, D. Lee, M. Uyar, An optimization technique for protocol conformance test generation based on UIO sequences and rural chinese postman tours, IEEE Trans. Commun. 39 (11) (1991) 1604–1615.

[38] J. Edmonds, E.L. Johnson, Matching, Euler tours and the Chinese postman, Math. Programm. 5 (1) (1973) 88–124.

[39] M.K. Kwan, Graphic programming using odd or even points, Chin. Math. 1 (3) (1962) 273–277.

[40] B.A. Malloy, J.F. Power, A Top-Down Presentation of Purdom's Sentence-Generation Algorithm, 2005 (Technical Report, NUIM-CS-TR-2005-04, Maynooth, Ireland).

[41] P. Purdom, A sentence generator for testing parsers, BIT Numer. Math. 12 (3) (1972) 366–375.

[42] L. Zheng, D. Wu, A sentence generation algorithm for testing grammars, in: Proceedings of the 33rd International Computer Software and Applications Conference (COMPSAC 2009), vol. 1, 20–24 July, Washington, DC, 2009, pp. 130–135.

[43] D. Hamlet, Foundation of software testing: dependability theory, in: Proceedings of the 2nd Symposium on Foundations of Software Engineering (SIGSOFT 1994), New York, NY, 1994, pp. 128–139.

[44] N. Nissanke, H. Dammag, Design for safety in safecharts with risk ordering of states, Saf. Sci. 40 (9) (2002) 753–763.

[45] N.G. Leveson, Software safety: why, what, and how, ACM Comput. Surv. 18 (2) (1986) 125–163.

[46] G.V. Bochmann, A. Petrenko, Protocol testing: review of methods and relevance for software testing, in: Proceedings of the International Symposium on Software Testing and Analysis (ISSTA 1994), New York, NY, 1994, pp. 109–124.

[47] T.S. Chow, Testing software design modeled by finite-state machines, IEEE Trans. Softw. Eng. SE-4 (3) (1978) 178–187.

[48] D.L. Parnas, On the use of transition diagrams in the design of a user interface for an interactive computer system, in: Proceedings of the 24th National Conference (ACM 1969), New York, NY, 1969, pp. 379–385.

[49] J. Offutt, L. Shaoying, A. Abdurazik, P. Ammann, Generating test data from state-based specifications, J. Softw. Test. Verif. Reliab. 13 (1) (2003) 25–53.

[50] R.K. Shehady, D.P. Siewiorek, A method to automate user interface testing using variable finite state machines, in: Proceedings of the 27th International Symposium on Fault-Tolerant Computing (FTCS 1997), 24–27 June, Washington, DC, 1997, pp. 80–88.

[51] L. White, H. Almezen, Generating test cases for GUI responsibilities using complete interaction sequences, in: Proceedings of the 11th International Symposium on Software Reliability Engineering (ISSRE 2000), Washington, DC, 2000, pp. 110–121.

[52] F. Redmill, J. Rajan, Human Factors in Safety-Critical Systems, Butterworth-Heniemann, 1997.

[53] B. Shneiderman, Designing the User Interface: Strategies for Effective Human-Computer Interaction, third ed., Addison-Wesley, Boston, MA, 1998.

[54] D.M. Cohen, S.R. Dalal, M.L. Fredman, G.C. Patton, The AETG system: an approach to testing based on combinatorial design, IEEE Trans. Softw. Eng. 23 (7) (1997) 437–444.

[55] K. Tai, Y. Lei, A test generation strategy for pairwise testing, IEEE Trans. Softw. Eng. 28 (1) (2002) 109–111.

[56] D.R. Kuhn, R. Kacker, Y. Lei, Combinatorial and Random Testing Effectiveness for a Grid Computer Simulator, 2008 (Technical Report, Gaithersburg, MD, 24 Oct.).

[57] D.R. Kuhn, R. Kacker, Y. Lei, Random vs. combinatorial methods for discrete event simulation of a grid computer network, in: Proceedings of Mod Sim World, 14–17 October, 2009, pp. 83–88.

[58] A. Gargantini, C. Heitmeyer, Using model checking to generate tests from requirements specification, in: Proceedings of the 7th European Software Engineering Conference held jointly with the 7th ACM SIGSOFT International Symposium on Foundations of Software Engineering (ESEC/FSE 1999), New York, NY, 1999, pp. 146–162.

[59] Y.-N. Shen, F. Lombardi, A.T. Dahbura, Protocol conformance testing using multiple UIO sequences, IEEE Trans. Commun. 40 (8) (1992) 1282–1287.

[60] F. Belli, C.J. Budnik, Test minimization for human-computer interaction, Appl. Intell. 26 (2) (2007) 161–174.

[61] F. Belli, C.J. Budnik, E. Wong, Basic operations for generating behavioral mutants, in: Proceedings of the 2nd Workshop on Mutation Analysis (MUTATION 2006), November, Washington, DC, 2006, pp. 9–18.

[62] S.C.P.F. Fabbri, J.C. Maldonado, M.E. Delamaro, P.C. Masiero, Mutation analysis testing for finite-state machines, in: Proceedings of the 5th International Symposium on Software Reliability Engineering (ISSRE 1994), 6–9 November, Washington, DC, 1994, pp. 220–229.

[63] S.C.P.F. Fabbri, J.C. Maldonado, T. Sugeta, P.C. Masiero, Mutation Testing Applied to Validate Specifications Based on Statecharts, in: Proceedings of the 10th International Symposium on Software Reliability Engineering (ISSRE 1999), Washington, DC, 1999, pp. 210–219.

[64] T.W. Williams, K.P. Parker, Design for testability—a survey, IEEE Trans. Comput. 31 (1) (1982) 2–15.

[65] D. Harel, A. Namaad, The STATEMATE semantics of statecharts, ACM Trans. Softw. Eng. Methodol. 5 (4) (1996) 293–333.

[66] Y.G. Kim, H.S. Hong, D.H. Bae, S.D. Cha, Test cases generation from UML state diagrams, IEE Proc. Softw. 146 (4) (1999) 187–192.

[67] L. Briand, Y. Labiche, A UML-based approach to system testing, Softw. Syst. Model. 1 (1) (2002) 10–42.

[68] F.B. Schneider, Implementing fault-tolerant services using the state machine approach: a tutorial, ACM Comput. Surv. 22 (4) (1990) 299–319.

[69] S.C.V. Raju, A. Shaw, A prototyping environment for specifying, executing and checking communicating real-time state machines, Softw. Pract. Exp. 24 (2) (1994) 175–195.

ABOUT THE AUTHOR

Fevzi Belli is a professor of Software Engineering at the University of Paderborn, Germany. In 1978, he completed his PhD in formal methods for verifying software systems and self-correction features in formal languages at Berlin Technical University. He spent several years as a software engineer in Munich, writing programs to test other programs, before he changed in 1989 to the University of Paderborn. He has an interest and experience in software reliability/fault tolerance, model-based testing, and test automation.

Mutlu Beyazıt received his M.Sc. degree in Computer Software from İzmir Institute of Technology (Turkey) in 2008. He also worked as a research assistant at İzmir Institute of Technology from 2005 to 2008. In 2009, he joined the Department of Computer Science, Electrical Engineering and Mathematics in the University of Paderborn where he is currently working as a research assistant and continuing his Ph.D. study. His primary interests lie in the area of model-based software and system testing.

Aditya Mathur's research spans software testing, reliability, and process control. His work, published in over 130 papers, relates to investigations into the effectiveness of testing techniques and their applicability to the testing of sequential and distributed software systems, methods for the estimation of software system reliability, and techniques and tools for managing a collection of Internet-enabled devices. In software process control he has formalized the feedback control of the software development process using methods from the discipline of automatic control widely practiced in engineering. He is the author of several textbooks including the recently published "Foundations of Software Testing." Aditya has consulted with and delivered numerous invited talks at American and Indian companies that engage in the development of embedded or other software.

Nimal Nissanke, MSc (Eng), MSc (appl. Maths), MSc (Comp), PhD (Eng), is an Emeritus Professor of Computer Science at London South Bank University, London, and is a Fellow of the British Computer Society. Though now retired, he continues his research in several areas, including formal methods and computer system security. He has published in areas such as formal methods, real-time systems, safety critical systems, including three self-authored books.

System Dependability: Characterization and Benchmarking

YVES CROUZET

LAAS-CNRS, Toulouse, Cedex 4, France
Université de Toulouse, UPS, INSA, INP, ISAE, UT1,
UTM, LAAS, Toulouse, Cedex 4, France

KARAMA KANOUN

LAAS-CNRS, Toulouse, Cedex 4, France
Université de Toulouse, UPS, INSA, INP, ISAE, UT1,
UTM, LAAS, Toulouse, Cedex 4, France

Abstract

This chapter presents briefly basic concepts, measures, and approaches for dependability characterization and benchmarking, and examples of benchmarks, based on dependability modeling and measurements. We put emphasis on commercial off-the-shelf (COTS) components on COTS-based systems. To illustrate the various concepts, techniques, and results of dependability benchmarking, we present two examples of benchmarks: one addressing the system and service level of a COTS-based fault tolerant system, and one dedicated to COTS software components. The first benchmark shows how dependability modeling can be used to benchmark alternative architectural solutions of instrumentation and control systems of nuclear power plants. The benchmarked measure corresponds to system availability. The second benchmark shows how controlled experiments can be used to benchmark operating systems taking Windows and Linux as examples. The benchmark measures are robustness, reaction time, and restart time.

ADVANCES IN COMPUTERS, VOL. 84
ISSN: 0065-2458/DOI: 10.1016/B978-0-12-396525-7.00004-6

93

1. Introduction

System performance is no longer the only factor that keeps customers satisfied. Dependability is increasingly playing a determinant role, as well, not only of life-critical systems but also for money-critical systems. Dependability assessment should be addressed from the early design and development phases of such systems. As a matter of fact, performance benchmarks greatly participated in improving system performance, as it is not conceivable nowadays to provide a system without indications on its performance attributes allowing users to appreciate the capacity of their computer systems properly. Moreover, some system vendors design and implement computer systems in such a way that they satisfy specific performance benchmark by construction.

Considering dependability, even though some system vendors provide information related to its dependability, this practice is seldom, and even when such information does exist it is provided in various forms according to the venders, making it very hard to compare alternative systems from the dependability point of view.

Benchmarking the dependability of a system consists in evaluating dependability or performance-related measures in the presence of faults, in a well-structured and standardized way. A dependability benchmark is intended to objectively characterize the system behavior in the presence of faults. Actually, despite the broad range of promising work on dependability benchmarking, we are far from having reached the consensus needed to get to the current situation of performance benchmarks. Dependability benchmarking is an emerging domain, and a great variety of benchmarks has been defined, for example, robustness benchmarks, fault-tolerance benchmarks, recovery benchmarks. Most of these dependability benchmarks have been defined in a noncoordinated way. No standardization results have been published to help in this process. Nevertheless, the work achieved so far is necessary to pave the way for standard dependability benchmarks, even though all actors agree on the fact that implementing dependability benchmarks is essential for competition.

One of the difficulties steams from the fact the spectrum of measures is wider for dependability benchmarks than for performance benchmarks. It is thus very important to agree both on the dependability benchmark measures of interest, and on the way they can be obtained in a nonambiguous manner. A way of reducing the spectrum is to address specific categories of systems, which help understanding and solving progressively the problems. Based on the fact that the current trend is to build systems composed of commercial off-the-shelf (COTS) components, a natural start is to address COTS and COTS-based systems. In this chapter, we will concentrate on COTS and COTS-based fault tolerant systems for critical systems.

The paradox with using COTS components is that, on the one hand, their large-scale usage increases the confidence that one may have in their general dependability but, on the other hand, this same "large-scale usage" argument may not constitute a sufficient dependability case for using COTS in critical applications. Thus, one is faced with providing further characterization and benchmarking of components over whose design one has had no control.

The chapter is composed of seven sections. In Section 2, we will present dependability measures that can be used for benchmarking fault tolerant system and components. As system benchmarking makes use of dependability assessment approaches based on modeling and on measurement, the basic assessment approaches will be presented in Section 3. Section 4 will address the benchmarking concepts and give examples of existing dependability and performance benchmarks. Sections 5 and 6 present two case studies related, respectively, to an example of

COTS-based systems for Instrumentation and Control system of nuclear power plants, and to COTS, taking as an example the case of operating systems (OSs). Finally, Section 7 concludes the chapter.

2. Dependability Measures

The dependability characteristics of a system or a component can be expressed either qualitatively, in terms of attributes and features describing the system capacities and properties, or in terms of quantitative measures. As the occurrence or activation of faults in a system may lead to performance degradation without leading to system failure, dependability, and performance are strongly related. Thus, the evaluation of system performance under faulty conditions, in addition to dependability measures, will allow characterizing completely the system behavior from the dependability point of view.

We distinguish two kinds of dependability measures: comprehensive and specific measures. Comprehensive measures characterize the system globally at the service delivery level while specific measures characterize particular aspects of a system or a component (e.g., the fault-tolerance mechanisms or the system behavior in presence of faults). In the following we first provide examples of comprehensive measures, then examine specific measures and finally we address performance-related measures.

2.1 Comprehensive Dependability Measures

Dependability is an integrative concept that encompasses the following basic attributes [1,2]:

- Availability: readiness for correct service.
- Reliability: continuity of correct service.
- Safety: absence of catastrophic consequences on the user(s) and the environment.
- Confidentiality: absence of unauthorized disclosure of information.
- Integrity: absence of improper system state alterations.
- Maintainability: ability to undergo repairs and modifications.

Several other dependability attributes have been defined that are either combinations or specializations of the six basic attributes listed above. Security is the concurrent existence of (a) availability for authorized users only, (b) confidentiality, and (c) integrity with "improper" taken as meaning "unauthorized." Dependability with respect to erroneous inputs is referred to as robustness.

The attributes of dependability may be emphasized to a greater or lesser extent depending on the application: availability is always required, although to a varying degree, whereas reliability, safety, and confidentiality may or may not be required. The extent to which a system possesses the attributes of dependability should be interpreted in a relative, probabilistic sense, and not in an absolute, deterministic sense: due to the unavoidable presence or occurrence of faults, systems are never totally available, reliable, safe, or secure.

The evaluation of these attributes leads to view them as measures of dependability. The associated measures are referred to as *comprehensive dependability measures* as (i) they characterize the service delivered by the system, (ii) they take into account all events impacting its behavior and their consequences and (iii) they address the system in a global manner, even though the notion of system and component is recursive and a system may be a component of another system.

Measures associated with the above attributes have been defined in Refs. [1,2] as follows:

- *Reliability* measures the continuous delivery of correct service or, equivalently, the time to failure.
- *Availability* measures the delivery of correct service with respect to the alternation of correct and incorrect service.
- *Maintainability* measures the time to service restoration since the last failure occurrence, or equivalently, measures the continuous delivery of incorrect service.
- *Safety*: when the state of correct service and the states of incorrect service due to noncatastrophic failure are grouped into a safe state (in the sense of being free from catastrophic damage, not from danger). Safety measures the continuous safeness, or equivalently, the time to catastrophic failure. As a measure, safety is thus reliability with respect to catastrophic failures.

The joint evaluation of performance and dependability leads to the notion of performability.

2.2   Specific Dependability Features and Measures

For some systems, the dependability can be expressed in terms of properties or features the system must satisfy in the presence of faults. For example:

- One feature could be for example "the system should be *fail-controlled*," meaning that the system should fail only in specific and controlled modes of failure, such as (i) fail-halt or fail-silent modes, when, to an acceptable extent, all failures lead to halt the system or to make it silent; or (ii) fail-safe mode, when failures are all minor ones, to an acceptable extent.

• Another feature could be "the system should be *Fail-safe/Fail-silent,*" meaning the system should be fail-safe after the first failure and fail-silent after the second failure

One has to assess to which extend these features, expressed in qualitative terms, are statistically satisfied.

Additionally, it may be interesting to assess specific aspects of system behavior without necessarily taking into account all the processes impacting its global behavior and without addressing the service delivery level. This concerns essentially features related to (i) system error detection and fault-tolerance capabilities, (ii) maintenance facilities, (iii) system evolution capacities. These features are of prime interest when building COTS-based systems where such information should be made available for system integrators, otherwise the latter cannot rely on the COTS components to build the system.

Without being exhaustive, we illustrate below the kind of features that are worth to be investigated in the context of dependability benchmarking.

Examples of features related to fault-tolerance capabilities:

- Detection and recovery of permanent hardware and/or software faults
- Detection and recovery of transient hardware and/or software faults
- Detection and recovery of successive faults
- Error containment (avoidance of error propagation)
- On-line fault diagnosis
- Protection against operational errors (accidental/intentional)
- Failure modes
- Recovery after power failure

Examples of features related to maintenance and evolution:

- On-line repair
- On-line backup
- Detection of inconsistent upgrade

It is worth to mention that features such as extendibility, scalability, and modularity may be considered as essential for a system, even though they are not directly related to dependability, but they may impact system dependability.

The list of features above is provided in a generic manner, and each feature has to be specified precisely to characterize the dependability of a system. In particular, one has to specify the exact nature and location of errors that can be detected, contained (whose effects can be confined) or tolerated. For example, a system may be tolerant to hardware faults without being tolerant to software faults.

In order to have an accurate knowledge about the system behavior, features should be completed by quantitative information. In particular, one has to know to which extent these features are fulfilled. This leads to associate to each feature one or more *specific dependability measures* to be quantified to describe its behavior accurately.

Usually features are assessed through their efficiency. The latter has two complementary dimensions: (i) a time dimension corresponding to the duration of the considered action (error detection, recovery or containment, fault diagnosis and system repair) and (ii) a conditional probability of success of an action, provided it has been initiated (referred to as coverage factor or coverage). For example, fault diagnosis coverage is defined as the probability that a fault is correctly diagnosed given the fact that an error is detected. However, for some systems, action duration or action coverage may have more impact and emphasis may thus be put only on the most influential dimension of the efficiency.

2.3   Performance-Related Measures

Classical performance measures include measures such as system response time and system throughput. In the context of dependability benchmarking, performance evaluation addresses the characterization of system behavior in the presence of faults or with respect to the additional fault-tolerance mechanisms. For example, some fault-tolerance mechanisms may have a very high coverage factor with a large time overhead in normal operation. It is interesting to evaluate such time overhead. Concerning the system behavior in the presence of faults, following fault occurrence or fault activation, either the system fails or a correct response is provided (correct value, delivered on time). Indeed, a correct value delivered too late with respect to the system specification is to be considered as a failure, mainly for hard real-time systems.

In the presence of errors, a system may still provide a correct response with a degraded performance. Hence, the response time and the throughput (which are at the origin pure performance measures) become dependability and performance-related measures characterizing the *system performance in the presence of faults*.

2.4   Comments on Features and Measures for Dependability Assessment

We have presented various dependability attributes and features and their associated measures as well as performance-related measures that allow characterization of the dependability of a system or a component. We have distinguished two kinds of dependability measures: comprehensive and specific measures. Comprehensive measures characterize the system globally at the service delivery level, taking into account all events impacting its behavior and their consequences on the application or service delivery. Specific measures characterize particular aspects of a system or a component related for example to system behavior in the presence of faults and fault-tolerance capabilities. Each measure characterizes one side of the multifaceted problem. The variety and number of comprehensive and specific measures show the complexity of dependability characterization.

Approaches for assessing the various measures will be presented in the next section.

3. Basic Dependability Assessment Approaches

During the system design and integration phases, dependability analysis and assessment, along with other performance and functional analyses, supports the selection of the most suitable system architecture with respect to the dependability requirements of the application. Section 2 presented measures of dependability to be assessed to characterize fault tolerant systems and their components. This section presents assessment approaches that can be used to assess these measures.

Assessment is usually carried out by means of three complementary approaches, based (i) on analytical modeling approaches, or (ii) on field data, resulting from the observation of real-life systems (i.e., field measurement), or (iii) on controlled, off-line, experiments (i.e., experimental measurement). Each kind of approach has its advantages and limitations. Obviously, whenever possible, results based on field data are most significant than those based on experimentation and modeling. Unfortunately, such analyzes are not always available because they require the collection of very specific data items, most of the time related to (hopefully) very rare events, hence requiring a long period of data collection to lead to statistically significant results.

Analytical modeling approaches are commonly used to support the selection of candidate systems for which the most significant dependability attributes, among those presented in the previous section, are compared. Modeling requires the knowledge of (i) the system functions, (ii) the system architecture used to fulfill these functions (in terms of components and interactions between the components), as well as in terms of fault-tolerance and recovery mechanisms embedded in the system to increase its dependability, and (iii) the maintenance strategy adopted during system operation in case of failures of multiple components. This knowledge is then used to model the system behavior as resulting from failure occurrence, error detection, error propagation or confinement, system recovery or reconfiguration, failure modes, maintenance facilities, etc. At the model level, these events and activities are expressed by means of event rates and conditional probabilities of success or failure, referred to as model parameters. Numerical values of the model parameters are needed to process the model. They are usually evaluated derived from measurement.

Field measurement is based on data collected on the system and its environment during its development, validation, and operational life. Data collected concern failure and maintenance processes: time of failure occurrence, nature of failures and impact on system services, faulty component, recovery time, repair duration, restart time, etc. This information allows evaluation of measures such as the mean time between failures or the system failure rate, the failure rates according to some specific (critical) failure modes, the system components' failure rates, and system availability.

Experimental measurements, typically performed off-line, on the system or on a prototype might complement very well-field measurement, mainly for parameters describing the system behavior in the presence of faults. As fault occurrences constitute rare events, injecting faults that mimic or simulate real faults in the system or in its environment allows the assessment of the fault-tolerance mechanisms, and, whenever possible, the improvement of these mechanisms.

In the context of COTS-based systems, the combined use of the three approaches is recommended, and generally provides very useful results for system providers, system integrators, and system users. Since COTS are generally widely used in several architectures, data collection either by system providers or users is achievable and can provide accurate and statistically meaningful results even over relatively short periods of time (compensated by a large number of systems). This is a very useful means for assessing COTS component's and COTS-based systems failures rates and failure modes. During the integration of the COTS-based system, controlled experiments are carried out to complement this information, related essentially to fault-tolerance mechanisms. Based on these two sources of information, dependability models are built and processed to derive dependability measures at the system and service level.

The rest of this section is dedicated to analytical modeling for assessing comprehensive dependability measures, and to controlled experimentation by means of fault injection techniques for assessing specific measures.

3.1   Assessment Based on Analytical Modeling

With respect to dependability modeling, the main difficulty results from the various dependencies between the components. These dependencies may result from functional or structural interactions between the components or from interactions due to system-level fault-tolerance mechanisms, reconfiguration, and maintenance strategies. State-space models, in particular Markov chains, are commonly used for dependability modeling of computing systems. They are able to capture various functional and stochastic dependencies among components and allow evaluation of various measures related to dependability and performance (i.e., performability measures) based on the same model, when a reward structure is associated to them (see also Chapter 1).

To master model construction and processing, the system is decomposed into subsystems and their submodels are built individually. Depending on the complexity of the system and the kind of dependencies to be modeled, two classes of approaches have been developed to build and solve the system model: compositional approaches or decomposition/aggregation approaches [3]. In the compositional approaches, the system model results from a modular composition of the submodels that is then solved as a whole. Most of the published work related to modular model construction concentrates on rules to be used to construct and interconnect the submodels. In the decomposition/aggregation approaches, the submodels are solved individually, and the obtained individual measures are aggregated to compute the dependability measures of the overall system. The first class of approaches is very convenient for systems having a high degree of dependency between its components while the second class of approaches provides an easy way to describe the behavior of systems that can be decomposed into sets of subsystems with a low degree of dependency, or without dependencies to make the computation tractable.

In the following, we present briefly examples of modeling approaches pertaining to the two classes. We put more emphasis on the former as, in Section 5, the case study will be based on a compositional approach, and more specifically on the approaches defined in Ref. [4] and Ref. [5].

3.1.1   Compositional Modeling Approaches

The most popular technique used to build dependability and performability state space models in a modular way are based on Petri nets (PNs), and more precisely Generalized Stochastic Petri Nets (GSPNs). Composition of PN consists in constructing PN models from a set of building blocks by applying suitable operators of places and/or transition superposition. Initially investigated for no timed models, composition approaches have been then explored for stochastic extensions of PNs. For example, Ref. [6] explored composition in the context of Stochastic Petri Nets (SPNs) and Ref. [7] proposed a systematic compositional approach to the construction of parallel hardware–software models. The GSPN composition rules are based on the concept of matching labels associated with transitions and places of a GSPN, and the superposition of transitions (places) with matching labels, each one belonging to a different GSPN. Also, composition operators have been defined to facilitate model composition. For example, in the context of stochastic activity networks (SANs) that constitute an extension to GSPNs [8], two composition operators are defined (*Join* and *Replicate*) to compose system models based on SANs.

When the modeled systems exhibit various dependencies that need to be explicitly described in the dependability models. Various modeling approaches have been proposed to facilitate the construction of large dependability models taking into account such dependencies. For example, the block modeling approach defined in Ref. [4] provides a generic framework for the dependability modeling of hardware and software fault-tolerant systems based on GSPNs. The proposed approach is modular: generic GSPN submodels called block nets are defined to describe the behavior of the system components and of the interactions between them. The system model is obtained by composition of these GSPNs. Composition rules are defined and formalized through the identification of the interfaces between the component and interaction block nets. In addition to modularity, the formalism brings flexibility and reusability thereby allowing for easy sensitivity analyses with respect to the assumptions that could be made about the behavior of the components and the resulting interactions. The main advantage of this approach lies in its efficiency for modeling several alternatives for the same system as illustrated for example in Ref. [9] and Section 5.

The efficiency of the block modeling approach can be further improved by using an incremental and iterative approach for the construction and validation of the models as suggested in Ref. [10]. At the initial iteration, the behavior of the system is described taking into account the failures and recovery actions of only one selected component, assuming that the others are in an operational nominal state. Dependencies between components are taken into account progressively at the following iterations. At each iteration, a new component is added and the GSPN model is updated by taking into account the impact of the additional assumptions on the behavior of the components that have been already included in the model. Similarly to the block modeling approach, submodels are defined for describing the components behaviors and specific rules and guidelines are defined for interconnecting the submodels. This approach has been successfully used to model the dependability of the French air traffic control computing system [11].

An iterative dependability modeling approach has been also proposed in Ref. [5] where the construction and validation of the GSPN dependability model is carried out progressively following the system development refinement process, to facilitate the integration of dependability modeling activities in the system engineering process. Three main steps are distinguished. The first step is dedicated to the construction of a functional-level model describing the system functions, their states and their interdependencies. In the second step, the functional-level model is transformed into a high-level dependability model based on the knowledge of the system's structure. A model is generated for each preselected candidate architecture. The third step is dedicated to the refinement of the high-level dependability model into a detailed dependability model for each selected architecture. Formal rules are defined to make the successive model transformations and refinements as systematic as possible taking into account three complementary aspects: (i) component decomposition, (ii) state/event fine-tuning, and (iii) stochastic distribution adjustments. This approach allows the integration of various dependencies at the right level of abstraction: functional dependency, structural dependency and those induced by nonexponential distributions. A case study is described in Ref. [12].

Actually, the approach presented in Ref. [5] can be seen as a special case of the more general class of techniques based on layered and multilevel modeling methods, where the modeled system is structured into different levels corresponding to different abstraction layers, with a model associated to each level. Various techniques based on this idea have been developed, see for example, Refs. [7,13–20].

3.1.2 Decomposition and Aggregation Approaches

The decomposition and aggregation techniques depend on the type of measures to be evaluated and on the modeling formalism. Generally approximate solutions are provided for the composition of the results derived from the submodels. A decomposition and aggregation theory for steady state analysis of general continuous time Markov Chains has been proposed in Ref. [21]. The quality of the approximation is related to the degree of coupling between the blocks into which the Markov chain matrix is decomposed. In Ref. [22], the authors present an extension of this technique specifically addressed to the transient analysis of large stiff Markov chains, where stiffness is caused by the simultaneous presence of "fast" and "slow" rates in the transition rate matrix.

Time-scale-based decomposition approaches have been applied to Non-Markovian stochastic systems in Ref. [23], and to GSPN models of systems containing activities whose durations differ by several orders of magnitude in Ref. [24]. For example, in Ref. [24] the GSPN model is decomposed into a hierarchical sequence of aggregated subnets each of which is characterized by a certain time scale. Then these smaller subnets are solved in isolation, and their solutions are combined to get the solution of the whole system. In Ref. [25], the overall model consists of a set of submodels whose interactions are described by an import graph.

The decomposition approach in Ref. [26] is based on a new set of connection formalisms that reduce the state-space size and solution time by identifying submodels that are not affected by the rest of the model, and solving them separately. The result from each solved submodel is then used in the solution of the rest of the model.

3.2   Assessment Based on Controlled Experiments

In the context of dependable and fault tolerant systems, controlled experiments are mainly used to analyze qualitatively or to assess the behavior of the system in the presence of faults. The aim is either to identify possible weaknesses in the system to be dealt with at the design level to improve system dependability, or to assess specific dependability measures to provide numerical values for performability models to allow accurate estimation of comprehensive measures.

In this context, controlled experiments are mainly based on fault injection techniques. The observation of the system behavior after fault occurrence allows assessment of conditional probabilities such as probability of error detection, probability of error containment or probability of error recovery.

Several surveys have been devoted to fault injection techniques that are more or less detailed (see e.g., Refs. [27–29] and Chapter 7 of Ref. [30]). In the rest of this section, we will briefly outline some techniques and tools for (i) injecting hardware faults, for (ii) injecting or emulating software faults, and for (iii) message-based fault injection.

3.2.1   Techniques for Injecting Hardware Faults

In this section, we describe four techniques for injecting or emulating hardware faults. The two first techniques are related to fault injection into real hardware systems, based respectively on hardware-implemented fault injection and on software-implemented fault injection. The two other techniques are related respectively to simulation-based fault injection and to hardware emulation-based fault injection

Hardware-implemented fault injection includes five techniques: pin-level fault injection, electromagnetic interferences, power supply disturbances, radiation-based fault injection and test port-based fault injection.

- In pin-level fault injection, faults are injected via probes connected to electrical contacts of integrated circuits or discrete hardware components. Many experiments and studies using pin-level fault injection were carried out during the 1980s and early 1990s, and several tools were developed, for example,

MESSALINE [31] and RIFLE [32]. A key feature of these tools was that they supported fully automated fault injection campaigns.

- Electromagnetic interferences are common disturbances in automotive vehicles, trains, airplanes, or industrial plants. Such techniques are widely used to stress digital equipment thanks to the use of a commercial burst generator in conformance with the IEC 801-4 standard (CEI/IEC).

- Power supply disturbances are rarely used for fault injection because of low repeatability. They have been used mainly as a complement to other fault injection techniques in the assessment of error detection mechanisms for small microprocessors [33].

- Radiation-based fault injection is a technique for analyzing the susceptibility of integrated circuits to soft errors, that is, bit-flips caused when highly ionizing particles hits sensitive regions within in a circuit. In space, soft errors are caused by cosmic rays, that is, highly energetic heavy-ion particles. The sensitivity of integrated circuits to heavy-ion radiation can be exploited for assessing the efficiency of fault-tolerance mechanisms Refs. [33] and [34]. In Ref. [35], the three techniques described above (pin-level fault injection, electromagnetic interferences, heavy-ion radiation) have been used for the validation of the MARS architecture.

- Test port-based fault injection techniques use built-in debugging and testing features, which can be accessed through special Input/Output-ports, included in modern equipments (microprocessors, boards), known as test access ports. Test ports are defined by standards such as Nexus (IEEE-ISTO 5001 standard [36]) for real-time debugging, or JTAG (IEEE 1149.1 Standard Test Access Port and Boundary-Scan Architecture [37]). Freescale provides a proprietary solution for debugging known as Background Debug Mode facility. The type of faults that can be injected via a test port depends on the debugging and testing features supported by the target microprocessor. Faults can be injected in all registers of the microprocessor. Using Background Debug Mode facilities and Nexus, faults can be injected in the main memory. Tools that support test port-based fault injection include GOOFI [38] supporting both JTAG-based and Nexus-based fault injection and INERTE [39] supporting Nexus-based fault injection. An environment for fault injection based on Background Debug Mode is presented in Ref. [40].

Software-implemented fault injection techniques allow injection of faults through the software executed on the target system. There are basically two approaches to emulate hardware faults by software: runtime injection and pre-runtime injection. In runtime injection, faults are injected while the target system executes a workload.

This requires a mechanism that stops the execution of the workload, invokes a fault injection routine, and restarts the workload. In pre-runtime injection, faults are introduced by manipulating either the source code or the binary image of the workload before it is loaded into memory. Numerous tools are capable of emulating hardware faults through software (see e.g., FIAT [41], FERRARI [42], FINE [43], DEFINE which was an extension of FINE [44], FTAPE [45], DOCTOR [46], Xception [47], and MAFALDA [48]).

Simulation-based fault injection can be performed at different levels of abstraction, the device level, logical level, functional block level, instruction set architecture level, and system level.

FOCUS [49] is an example of a simulation environment that combines device-level and gate-level simulation for fault sensitivity analysis of circuits with respect to soft errors.

At the logic level and the functional block level, circuits are usually described in a hardware description language (HDL or VHDL). Several tools have been developed that support automated fault injection experiments with HDL models, for example, MEFISTO [50] and the tool described in Ref. [51]. There are different methods for implementing fault injection, by modifying the VHDL code [52] or modifying the HDL simulator, or commanding the simulator through scripts.

DEPEND [53] is a tool for simulation-based fault injection at the functional level: a simulation model in DEPEND consists of number of interconnected modules, or components, such as CPUs, communication channels, disks, software systems, and memory.

Hardware emulation-based fault injection is based on the use of large Field Programmable Gate Arrays (FPGAs) circuits. This technique provides means for conducting model-based fault injection for analyzing the impact of faults in hardware circuits [54]. It has all the advantages of simulation-based fault injection such as high controllability and high repeatability, but requires less time for conducting a fault injection campaign compared to software simulation.

Fault injection can be performed in hardware emulation models through compile time reconfiguration and runtime reconfiguration. An approach for compile-time instrumentation for injection of single event upsets (soft errors) is described in Ref. [55]. One disadvantage of compile-time reconfiguration is that the circuit must be resynthesized for each reconfiguration, which can impose a severe overhead on the time it takes to conduct a fault injection campaign. In order to avoid resynthesizing the target circuit, a technique for runtime reconfiguration is proposed in Ref. [56]. This technique relies on directly modifying the bit-stream that is used to program the FPGA-circuit. A tool for conducting hardware emulation-based fault injection called FADES is presented in Ref. [57,58].

3.2.2   Techniques for Injecting or Emulating Software Faults

There are two fundamental approaches to injecting software faults into a computer system: fault injection and error injection [59].

- In the *error injection* approach, there are two common techniques for emulating software faults by error injection: program state manipulation and parameter (involving changing variables, pointers, and other data stored in main memory) or CPU-registers corruption (modification of function parameters, procedures, and system calls). Several tools, developed for hardware fault injection through software-implemented fault injection, can potentially be used to emulate software faults since they are designed to manipulate the system state (e.g., FIAT, FERRARI, FTAPE, DOCTOR, Xception, and MAFALDA).

- *Fault injection* imitates mistakes of programmers by changing the code executed by the target system, while error injection attempts to emulate the consequences of software faults by manipulating the state of the target system. In the fault injection approach, software faults are injected into a system by mutations (i.e., by manipulating the source code, the object code or the machine code). FINE [43] and DEFINE [44] were among the first tools that supported emulation of software faults by mutations. The mutation technique used by these tools requires access to assembly language listings of the target program. SESAME is another tool using mutation as the target fault model, allowing fault injection into software written in assembly languages, procedural languages (Pascal, C), data-flow languages (LUSTRE), as well as declarative languages [60]. A technique, referred to as Generic Software Fault Injection Technique, for emulation of software faults by mutations at the machine-code level is presented in Ref. [61]. This technique can be used as a basis for faultload definition for dependability benchmarking [59].

3.2.3   Message-Based Fault Injection

Message-based fault injection technique is dedicated to test protocols in fault-tolerant distributed systems. The aim of this type of testing is to reveal design and implementation faults in the tested protocol. The tests are performed by manipulating the content and/or the delivery of messages sent between nodes in the target system. In this context, several fault injection tools and frameworks have been developed.

The experimental environment for fault-tolerance algorithms [62] is an early example of a fault injector for message-based fault injection. The tool inserts fault injectors in each node of the target system and implements different fault types, including message omissions, sending a message several times, generating spontaneous messages, changing the timing of messages, and corrupting the contents of messages. A similar environment is provided by the DOCTOR tool [46], which can cause messages to be lost, altered, duplicated, or delayed.

Specifying test cases is a key problem in testing of distributed fault-handling protocols. A technique for defining test cases of protocols from Petri-net models is described in Ref. [63]. An approach for defining test cases from an execution tree description is presented in Ref. [64].

A tool for testing distributed applications and communication protocols called ORCHESTRA is described in Ref. [51,65]. This tool inserts a probe/fault injection layer between any two consecutive layers in a protocol stack. Results from message-based fault injection assessment of several implementations of CORBA middleware are reported in Ref. [66].

3.3   Summary and Relationships Between the Assessment Approaches

Assessment of comprehensive dependability measures can be carried out, even before system building, based on analytical modeling. Modeling requires the knowledge of the following:

- System functions and structure.
- System nominal and degraded operational modes, system failure modes, as well as component failure modes.
- The most significant error detection and fault-tolerance capabilities.
- Maintenance facilities (e.g., on-line repair and backup possibilities, maintenance policy).

For modeling purposes, the above sets of information are expressed in terms of event occurrence rates and conditional probabilities. Events refer for example to fault occurrence and activation, error propagation and system repair or restart. Conditional probabilities are usually related to system behavior after event occurrence. For example, if the event is fault occurrence and activation, the conditional probabilities describe the reaction of the system to faults (i.e., probability of error detection, probability of error containment or probability of error recovery).

The evaluation of dependability entails additionally the knowledge of the numerical values of the model parameters (event rates and conditional probabilities). From a practical point of view:

- Fault occurrence and activation rates are generally obtained from field measurement related to the same system if it is already in operation or, most probably, from similar previous systems that have already been in operation for a long time or in a large number.
- Conditional probabilities can be obtained from experimentation: from field data, whenever possible or from controlled experiments.

When the parameter values are not available, approximate values can be attributed in a first step. Sensitivity analyses allow identification of the most salient ones for the considered measure(s), to be evaluated from controlled experiments such those presented in Section 3.2.

4. Benchmarking Concepts and Examples

Benchmarking is widely used to measure computer performance in a deterministic and reproducible manner, allowing users to appreciate the capacity of their computer systems properly, while benchmarking of system dependability is hardly emerging. Benchmarking the dependability of a system consists in evaluating dependability or performance-related measures in the presence of faults, in a well-structured and standardized way. A dependability benchmark is intended to objectively characterize the system behavior in the presence of faults.

To be meaningful and objective, a dependability benchmark should satisfy a set of properties. In particular, a benchmark must be at least representative and cost-effective, to be accepted by the community. In addition, when the benchmark is based on experimentation, the experiments should be repeatable (in statistical terms), portable, and nonintrusive. These properties have to be addressed from the earliest phases of the benchmark specification as they have a significant impact on the benchmark nature and objectives, and they should be checked after the benchmark design and implementation. These properties contribute to shift the benchmarks from *ad hoc* to standard approaches to dependability assessment.

Performance and dependability benchmarks share a common feature: the definition of an appropriate *workload*, representing a synthetic or a realistic operational profile. The selection of such a workload constitutes a major difficulty as an agreement between system vendors and potential users should be reached to expect recognition and adoption of any performance benchmark. It is the main (and the only) complexity of performance benchmarks. Actually, several workloads for performance benchmarks have been used as workloads for dependability benchmarks, to which faultloads have been superposed (see e.g., Chapters 5, 6, and 12 of Ref. [67]).

Dependability benchmarks characterize the system behavior in the presence of faults, or under abnormal conditions or perturbations. Thus, in addition to the definition of appropriate workloads, they require the definition of suitable "perturbations," referred to as *faultload*. This is not an easy task since the faultload is intended to simulate faults that could be internal or external to the system being benchmarked.

A further difficulty steams from the fact that several benchmark measures may be of interest (cf. Section 2) for characterizing the system either in a comprehensive way (with respect to the service delivered) or according to specific features (e.g., fault-tolerance mechanisms). This adds an extra complexity. As a result, a great variety of benchmarks has been defined, for example, robustness benchmarks, recovery benchmarks, availability benchmarks.

The results of performance and dependability benchmarks can be useful for both the end-users and vendors. Considering the case of dependability benchmarks, the results can help to:

- Characterize the dependability of a component or a system, qualitatively or quantitatively.
- Track dependability evolution for successive versions of a product.
- Identify weak parts of a system, requiring more attention and perhaps needing some improvements by tuning a component to enhance its dependability, or by tuning the system architecture (e.g., adding fault tolerance) to ensure a suitable dependability level.
- Compare the dependability of alternative or competitive solutions according to one or several dependability attributes.

Performance benchmarks are essentially based on experimentation. Performing a performance benchmark consists in executing the workload associated to the benchmark, under particular conditions that are specified within the benchmark.

Dependability benchmarks can be based on modeling or experimentation or both, using the assessment approaches presented in Section 3, depending on the measure to be assessed by the benchmark. More specifically, comprehensive measures are usually obtained from the processing of dependability models. The latter require the knowledge of numerical values of some parameters, some of which are to be provided by controlled experiments, the others being made available by system providers, or are already known (published data), or can be obtained from field data. Typical measures (or parameters) that can be obtained from controlled experiments have been presented in Section 2.2. Such experimental benchmark measures, for fault tolerant systems may correspond to (i) efficiency of the fault-tolerance mechanisms, (ii) switching time between the primary and the secondary computer of a fault-tolerant system, (iii) latency of error detection mechanisms, (iv) system restart time, or the (v) system failure modes.

At the component level, experimental benchmark measures address for example the failure modes of the component, its robustness, or its restart time. In the rest of this section, we present few examples of performance benchmarks and dependability benchmarks.

4.1   Examples of Performance Benchmarks

A performance benchmark is a test that measures the performance of a computer system or a component on a well-defined task or set of tasks. The task or set of tasks is normally defined by a workload and the measures are specific of each benchmark. A set of rules specifies the way the test must be conducted to reach valid benchmark results.

There are three major organizations in the performance benchmarking: EEMBC (Embedded Microprocessor Benchmark Consortium), SPEC (Standard Performance Evaluation Corporation) and TPC (Transaction Processing Performance Council). They are nonprofit organizations and their members include most of the major companies in the computer industry. In the following, we give an overview of a few benchmark developed by these organizations.

4.1.1   EEMBC Benchmarks

EEMBC [68], the Embedded Microprocessor Benchmark Consortium, was formed in 1997 to develop meaningful performance benchmarks for the hardware and software used in embedded systems. Through the combined efforts of its members, EEMBC benchmarks have become an industry standard for evaluating the capabilities of embedded processors, compilers, and Java implementations according to objective, clearly defined, application-based criteria.

Since releasing its first certified benchmark scores in April 2000, EEMBC scores have effectively replaced the obsolete Dhrystone mips, especially in situations where real engineering value is important. EEMBC benchmarks reflect real-world applications and the demands that embedded systems encounter in these environments. The result is a collection of "algorithms" and "applications" organized into benchmark suites targeting telecommunications, networking, digital media, Java, automotive/industrial, consumer, and office equipment products. An additional suite of algorithms specifically targets the capabilities of 8- and 16-bit microcontrollers.

EEMBC's certification rules represent another break with the past. For a processor's scores to be published, the EEMBC Technology Center must execute benchmarks run by the manufacturer. EEMBC certification ensures that scores are repeatable and obtained according to EEMBC's rules.

4.1.2   SPEC Benchmarks

SPEC [69] was founded in 1988 and has more than 60 members today, including most of the major computer industry companies. SPEC benchmarks consist of a standardized source code taken form established applications (i.e., real-life applications) and modified by SPEC to improve portability and accommodate some specific requirements of performance benchmarking [70]. In most of the cases, the workload of a SPEC benchmark includes several applications that are run in sequence one after the other. Typically, to run a SPEC benchmark, all what is required is to compile the workload for a specific system and then tune the system for the best results. Two benchmarks are of particular interest, SPEC CPU and SPECjvm, addressing the CPU and JVM (that is used in Section 6).

- SPEC CPU2006 is a suite of compute-intensive benchmarks that measures performance of the computer processor, memory, and compiler. It includes two benchmarks suites: CINT2006 for measuring and comparing compute-intensive integer performance, and CFP2006 for measuring and comparing compute-intensive floating point performance. CINT2006 consists of 12 applications and CFP2006 includes 17 applications. All the applications are real applications and they are written in several languages such as C, C++, and Fortran. Each of these benchmark suites includes four metrics: two speed metrics, corresponding to the execution time of the applications compiled respectively with conservative and aggressive compiler optimization choices, and two throughput metrics, corresponding to the rate of execution of the applications in a given time using again conservative and aggressive compiler optimization choices.

- SPECjvm2008 is a benchmark suite for measuring the performance of a Java Runtime Environment (JRE), containing several real life applications and benchmarks focusing on core java functionality. The suite focuses on the performance of the JRE executing a single application; it reflects the performance of the hardware processor and memory subsystem, but has low dependence on file I/O and includes no network I/O across machines. The SPECjvm2008 workload mimics a variety of common general purpose application computations. These characteristics reflect the intent that this benchmark will be applicable to measuring basic Java performance on a wide variety of both client and server systems.

4.1.3   TPC Benchmarks

The Transaction Processing Performance Council (TPC) is a nonprofit corporation formed by the major vendors of systems and software from the transaction processing and database market. The goal of TPC is to define and disseminate performance benchmarks for transaction processing systems. Detailed and latest information on TPC organization and TPC benchmarks can be obtained from TPC's web site [71].

All TPC benchmarks include two kinds of measures: performance and price/performance measures. The performance measure is a transaction rate (e.g., number of transactions per minute) and the price/performance measures are based on a detailed set of pricing rules that take into account the price of purchasing the system (hardware and software) and the maintenance costs for a given period.

Unlike SPEC benchmarks, that heavily rely on the source code of the workload, TPC transactions are defined by a very detailed specification. So, to run a TPC benchmark it is necessary to implement the specification in the target system, which means that it is necessary to program the transactions and all the aspects defined in a functional way in the benchmark specification.

The TPC has currently four benchmarks: TPC-C for OLTP (On-Line Transaction Processing) systems, TPC-W for transactional Web systems such as e-commerce systems, and two benchmarks for decision support systems, the TPC-H for *ad hoc* decision support queries (queries may not be known in advance) and the TPC-R for business reporting and decision support queries (when preknowledge of the queries is assumed and may be used for optimization).

4.2   Examples of Dependability Benchmarks

Currently, most of the published work on dependability benchmarking resulted from individual effort of institutions, without the involvement of a standardization body. Pioneer work on dependability benchmarking is published in Ref. [45] for fault tolerant systems (that has then be followed by Refs. [72–74]), and in Ref. [75] for OSs. Regarding OSs, the dependability benchmarks developed are robustness benchmark either with respect to faulty applications [76–81], or with respect to faulty device drivers [82,83].

As far as we are aware, the only two groups who have worked collectively towards dependability benchmarking are DBench, a European project on Dependability Benchmarking, partially supported by the European Commission [84], and the Special Interest Group on Dependability Benchmarking [85], founded by the IFIP Working Group 10.4 on Dependable Computing and Fault Tolerance.

DBench has developed a framework for defining dependability benchmarks for computer systems, with emphasis on (i) *Off-the-Shelf components,* commercial or not, and on (ii) systems based on Off-the-Shelf components, via experimentation and modeling. The use of dependability benchmarks in the development/integration of such composite systems seems very useful for component selection and to assess dependability measures of the whole system. To exemplify how the benchmarking issues can actually be handled in different application domains, five examples of benchmarks and their associated prototypes (i.e., actual implementations of the benchmarks) have been developed within DBench. They concern general-purpose OSs, embedded systems (automotive and space applications) and transactional systems [86]. These benchmarks addressed specifically system integration and share the following common characteristics:

- The benchmark is performed during the *integration phase* of a system including the benchmark target (or when the system is available for *operational phase*).
- The benchmark performer is someone (or an entity) who has no in depth knowledge about the benchmark target and who is aiming at (i) obtaining valuable information about the target system dependability, and (ii) publicizing information on the benchmark target dependability in a standardized way.
- The primary users of the benchmark results are the *integrators* of the system including the benchmark target (or the end-users of the benchmark target).

Dependability benchmarking is without doubt a valuable support for system integration, mainly for COTS-based systems.

The work of the Special Interest Group on Dependability Benchmarking led to the publication of the first (and unique) book on dependability benchmarking, published in 2008 [67]. The OS benchmark presented in Section 6 is a subset of a benchmark published in that book in Chapter 12. This book consists of 16 chapters, prepared by researches and engineers working on the dependability field for several years and more specifically on dependability benchmarking during the more recent years. These chapters illustrate the current multiplicity of approaches to dependability benchmarking, and the diversity of benchmark measures that can be evaluated. Chapters 1–6 examine system-level benchmarks, which focus on various aspects of dependability using different measurement methods. Chapters 7–16 focus on benchmarks for system components: control algorithms (Chapter 7), intrusion detectors (Chapter 8), fault-tolerance algorithms (Chapter 9), OSs (Chapters 10–15), and microprocessors (Chapter 16). More details on these chapters are given in the Appendix.

5. Case Study: Benchmarking COTS-based Systems

In this section we illustrate the kind of results that can be obtained based on dependability modeling for benchmarking COTS-based systems. More specifically, our aim is to show how analytical modeling can be used to support benchmarking

COTS-based, fault tolerant, alternative architectures. In these architectures, fault tolerance can be ensured by three classical replication (or redundancy) techniques, namely passive replication, semiactive replication and active replication.

In a passive replication, only one of the n parallel replicas ($n \geq 2$) processes the input messages and provides output messages (active replica). The other (passive) replicas do not process the input messages. In case of unavailability of the active replica, one of the passive replicas becomes active.

In a semiactive redundancy, only one of the two replicas (i.e., the primary replica) processes all input messages and provides output messages. The other replica (secondary) is active since it also processes the input messages even though it does not provide any output messages. In case of fault occurrence or activation in the primary, a switch from the primary to the secondary replica is performed.

In an active redundancy, the three replicas process all input messages concurrently so that their internal states are closely synchronized, in the absence of faults. The outputs can be taken from any replica as long as at least two replicas are in the nominal state. In case of fault occurrence or activation, the error is masked.

The case study concerns *instrumentation and control* (I&C) systems available as COTS systems from several providers for power plants (more details can be found in Ref. [12]). The starting point of our work was to help, based on dependability evaluation, a stakeholder of an I&C system in selecting and refining systems proposed by various contractors in response to a Call for Tender.

In the rest of this section, we first present the main functions of an I&C system and examples of three different candidate COTS-based hypothetical systems constituting a set of different possible realizations for the considered I&C application. Examples of PNs models are given in Section 5.2 and an assessment result is given in Section 5.3.

5.1   Presentation of the Considered I&C Systems

The main functions of an I&C system are given in Fig. 1, in which the arrows represent the interactions between these functions. The three system architectures considered are depicted in Fig. 2. These systems have been selected for their diversity of architectures and of redundancy techniques. For example in System 1, every computer executes a single function, while in System 2 and System 3, some computers execute more than one function.

System 1 is composed of 13 nodes (each one executing a single function), connected via a Local Area Network (LAN). Nodes 1–10 are composed of a computer each. Nodes 11–13 are fault-tolerant: they are composed of two redundant computers each. Also, nodes 12 and 13 are complementary (i.e., they interface complementary parts of the I&C system).

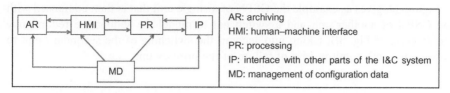

FIG. 1. Main functions of the I&C system. (For color version of this figure, the reader is referred to the Web version of this chapter.)

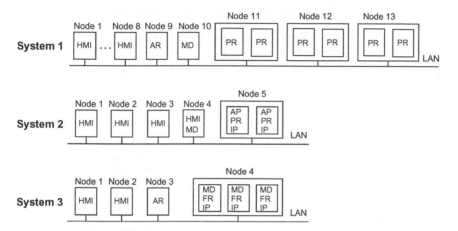

FIG. 2. Three examples of architectures based on COTS computers.

System 2 is composed of five nodes connected by a LAN. Note that while HMI is executed on four nodes, node 5 runs three functions. Nodes 1–4 are composed of one computer each. Node 5 is fault-tolerant: It is composed of two redundant computers.

In System 3, nodes 1–3 are composed of a single computer each running a single function. Node 4 is fault-tolerant: it is composed of three redundant computers (i.e., forming a triple-modular redundancy).

Table I summarizes the redundancy type of each node. Nonredundant nodes are referred to as single nodes. We assume that each hardware computer hosts a single software component, forming a COTS unit referred to a unit.

5.2 Modeling of the I&C Systems

To simplify the model's construction for the three systems, we have built a library of basic models for the efficient modeling and refinement of the given systems, with minimal modifications (see Ref. [5]).

Figure 3A gives as example the GSPN of a single unit that is then composed with the GSPN of another unit and a switch net to model the semiactive redundancy architecture of Fig. 3B, taking into account the switching of the secondary unit to become the active unit in case of failure of the primary unit.

TABLE I
REDUNDANCY TYPE OF THE THREE ARCHITECTURES

System	Node	Type of redundancy	Recovery
System 1	#1–8	Passive	–
	#9–10	Single	–
	#11–12	Semiactive	Switch
System 2	#1–3	Passive	–
	#4	Single	–
	#5	Semiactive	Switch
System 3	#1–2	Passive	–
	#3	Passive	–
	#4	Active	Masking

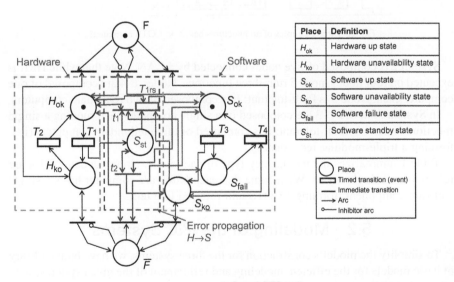

Place	Definition
H_{ok}	Hardware up state
H_{ko}	Hardware unavailability state
S_{ok}	Software up state
S_{ko}	Software unavailability state
S_{fail}	Software failure state
S_{St}	Software standby state

Place
Timed transition (event)
Immediate transition
Arc
Inhibitor arc

A One COTS unit

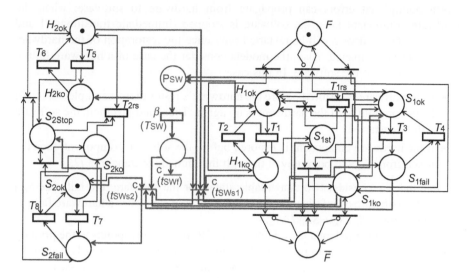

B Semiactive redundancy

Transition	Rate	Definition
T1 / T5	λ_h	Primary/secondary hardware fault occurrence
T2 / T6	v_h	Primary/secondary hardware repair
T3 / T7	λ_s	Primary/secondary software fault activation
T4 / T8	v_s	Primary/secondary software re-initialization after software failure
T1 / T5	ρ_s	Primary/secondary software restart after hardware repair
Tsw	β	Switch from the primary to the secondary

Fɪɢ. 3. GSPNs for single and semiactive redundancy architectures. (A) One COTS unit. (B) Semi-active redundancy. (For color version of this figure, the reader is referred to the Web version of this chapter.)

Figure 3A assumes that function F is carried out by a hardware component H and a software component S. F and $\bar{F}$ markings depend upon the markings of H and S (F up state is the combined results of H and S up states, while F failure (marking of $\bar{F}$) results from H or S unavailability). For each component, we consider two states: nominal (ok) and unavailable (ko). Transitions between these two states are ruled by events of failure (transitions $T1$ and $T3$) and restoration (transitions $T2$ and $T4$). It is worth noting that errors can propagate from hardware to software: when the hardware component fails, the software is stopped (immediate transitions $t1$ and place S_{st}). The software will be restarted only once the restoration of the hardware component is completed. Also, the models consider the case of a hardware failure after the failure of the software. In this case:

- if the software is restored before the hardware's restoration is completed, it will be put on hold until the hardware is up again. Then, and just then, the software will be restarted,
- if the hardware component is restored before the software component, then the token from S_{st} will be removed through the immediate transition $t2$.

Note that we consider two unavailable states for the software: the fail state S_{fail} (due to the software own failure) and the software stop state after a hardware failure, corresponding to S_{st}. $S_{ko}=S_{fail} \cup S_{st}$.

In the semiactive redundancy GSPN of Fig. 3B, unit 1 corresponds to the primary while unit 2 corresponds to the secondary unit. If the primary unit fails due to the failure of one of its components, the internal fault-tolerance mechanisms switch over to the secondary unit that becomes primary. The switching event is represented by transition TSW whose rate is β (the switching time is $1/\beta$). The coverage factor (i.e., the conditional probability that the switch succeeds given the failure of the primary) is c (immediate transitions tSWs1 and tSWs2). Thus, the switch fails and the function is lost with probability $\bar{c} = 1 - c$ (immediate transition tSWf).

5.3   Comparison of System 1 and System 2

To show the kind of results that can be provided to the stakeholder when using analytical models for benchmarking and comparing alternative solutions, we perform a comparative analysis of System 1 and System 2 unavailability, using the SURF-2 tool [87] to process the models.

Figure 4 presents the annual unavailability of System 1 and System 2, as a function of the switching time $(1/\beta)$ for $c=0.95$ and $c=0.98$, expressed in hours per year. For large values of the switching time, System 1 is more sensitive to this variation than System 2. This can be explained by the fact that System 1 has three components dependent on these two parameters, whilst System 2 has only one.

Also, we notice that for a small switching time $(1/\beta=30s$ or $1min)$, System 1 annual unavailability is smaller than System 2's. However, for larger values of the switching time $(1/\beta=5$ or $10min)$, this trend is reversed.

If we consider the same system for the two values of c, it can be seen that System 1 is more sensitive to c than System 2. Improving c from 0.95 to 0.98, the

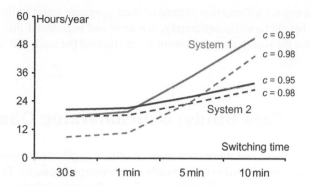

FIG. 4. Comparison of System 1 and System 2 annual unavailability. (For color version of this figure, the reader is referred to the Web version of this chapter.)

unavailability is reduced by at least 10h per year for System 1, while it is only reduced by 2–3h for System 2. Hence the values of c and $1/\beta$ impact more System 1 than on System 2.

5.4   Integration of the Results in the Dependability Benchmarking Process

Assuming that the considered values of the failure and repair rates are not far from reality (they are either provided by the COTS providers or obtained from similar systems), the kind of conclusions the stakeholder can make are, for example:

- If the switching time, $1/\beta$, is around 10min, then for all values of the c parameter, the safest case is obtained for System 2.
- If the switching time is around 1min, then for all values of the c parameter, the safest case is obtained for System 1.

The above analysis shows that it is really important to have the most realistic and accurate numerical values for parameters c and β, to allow a fair and relevant comparison of the systems.

Referring to Section 2, unavailability is a comprehensive measure; c and β are specific measures characterizing the fault-tolerance mechanisms, respectively the coverage factor and the duration of switching from secondary to primary in case of failure of the primary. The best way to assess accurately the two parameters is to perform controlled experiments, based on fault injection, where faults simulate hardware and software faults of the components, aiming at activating the recovery mechanisms to collect information related to their coverage and duration. This calls for a specific benchmark. Unfortunately, we have not performed this benchmark, and we hope that the stakeholder for whom we performed the study did such analysis to refine the offers.

6. Case Study: Benchmarking OSs

COTS OSs are more and more used even in critical application domains. Choosing the OS that is best adapted to one's needs is becoming a necessity. In this section, we consider OSs belonging to Windows and Linux families. In our previous work, we have considered three workloads: the TPC-C Client performance benchmark for transactional systems in Ref. [76], PostMark that is a file system performance benchmark in Ref. [79] and the Java Virtual Machine (JVM) in Ref. [78]. In this section, we summarize part of the results obtained with the JVM workload. Before presenting the results, we first describe the specification of the OS benchmark and their implementation for Windows and Linux families.

6.1 Specification of the Benchmark

A dependability benchmark is specified through the definition of (i) the benchmark target, (ii) measures to be evaluated, (iii) benchmark execution profile to be used to activate the OS, (iv) guidelines for conducting benchmark experiments and implementing the benchmark. The benchmark results are useful and interpretable only if all the above benchmark elements are supplied together with the results. These elements are summarized hereafter.

6.1.1 Benchmarking Target

An OS is a generic software layer providing basic services to the applications through the API, and communication with peripherals devices via device drivers. The benchmark target corresponds to the OS with the minimum set of device drivers necessary to run the OS under the benchmark execution profile. However, the benchmark target runs on a hardware platform whose characteristics impact the results. Thus, all benchmarks must be performed on the same hardware platform.

Although, in practice, the benchmark measures characterize the target system and the hardware platform, we state simply that the benchmark results characterize the OS as a COTS.

Our benchmark addresses the user perspective, that is, it is intended to be performed by (and to be useful for) someone who has no thorough knowledge about the OS and whose aim is to improve her/his knowledge about its behavior in the presence of faults. In practice, the user may well be the developer or the integrator of a system including the OS.

As a consequence, the OS is considered as a "black box." The only required information is its description in terms of system calls and in terms of services provided.

6.1.2   Benchmark Measures

The OS receives a corrupted system call. After execution of such a call, the OS is in one of the states defined in Table II.

It is worth to mention that *Panic* and *Hang* situations (SPc, SHg) are actual states in which the OS can stay for a while. SEr and SXp characterize events. They are easily identified when the OS provides an error code or notifies an exception.

The benchmark measures include a robustness measure and two temporal measures. They are defined in Table III.

Although under nominal operation the OS restart time is almost deterministic, it may be impacted by the corrupted system call. The OS might need additional time to make the necessary checks and recovery actions, depending on the impact of the fault applied.

The OS *reaction time* and *restart time* are also evaluated by experimentation in absence of faults for comparison purposes. They are respectively denoted $\tau reac$ and τres.

TABLE II
OS STATES

SEr (error code)	The OS generates an error code that is delivered to the application.
SXp (exception)	In the user mode: the OS processes the exception and notifies the application. For some critical situations, the OS aborts the application. In the kernel mode: an exception is automatically followed by a panic state (e.g., blue screen for Windows and oops messages for Linux). The latter exceptions are included in the panic state and the term exception refers only to the first case of user mode exception.
SPc (panic)	The OS is still "alive" but it is not servicing the application. In some cases, a soft reboot is sufficient to restart the system.
SHg (hang)	A hard reboot of the OS is required.
SNS (no signaling)	The OS does not detect the erroneous parameter and executes the erroneous system call. SNS is presumed when none of the previous situations is observed.

TABLE III
BENCHMARK MEASURES

OS Robustness, OSR	The percentages of experiments leading to any of the states listed above. OSR is a vector composed of five elements
OS Reaction Time, Treac	The average time necessary for the OS to respond to a system call in presence of faults, either by notifying an exception or by returning an error code or by executing the required instructions
OS Restart Time, Tres	The average time necessary for the OS to restart after the execution of the workload in the presence of faults

6.1.3 Benchmark Execution Profile

In the current benchmark, the workload is JVM, solicited through a small program activating 76 system calls for Windows family and 31–37 system calls for Linux Family.

The faultload consists of corrupted parameters of system calls. For Windows, system calls are provided to the OS through the Win32 environment subsystem. In Linux OSs, these system calls are provided to the OS via the POSIX API. During runtime, the system calls activated by the workload are intercepted, corrupted, and reinserted.

The parameter corruption technique relies on thorough analyzes of system call parameters to define selective substitutions to be applied to these parameters (similarly to the one used in Ref. [88]). A parameter is either a data or an address. The value of a data can be substituted either by an out-of-range value or by an incorrect (but not out-of-range) value, while an address is substituted by an incorrect (but existing) address (that could contain an incorrect or out-of-range data). We use a mix of these three techniques. More details can be found in Ref. [79].

6.1.4 Benchmark Conduct

A benchmark controller is required to control the benchmark experiments, mainly in case of OS Hang or Panic states or workload hang or abort states, as such states cannot be reported by the machine hosting the benchmark target itself. Hence, we need at least two computers as shown in Fig. 5. The Target Machine hosts the benchmarked OS and the workload; and the Benchmark Controller is in charge of diagnosing and collecting part of benchmark data.

The two machines perform the following: (i) restart of the system before each experiment and launch of the workload, (ii) interception of system calls with

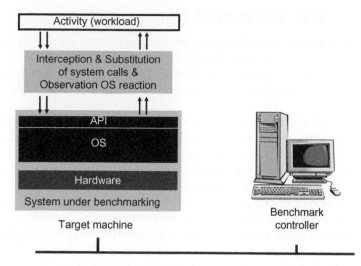

FIG. 5. Benchmark environment. (For color version of this figure, the reader is referred to the Web version of this chapter.)

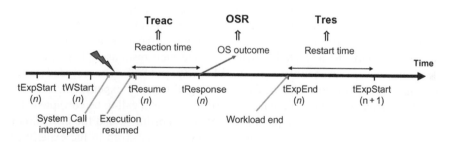

FIG. 6. Benchmark execution sequence in case of workload completion. (For color version of this figure, the reader is referred to the Web version of this chapter.)

parameters, (iii) corruption of system call parameters, (iv) reinsertion of corrupted system calls, (v) observation and collection of OS states. The experiment steps in case of workload completion are illustrated in Fig. 6 and will be detailed in the next section. In case of workload noncompletion state (i.e., the workload is in abort or hang state), the end of the experiment is governed by a watchdog timeout, fixed to three times the workload execution time without faults.

6.2   Benchmark Implementation

In order to obtain comparable results, all the experiments are run on the same target machine, composed of an Intel Pentium III Processor, 800 MHz, and a memory of 512 MB. The hard disk is 18 GB, ULTRA 160 SCSI. The benchmark controller in both prototypes for Windows and Linux is a Sun Microsystems workstation.

To intercept Win32 functions, we use the Detours tool [89], a library for intercepting arbitrary Win32 binary functions on X86 machines. We added three modules for (i) substituting parameters of system calls by corrupted values (ii) observing the reactions of the OS after execution of a corrupted system call, and (iii) collecting the required measurements.

To intercept POSIX system calls, we used another interception tool, Strace [90] to which we added modules similar to those added to Detours.

Before each benchmark run (i.e., execution of the series of experiments related to a given OS), the target kernel is installed, and the interceptor is compiled for the current kernel (interceptors are kernel dependent both for Windows and Linux). Once the benchmarking tool is compiled, it is used to identify the set of system calls activated by the workload. Parameters of these system calls are then analyzed and a database of corrupted values is built accordingly.

At the beginning of each experiment, the target machine records the experiment start instant tExpStart and sends it to the benchmark controller along with a notification of experiment start-up. The workload starts its execution. The Observer module records, in the experiment execution trace, the start-up instant of the workload, tWStart, the activated system calls and their responses. This trace also collects the relevant data concerning states SEr, SXp, and SNS. The recorded trace is sent to the benchmark controller at the beginning of the next experiment.

The parameter substitution module identifies the system call to be corrupted. The execution is then interrupted, a parameter value is substituted and the execution is resumed with the corrupted parameter value (tResume is saved in the experiment execution trace). The state of the OS is monitored so as to diagnose SEr, SXp, SNS. The corresponding OS response time (tResponse) is recorded in the experiment execution trace. For each run, the OS reaction time after the experiment is calculated as the difference between tResponse and tResume. At the end of the execution of the workload, the OS notifies the end of the experiment to the benchmark controller by sending an end signal along with the experiment end instant, tExpEnd. If the workload does not complete, then tExpEnd is governed by the value of a watchdog timer. If, at the end of the watchdog timer, the benchmark controller has not received the end signal from the OS, it then attempts to connect to the OS. If this connection is successful, and if the soft reboot is successful, then a workload abort or hang state is diagnosed. If the soft reboot is unsuccessful, then a panic state, SPc, is deduced and a hard reboot is required. Otherwise SHg is assumed.

At the end of a benchmark execution, all files containing raw results corresponding to all experiments are on the benchmark controller. A processing module extracts automatically the relevant information from these files (two specific modules are required for Windows and Linux families). The relevant information is then used to evaluate automatically the benchmark measures (the same module is used for Windows and Linux).

6.3 Benchmark Results

Three versions of Windows OSs are benchmarked: Windows NT4 Workstation with SP6, Windows 2000 Professional with SP4, and Windows XP Professional with SP1.[1] Windows 2000 Professional and Windows NT4 Workstation will be referred to as Windows 2000 and Windows NT4, respectively. Four Linux OSs (Debian distribution) are benchmarked: Linux 2.2.26, Linux 2.4.5, Linux 2.4.26 and Linux 2.6.6. Each of them is a revision of one of the stable versions of Linux (2.2, 2.4, 2.6).

For Windows, the number of system calls activated by the workload is 76 for the three versions, and the number of experiments ranges from 1282 to 1294. For Linux, the number of system calls activated by the workload ranges from 31 for Linux 2.6.6 to 37 for Linux 2.6.26, and the number of experiments ranges from 408 for Linux 2.4.X to 457 for Linux 2.2.26 (it is 409 for Linux 2.6.6).

The robustness measure, OSR, is given in Fig. 7. It shows that all OSs of the same family are equivalent. It also shows that none of the catastrophic states (Panic or Hang OS states) occurred for all Windows and Linux OSs. Linux OSs notified more error codes (58–66%) than Windows (25%), while more exceptions were raised with Windows (22–23%) than with Linux (7–10%). More no-signaling cases have been observed for Windows (52–54%) than for Linux (27–36%).

These results are in conformance with our previous results, related to Windows using TPC-C Client [76] and to Windows and Linux using PostMark [79]. In Ref. [81], it was observed that on the one hand Windows 95, 98, 98 SE and CE had a few catastrophic failures and on the other hand Windows NT, Windows 2000 and Linux are more robust and did not have any catastrophic failures as in our case.

The reaction times in the presence of faults (and without fault) are given in Table IV. Note that for the Windows family, XP has the lowest reaction time, and for the Linux family, 2.6.6 has the lowest one. However, the reaction times of Windows NT and 2000 are very high. A detailed analysis showed that the large

---

[1] In our previous work we have also considered the server versions of the same Operating Systems.

Windows family

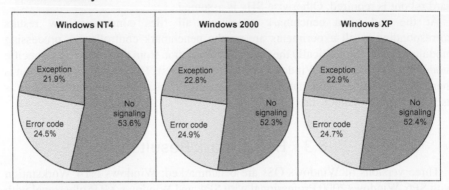

Linux Family

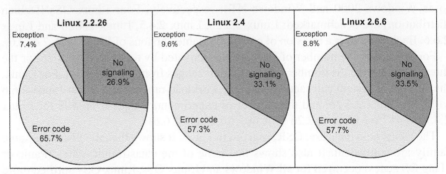

Fig. 7. OS Robustness, OSR. (For color version of this figure, the reader is referred to the Web version of this chapter.)

response time for Windows NT and 2000 are mainly due to system calls LoadLibraryA, LoadLibraryExA, and LoadLibraryEXW. Not including these system calls when evaluating the average of the reaction time in the presence of faults leads respectively to 388, 190, and 214 μs for NT4, 2000 and XP (the associated average reaction times without fault become respectively 191, 278, and 298 μs). For Linux, the high values of the reaction times in presence of faults are also due to three system calls (execve, getdents64, nanosleep). Not including the reaction times associated to these system calls leads respectively to 88, 241, 227, and 88 μs for Linux 2.2.26, 2.4.5, 2.4.26, and 2.6.6.

The restart times are shown in Table V. The average restart time without faults, τ_{res}, is always lower than the benchmark restart time (with faults), Tres, but the

TABLE IV
OS REACTION TIMES

Windows family					
Windows NT4		Windows 2000		Windows XP	
Mean	Standard deviation	Mean	Standard deviation	Mean	Standard deviation
τreac	44,035 μs		9504 μs		564 μs	
Treac	12,543 μs	154,317 μs	306 μs	1047 μs	318 μs	940 μs

Linux family							
Linux 2.2.26		Linux 2.4.5		Linux 2.4.26		Linux 2.6.6	
Mean	Standard deviation	Mean	Standard deviation	Mean	Standard deviation	Mean	Standard deviation
τreac	2951 μs		2847 μs		2255 μs		865 μs	
Treac	202 μs	583 μs	557 μs	2257 μs	544 μs	2223 μs	505 μs	2198 μs

TABLE V
OS RESTART TIMES

Windows Family					
Windows NT4		Windows 2000		Windows XP	
Mean	Standard deviation	Mean	Standard deviation	Mean	Standard deviation
τres	90 s		88 s		67 s	
Tres	91 s	3 s	89 s	5 s	71 s	5 s

Linux Family							
Linux 2.2.26		Linux 2.4.5		Linux 2.4.26		Linux 2.6.6	
Mean	Standard deviation	Mean	Standard deviation	Mean	Standard deviation	Mean	Standard deviation
τres	64 s		74 s		79 s		77 s	
Tres	71 s	37 s	79 s	23 s	83 s	24 s	82 s	27 s

difference is not significant. The standard deviation is very large for all OSs. Linux 2.2.26 and Windows XP have the lowest restart time (71 s, in the absence of fault) while Windows NT and 2000 restart times are around 90 s and those of Linux versions 2.4.5, 2.4.26, and 2.6.6 are around 80 s.

It is worth to mention that the average restart times mask interesting phenomena. Detailed analyzes show that all OSs of the same family have similar behavior and that the two families exhibit very different behaviors.

For Windows, there is a correlation between the restart time and the workload state at the end of the experiment. When the workload is completed, the restart time is almost the same as the average restart time without substitution. On the other hand, the restart time is statistically larger for all experiments with workload abort/hang. Moreover, statistically, the same system calls lead to workload abort/hang. This is illustrated in Fig. 8 in which the benchmark experiments are executed in the same order for the three Windows versions. Similar behaviors have been observed when using TPC-C [76] and PostMark workloads [79].

Linux restart time is not affected by the workload state. Detailed restart time analyses show high values appearing periodically. These values correspond to a check-disk performed by the Linux kernel every 26 restarts (which explains the important standard deviation on this measure). This is illustrated in Fig. 9 for Linux 2.2.26, as an example. The same behavior has been observed when using the PostMark workload [79].

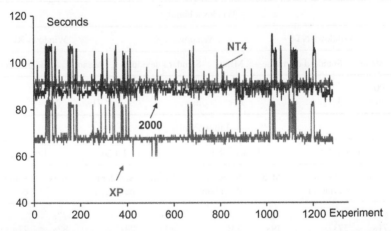

Fig. 8. Detailed restart time for Windows. (For color version of this figure, the reader is referred to the Web version of this chapter.)

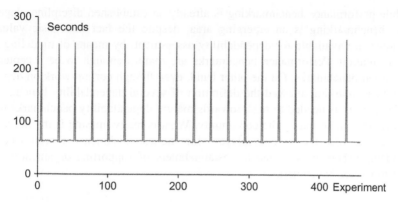

F̲ɪɢ̲. 9. Detailed restart time for Linux 2.2.26. (For color version of this figure, the reader is referred to the Web version of this chapter.)

7. Conclusion

This chapter was dedicated to system dependability characterization and benchmarking, based on modeling and on measurement. We put emphasis on COTS-based fault tolerant systems and on COTS systems. Before presenting the benchmarking concepts, we gave an overview of the kind of benchmark measures and features that can be used to characterize and benchmark a system. Then we presented the basic approaches that can be used to assess the benchmark measures. Whenever appropriate we made reference to performance benchmarks as they can provide good starting means for building dependability benchmarks. To illustrate the various concepts, techniques, and results involved in dependability benchmarking we presented two case studies: one addressing the system and service level of a COTS-based fault tolerant system, and one dedicated to a COTS software component. The first case study shows how dependability modeling can be used to benchmark alternative architectural solutions of instrumentation and control systems for nuclear power plants. The benchmarked measure corresponds to system availability. The second case study shows how controlled experiments can be used to benchmark OSs. The benchmark measures are robustness, reaction time and restart time.

To sum up, dependability benchmarks allow characterization of system dependability. They can provide a good means for comparison between alternative systems. They can also be used for guiding development efforts of system providers, and for supporting acquisition choices of system purchasers, or for comparing the dependability of new versions of a system with respect to previous ones.

While performance benchmarking is already an established discipline, dependability benchmarking is an emerging area, despite the fact that basic valuable techniques are available for dependability assessment, by means of modeling and experimentation. Performance benchmarks are mature enough to be accepted as competition benchmarks. On the other hand, even though current work on dependability benchmarking allowed the definition of several dependability benchmarks, still some work is needed to push towards mature dependability benchmarks to be accepted and supported by the community. What is really missing is the necessary agreement among the various players for the establishment of well-accepted dependability benchmarks, and the establishment of supporting organizations, as for performance benchmarks.

Appendix.   Brief Overview of the Chapters[2] in Dependability Benchmarking for Computer Systems

Chapter 1 describes an autonomic computing benchmark which measures system resiliency. In common with other benchmarks, it has a quantitative throughput metric to capture the impact of disturbances. The autonomic computing benchmark also has a qualitative metric representing the level of human interaction needed to detect, analyze, and recover from disturbances.

Chapter 2 contains three benchmarks which analytically measure reliability, availability, and serviceability of a system. All three are intended to allow a consistent dependability feature versus cost analysis for widely varying system architectures.

Chapter 3 covers two quantitative benchmarks which concentrate on the recovery of standalone systems and enterprise clusters. Recovery is broadly defined to be the time required for a system to return to service. For each benchmark, a scoring and weighting methodology is described.

The benchmark in Chapter 4 changes the physical environment around the system in order to quantitatively measure susceptibility to silent data corruption.

Chapters 5 and 6 include performance measurements in the presence of faults, providing performance degradation (due to faults) and availability measures to end-users of On-Line Transaction Processing and Web Serving systems. Chapter 5 discusses a benchmark for On-Line Transaction Processing which focuses on

---

[2] The description is as it appears in the Preface of the book itself [67].

availability using direct experimental measures. Chapter 6 includes a measurement-based benchmark for Web Servers which encompasses availability, accuracy, resilience, and service degradation.

Chapter 7 is dedicated to the benchmark of automotive control applications running inside engine control units. It addresses the safety of the software applications from the perspective of the engine they control. It is aimed at supporting the selection or the purchase of automotive applications for electronic controller units.

In Chapters 8 and 9, the systems under benchmarks are respectively the intrusion detection mechanisms and fault-tolerance algorithms.

Chapter 8 discusses issues that should be addressed when benchmarking intrusion detectors in the cyber domain. It is worth to mention that no intrusion detector benchmark is currently available, and that this chapter does not develop a benchmark *per se*.

Chapter 9 addresses Byzantine protocols dedicated to Byzantine-fault tolerance. The benchmark is aiming at assessing the effectiveness of Byzantine-fault tolerance implementation. It is illustrated on a specific protocol, the Castro-Liskov protocol.

Chapters 10–15 exemplify the multifaceted feature of dependability benchmarking, illustrated on operating systems. The benchmarks presented mainly differ by the nature of faults considered: Chapter 10 addresses internal faults, while Chapters 11–15 are concerned with external faults. Chapters 11–13 address faults in the software application, Chapter 14 faults in device drivers, and Chapter 15 faults in the hardware platforms.

Chapter 10 defines a benchmark that captures the user's expectations of product reliability during common user experiences. While the benchmark can be applied to any software product, this chapter focuses on the application of this benchmark for operating systems development. Its aim is to help the operating system developer to improve, during its development, the operating system's reliability.

Chapters 11–14 present benchmarks based on experimentation. They consider the operating system as a black box, solicit it only through its available inputs and observe its behavior only through the operating system outputs. The ultimate objective of end-user's benchmarks is to improve the application software, or the device drivers, or the hardware platform. However, the benchmark results may indicate weaknesses in the operating system that the operating system developer may use, with further analyzes, to improve the operating system.

Chapter 11 is dedicated to the Ballista project, the first operating system robustness testing approach. It reexamines the design decisions made, and the lessons learned from a decade of robustness testing research.

Chapter 12 elaborates on the Ballista approach and develops a benchmark evaluating, in addition to the operating system robustness, two measures, the system response time and restart time in the presence of faults.

Chapter 13 focuses on real-time kernels. It characterizes the response time predictability, based on the divergence of the response time in the presence of fault, and the frequency of out-of-boundary responses times.

Chapter 14 concentrates on failures modes of the operating systems induced by faulty drivers. Additionally, it evaluates three complementary measures: responsiveness, availability, and workload safety.

Chapter 15 considers in a first step the operating system as a black box, and develops an end-user benchmark, then shows how this benchmark can be complemented to help the operating system developer to improve the operating system's dependability.

Chapter 16 is dedicated to microprocessors benchmarks, with respect to electrical charge induced by high energy particles, referred to as soft errors. As the benchmark presented does not require any specific knowledge about the microprocessors. It can be used by the manufacturers or end-users.

REFERENCES

[1] A. Avizienis, J.-C. Laprie, B. Randell, Fundamental Concepts of Dependability, 2001 (LAAS Research Report, N°1145, April).

[2] J.-C. Laprie, Dependable computing: concepts, limits, challenges, 25th International Symposium on Fault-Tolerant Computing (FTCS-25), Special Issue (Pasadena, CA, USA), IEEE Computer Society Press, 1995, pp. 42–54.

[3] M. Kaaniche, P. Lollini, A. Bondavalli, K. Kanoun, Modeling the resilience of large and evolving systems, Int. J. Perform. Eng. 4 (2) (2008) 153–168.

[4] K. Kanoun, M. Borrel, Fault-tolerant system dependability—explicit modeling of hardware and software component-interactions, IEEE Trans. Reliab. 49 (4) (2000) 363–376.

[5] C. Betous-Almeida, K. Kanoun, Construction and stepwise refinement of dependability models, Perform. Eval. 56 (2004) 277–306.

[6] P. Buchholz, A notion of equivalence for stochastic Petri nets, 16th International Conference on Application and Theory of Petri Nets, Torino, Italy, 1995, pp. 161–180.

[7] S. Donatelli, G. Franceschinis, The PSR methodology: integrating hardware and software models, 17th Int. Conf. on Application and Theory of Petri Nets, ICATPN '96, Osaka, Japan, Springer-Verlag, 1996.

[8] J.F. Meyer, W.H. Sanders, Specification and construction of performability models, Int. Workshop on Performability Modeling of Computer and Communication Systems, Mont Saint Michel, France, 1993, pp. 1–32.

[9] K. Kanoun, M. Borrel, T. Morteveille, A. Peytavin, Modeling the dependability of CAUTRA, a subset of the French air traffic control system, IEEE Trans. Comput. 48 (5) (1999) 528–535.

[10] N. Fota, M. Kâaniche, K. Kanoun, Incremental approach for building stochastic Petri nets for dependability modeling, in: D.C. Ionescu, N. Limnios (Eds.), Statistical and Probabilistic Models in Reliability, Birkhäuser, 1999, pp. 321–335.

[11] N. Fota, M. Kâaniche, K. Kanoun, Dependability evaluation of an air traffic control computing system, Perform. Eval. 35 (3–4) (1999) 553–573.

[12] C. Betous-Almeida, K. Kanoun, Dependability modeling of instrumentation and control systems: a comparison of competing architectures, Saf. Sci. 42 (2004) 457–480.

[13] S. Bernardi, S. Donatelli, Building Petri net scenarios for dependable automation systems, 10th International Workshop for Petri Nets and Performance Models (PNPM'2003), Urbana-Champaign, IL, USA, 2003, pp. 72–81.

[14] S. Bernardi, Building Stochastic Petri Net models for the Verification of Complex Software Systems, 2003 PhD, Universita di Torino.

[15] A. Bondavalli, M. Nelli, L. Simoncini, G. Mongardi, Hierarchical modeling of complex control systems: dependability analysis of a railway interlocking, J. Comput. Syst. Sci. Eng. 16 (4) (2001) 249–261.

[16] Y.-S. Dai, Y. Pan, X. Zou, A hierarchical modeling and analysis for grid service reliability, IEEE Trans. Comput. 56 (5) (2007) 681–691.

[17] M. Kaâniche, K. Kanoun, M. Rabah, Multi-level modeling approach for the availability assessment of e-business applications, Softw. Pract. Exp. 33 (14) (2003) 1323–1341.

[18] P. Lollini, A. Bondavalli, F. Di Giandomenico, A modeling methodology for hierarchical control systems and its application, J. Braz. Comput. Soc. 10 (3) (2005) 57–69.

[19] M. Nelli, A. Bondavalli, L. Simoncini, Dependability modeling and analysis of complex control systems: an application to railway interlocking, European Dependable Computing Conference (EDCC-2), Taormina, Italy, Springer-Verlag, 1996, pp. 93–110.

[20] M. Rabah, K. Kanoun, Performability evaluation of multipurpose multiprocessor systems: the "separation of concerns" approach, IEEE Trans. Comput. 52 (2) (2003) 223–236.

[21] P.-J. Courtois, Decomposability—Queuing and Computer System Applications, Academic Press, New York, 1977.

[22] A. Bobbio, K. Trivedi, An aggregation technique for the transient analysis of Stiff Markov chains, IEEE Trans. Comput. C-35 (9) (1986) 803–814.

[23] S. Haddad, P. Moreaux, Approximate analysis of non-Markovian stochastic systems with multiple time scale delays, 12th Annual Meeting of the IEEE International Symposium on Modeling, Analysis, and Simulation of Computer and Telecommunication Systems (MASCOTS) Volendam, NL, 2004.

[24] H.H. Ammar, S.M. Rezaul Islam, Time scale decomposition of a class of generalized stochastic Petri net models, IEEE Trans. Softw. Eng. 15 (6) (1989) 809–820.

[25] G. Ciardo, K.S. Trivedi, Decomposition approach to stochastic reward Net models, Perform. Eval. 18 (1) (1993) 37–59.

[26] D. Daly, W.H. Sanders, A connection formalism for the solution of large and stiff models, 34th Annual Simulation Symposium, 2001, pp. 258–265.

[27] A. Benso, P. Prinetto, Fault Injection Techniques and Tools for Embedded Systems Reliability Evaluation, Kluwer Academic Publishers, Boston, MA, 2003.

[28] M.-C. Hsueh, T.K. Tsai, R.K. Iyer, Fault injection techniques and tools, Computer 30 (1997) 75–82.

[29] H. Ziade, R. Ayoubi, R. Velazco, A survey on fault injection techniques, Int. Arab J. Inform. Technol. 1 (2) (2004) 171–186.

[30] Aad van Moorsel, E. Alberdi, R. Barbosa, R. Bloomfield, A. Bondavalli, J. Durães, et al., State of the Art, Deliverable no. D2.2 of the Project AMBER (Assessing, Measuring, and Benchmarking Resilience), FP7-216295, June 2009, 250p., available at: http://eden.dei.uc.pt/~rbarbosa/files/md_242_amber_d2.2_stateoftheart_v2.0final_submit.pdf.

[31] J. Arlat, M. Aguera, L. Amat, Y. Crouzet, J.-C. Fabre, J.-C. Laprie, et al., Fault injection for dependability validation—a methodology and some applications, IEEE Trans. Softw. Eng. 16 (1990) 166–182.

[32] H. Madeira, M. Rela, F. Moreira, J.G. Silva, A general purpose pin-level fault injector, Proceedings of the European Dependable Computing Conference, Berlin, Germany, 1994, pp. 199–216.

[33] J. Karlsson, U. Gunneflo, P. Liden, J. Torin, Two fault injection techniques for test of fault handling mechanisms, Proceedings International Test Conference, Nashville, TN, USA, Oct, 1991, pp. 140–149.

[34] U. Gunneflo, J. Karlsson, J. Torin, Evaluation of error detection schemes using fault injection by heavy-ion radiation, Proceedings of the 19th International Symposium on Fault-Tolerant Computing (FTCS-19), Chicago, IL, USA, 1989, pp. 340–347.

[35] J. Arlat, Y. Crouzet, J. Karlsson, P. Folkesson, E. Fuchs, G.H. Leber, Comparison of physical and software-implemented fault injection techniques, IEEE Trans. Comput. 52 (2003) 1115–1133.

[36] IEEE-ISTO 5001, The Nexus 5001 ForumTM Standard for a Global Embedded Processor Debug Interface, IEEE-ISTO, Piscataway, NJ, 2003.

[37] IEEE Std, 1149.1-2001—IEEE Standard Test Access Port and Boundary-Scan Architecture, IEEE, Piscataway, NJ, 2001.

[38] D. Skarin, R. Barbosa, J. Karlsson, GOOFI-2: a tool for experimental dependability assessment, Proceedings of IEEE/IFIP International Conference on Dependable Systems and Networks (DSN 2010), Chicago, IL, USA, June 28–July 1, 2010, pp. 557–562.

[39] P. Yuste, D. de Andres, L. Lemus, J. Serrano, P. Gil, INERTE: integrated NExus-based real-time fault injection tool for embedded systems, Proceedings of the International Conference on Dependable Systems and Networks (DSN-2003), San Francisco, CA, USA, June, 2003, p. 669.

[40] M. Rebaudengo, M. Sonza Reorda, Evaluating the fault tolerance capabilities of embedded systems via BDM, Proceedings of the 17th IEEE VLSI Test Symposium, Dana Point, CA, USA, Apr, 1999, pp. 452–457.

[41] J.H. Barton, E.W. Czeck, Z.Z. Segall, D.P. Siewiorek, Fault injection experiments using FIAT, IEEE Trans. Comput. 39 (1990) 575–582.

[42] G.A. Kanawati, N.A. Kanawati, J.A. Abraham, FERRARI: a tool for the validation of system dependability properties, Proceedings of the 22nd International Symposium on Fault-Tolerant Computing, Boston, MA, USA, July, 1992, pp. 336–344.

[43] W.I. Kao, R.K. Iyer, D. Tang, FINE: a fault injection and monitoring environment for tracing the Unix system behavior under faults, IEEE Trans. Softw. Eng. 19 (1993) 1105–1118.

[44] W.I. Kao, R.K. Iyer, DEFINE: a distributed fault injection and monitoring environment, in: D. Pradhan, D. Avresky (Eds.), Fault-tolerant parallel and distributed systems, IEEE Computer Society Press, 1995, pp. 252–259.

[45] T.K. Tsai, R.K. Iyer, D. Jewitt, An approach towards benchmarking of fault-tolerant commercial systems, in: Proceedings of the 26th International Symposium on Fault-Tolerant Computing (FTCS-26), Sendai, Japan, IEEE CS Press, 1996, pp. 314–323.

[46] S. Han, K.G. Shin, H.A. Rosenberg, DOCTOR: an integrated software fault injection environment for distributed real-time systems, Proceedings of the International Computer Performance and Dependability Symposium, Erlangen, Germany, 1995, pp. 204–213.

[47] J. Carreira, H. Madeira, J.G. Silva, Xception: a technique for the experimental evaluation of dependability in modern computers, IEEE Trans. Softw. Eng. 24 (1998) 125–136.

[48] J. Arlat, J.-C. Fabre, M. Rodríguez, F. Salles, Dependability of COTS microkernel-based systems, IEEE Trans. Comput. 51 (2) (2002) 138–163.

[49] G.S. Choi, R.K. Iyer, FOCUS: an experimental environment for fault sensitivity analysis, IEEE Trans. Comput. 41 (1992) 1515–1526.

[50] E. Jenn, J. Arlat, M. Rimen, J. Ohlsson, J. Karlsson, Fault injection into VHDL models: the MEFISTO tool, Proceedings of the 24th International Symposium on Fault-Tolerant Computing, Pasadena, CA, USA, 1994, pp. 66–75.

[51] S. Dawson, F. Jahanian, T. Mitton, Testing of fault-tolerant and real-time distributed systems via protocol fault injection, Proceedings of the International Symposium on Fault Tolerant Computing, Sendai, Japan, Jun, 1996, pp. 404–414.

[52] M. Assaf, S. Das, E. Petriu, L. Jin, C. Jin, D. Biswas, et al., Hardware and software co-design in space compaction of cores-based digital circuits, in: proceedings of the 21st IEEE Instrumentation and Measurement Technology Conference (IMTC 04), Como, Italy, May 2004, vol. 2, 2004, pp. 503–1508.

[53] K. Goswami, DEPEND: a simulation-based environment for system level dependability analysis, IEEE Trans. Comput. 46 (1997) 60–74.

[54] C. Kwang-Ting, H. Shi-Yu, D. Wei-Jin, Fault emulation: a new methodology for fault grading, IEEE Trans. CAD Integr. Circuits Syst. 18 (1999) 1487–1495.

[55] P. Civera, L. Macchiarulo, M. Rebaudengo, M. Sonza Reorda, M. Violante, New techniques for efficiently assessing reliability of SOCs, Microelectronics J. 34 (2003) 53–61.

[56] L. Antoni, R. Leveugle, B. Feher, Using run-time reconfiguration for fault injection applications, IEEE Trans. Instrum. Meas. 52 (5) (2003) 1468–1473.

[57] D. de Andrés, J.C. Ruiz, D. Gil, P. Gil, Run-time reconfiguration for emulating transient faults in VLSI systems, Proceedings of the IEEE/IFIP International Conference on Dependable Systems and Networks (DSN-2006), Philadelphia, Pennsylvania, USA, June, 2006, pp. 291–300.

[58] D. de Andrés, J.C. Ruiz, D. Gil, P. Gil, Fault emulation for dependability evaluation of VLSI systems, IEEE Trans. VLSI Syst. 16 (2008) 4.

[59] J. Durães, Faultloads Based on Software Faults for Dependaility Benchmarking, 2006 (PhD Thesis, Department of Information Engineering, University of Coimbra).

[60] Y. Crouzet, H. Waeselynck, B. Lussier, D. Powell, The SESAME experience: from assembly languages to declarative models, Proceedings of the 2nd Workshop on Mutation Analysis (Mutation' 2006), IEEE, Raleigh, USA, Nov, 2006, p. 10.

[61] J. Durães, H. Madeira, Emulation of software faults by educated mutations at machine-code level, Proceedings of the 13th International Symposium on Software Reliability Engineering (ISSRE'02), Annapolis, Maryland, USA, Nov, 2002, pp. 329–340.

[62] K. Echtle, M. Leu, The EFA Fault Injector for Fault-Tolerant Distributed System Testing, IEEE Workshop on Fault-Tolerant Parallel and Distributed Systems, Amherst, MA, USA, 1992, pp. 28–35.

[63] K. Echtle, M. Leu, Test of fault tolerant distributed systems by fault injection, in: D. Pradhan, D. Avresky (Eds.), Fault-tolerant parallel and distributed systems, IEEE Computer Society Press, 1995, pp. 244–251.

[64] D. Avresky, J. Arlat, J.C. Laprie, Y. Crouzet, Fault injection for formal testing of fault tolerance, IEEE Trans. Reliab. 45 (3) (1996) 443–455.

[65] S. Dawson, F. Jahanian, T. Mitton, A software fault injection tool on real-time mach, Proceedings of the 16th IEEE Real-Time Systems Symposium, Pisa, Italy, Dec, 1995, pp. 130–140.

[66] E. Marsden, J.-C. Fabre, J. Arlat, Dependability of CORBA systems: service characterization by fault injection, Proceedings of the 21st IEEE Symposium on Reliable Distributed Systems (SRDS 2002), Osaka, Japan, Oct, 2002, pp. 276–285.

[67] K. Kanoun, L. Spainhower (Eds.), Dependability Benchmarking for Computer Systems, Wiley-IEEE Computer Society Press, 2008. http://eu.wiley.com/WileyCDA/WileyTitle/productCd-047023055X.html, 362 pp.

[68] Embedded Microprocessor Benchmarking Consortium, Web Site: http://www.eembc.org/.

[69] Web Site of the Standard Performance Evaluation Corporation: http://www.spec.org/.

[70] E. Rudolf (Ed.), Performance Evaluation and Benchmarking With Realistic Applications, MIT Press, 2001.

[71] Web Site of the Transaction Processing Performance Council: http://www.tpc.org/.

[72] D. Wilson, B. Murphy, L. Spainhower, Progress on defining standardized classes of computing the dependability of computer systems, Proceedings of the DSN 2002 Workshop on Dependability Benchmarking, Washington, D.C., USA, 2002, pp. F1–F5.

[73] J. Zhu, J. Mauro, I. Pramanick, Robustness benchmarking for hardware maintenance events, Proceedings of the International Conference on Dependable Systems and Networks (DSN 2003), IEEE CS Press, San Francisco, CA, USA, 2003, pp. 115–122.

[74] J. Zhu, J. Mauro, I. Pramanick, R3—a framework for availability benchmarking, Proceedings of the International Conference on Dependable Systems and Networks (DSN 2003), San Francisco, CA, USA, 2003, pp. B86–B87.

[75] A. Mukherjee, D.P. Siewiorek, Measuring software dependability by robustness benchmarking, IEEE Trans. Softw. Eng. 23 (6) (1997) 366–376.

[76] A. Kalakech, T. Jarboui, J. Arlat, Y. Crouzet, K. Kanoun, Benchmarking operating system dependability: Windows 2000 as a case study, Proceedings of the 2004 Pacific Rim International Symposium on Dependable Computing (Papeete, Tahiti, French Polynesia), 2004, pp. 261–270.

[77] A. Kalakech, K. Kanoun, Y. Crouzet, J. Arlat, Benchmarking the dependability of Windows NT, 2000 and XP, Proceedings of the International Conference on Dependable Systems and Networks (DSN-2004), Florence, Italy, 2004, pp. 681–686.

[78] K. Kanoun, Y. Crouzet, Dependability benchmarking for operating systems, Int. J. Perform. Eng. 2 (3) (2006) 275–287.

[79] K. Kanoun, Y. Crouzet, A. Kalakech, A.-E. Rugina, P. Rumeau, Benchmarking the dependability of Windows and Linux using postmark workloads, Proceedings of the 16th International Symposium on Software Reliability Engineering (ISSRE-2005) (Chicago, USA), 2005.

[80] P. Koopman, J. DeVale, Comparing the robustness of POSIX operating systems, Proceedings of the 29th International Symposium on Fault-Tolerant Computing (FTCS-29) (Madison, WI, USA), IEEE CS Press, 1999, pp. 30–37.

[81] C. Shelton, P. Koopman, K.D. Vale, Robustness testing of the Microsoft Win32 API, Proceedings of the International Conference on Dependable Systems and Networks (DSN-2000) (New York, NY, USA), IEEE CS Press, 2000, pp. 261–270.

[82] A. Albinet, J. Arlat, J.-C. Fabre, Characterization of the impact of faulty drivers on the robustness of the Linux kernel, International Conference on Dependable Systems and Networks (Florence, Italy), 2004, pp. 867–876.

[83] J. Durães, H. Madeira, Characterization of operating systems behavior in the presence of faulty drivers through software fault emulation, Proceedings of the 2002 Pacific Rim International Symposium on Dependable Computing (PRDC-2002) (Tsukuba City, Ibaraki, Japan), 2002, pp. 201–209.

[84] European Project on Dependability Benchmarking, IST-2000-25425, http://www.laas.fr/DBench.

[85] Special Interest Group on Dependability Benchmarking of the IFIP Working Group 10.4 http://homepages.laas.fr/kanoun/ifip_wg_10_4_sigdeb/.

[86] K. Kanoun, et al., Project Full Final Report 2004, Project Reports Section, http://www.laas.fr/DBench.

[87] C. Béounes, M. Aguera, J. Arlat, S. Bachmann, C. Bourdeau, J.-E. Doucet, et al., SURF-2: a program for dependability evaluation of complex hardware and software systems, 23rd International Symposium on Fault-Tolerant Computing (FTCS-23), Toulouse, France, 1993, pp. 668–673.

[88] P. Koopman, J. Sung, C. Dingman, D. Siewiorek, T. Marz, Comparing operating systems using robustness benchmarks, Proceedings of the 16th International Symposium on Reliable Distributed Systems, Durham, USA, 1997, pp. 72–79.

[89] G. Hunt, D. Brubaher, Detours: binary interception of Win32 functions, 3rd USENIX Windows NT Symp., Seattle, Washington, USA, 1999, pp. 135–144.

[90] R. McGrath, W. Akkerman, Source Forge Strace Project, 2004. http://sourceforge.net/projects/strace.

ABOUT THE AUTHOR

Dr. Yves Crouzet is Chargé de Recherche at LAAS-CNRS (French National Centre for Scientific Research - Laboratory for Analysis and Architecture of Systems), member of the Dependable Computing and Fault Tolerance research group (http://www.laas.fr/TSF-EN/). His main research interests concern the design and realization of dependable VLSI circuits, the design of dependable computer architectures for critical embedded systems, the validation of software testing methods by mutation analysis, and the experimental assessment of dependable systems by means of fault injection. He is a member of the IEEE TC on Dependable Computing and Fault Tolerance and of the French SEE WG on Design and Validation for Dependability.

Dr. Karama Kanoun is Directeur de Recherche at LAAS-CNRS, in charge of the Dependable Computing and Fault Tolerance Research Group (http://www.laas.fr/~kanoun/). She was Visiting Professor at the University of Illinois, Urbana Champaign, USA in 1998. Her research interests include modeling and evaluation of computer system dependability considering hardware as well as software, and dependability benchmarking. She has authored or co-authored more than 150 conference and journal papers, 5 books and 10 book chapters. She has also co-directed the production of a book on Dependability Benchmarking (Wiley and IEEE Computer Society, 2008).

Dr. Kanoun is Chair of the Special Interest Group on Dependability Benchmarking of the International Federation for Information Processing (IFIP), and vice-Chair of the IFIP working group 10.4 on Dependable Computing and Fault Tolerance. She was the Principal Investigator of the DBench European project (Dependability Benchmarking), and managed the European Network of Excellence ReSIST, Resilience Survivability in IST.

ABOUT THE AUTHORS

Pragmatic Directions in Engineering Secure Dependable Systems

M. FARRUKH KHAN

Department of Computer Science,
Texas Southern University, Houston, Texas, USA

RAYMOND A. PAUL

Command & Control Policy Directorate
Office of the Secretary of Defense (OSD/NII)
Department of Defense, Washington, DC

Abstract

All large and complex computer and communications systems have an intrinsic requirement to be *dependable* since their failure can cause significant losses in terms of life or treasure. Such the systems are expected to have the attributes of *reliability, availability, safety, confidentiality, survivability, integrity,* and *maintainability.*

   Current software and hardware systems continue to evolve in complexity at rapid rates. Although the increase in the complexity of single artifact (such as number of logical decision points in a software package) can often be tracked with Moore's Law like approximations, systems constructed out of larger number of smaller subsystems defy such classifications. The reason for this added complexity is that interactions between the subsystems explode exponentially in the size of the parent system. Yet all component interactions must be addressed exhaustively to predict accurate behavior of the whole system. The challenge that we face is that it is seldom possible to model or test all such interactions in a given system. As a result, building dependable complex systems with realistic assessment of risks of failure is an extremely difficult endeavor. Attempts have been made to ameliorate the difficulty in the engineering of dependable complex systems using lessons from engineering methodologies in other domains.

ADVANCES IN COMPUTERS, VOL. 84
ISSN: 0065-2458/DOI: 10.1016/B978-0-12-396525-7.00005-8

141

We discuss key attributes of dependable complex systems, with a special emphasis on security where information is involved. We review classical approaches to designing, building, and maintaining dependable complex systems. We present promising features and novel ideas applicable to the lifecycle of dependable complex systems. Most of our discussion is focused within the domain of hardware and software systems. Over time, practitioners in dependable engineering have learned lessons from previous experience and continue to present prescriptive approaches discovered through research and analysis. These lessons and approaches are often applicable to other engineering domains such as construction, transportation, and industrial control.

We look at specific engineering challenges and proposed solutions pertaining to the following general domains, with occasional examples from any branch of engineering:

- dependable hardware/software systems;
- secure dependable systems;
- dependable cloud infrastructure and applications.

Finally, we conclude with the observation that several approaches are applicable across all these domains and identify accessible techniques that have good potential to increase the dependability of systems. These approaches can be considered as axiomatic in building any future complex systems with a high degree of dependability.

1. Introduction

Dependable computing and communication systems provide extensive facilities that allow reliable, safe and secure dissemination, exchange, and archiving of critical information. During the past half a century, reliability and availability of computer systems have increased by an order of magnitude during each decade [1]. As far as technological feasibility is concerned, communication bandwidths and computational prowess have advanced sufficiently to bring significant number of new e-commerce and e-government applications into the realm of possible deployment. Systems are built and verified to perform specific functions or services, as detailed in functional specifications by engineers. Dependable systems perform according to specifications under most environmental constraints, and under expected stresses.

If functions in the system specification are not performed, or performed incorrectly, then some type of *failure* is perceived to have taken place [1]. Dependable systems have relatively small number of failures. The acceptable levels of failures of a system vary with specific applications. Commonly used measures include *mean time between failures*, MTBF, and availability or uptime, as a percent of total operational time. The levels could be take other forms, such as probability of a critical failure in an operational ship, or probability of exceeding the maximum threshold for a contaminant in drinking water supply, or probability of going outside the maximum and minimum pressures in a Boric acid safety tank for a nuclear reactor. In any domain, users, stakeholders, and policymakers need to determine the acceptable probabilities of failure.

Other concepts that are very closely related to dependability have been used in the literature, and briefly mentioned here. *Trustworthiness* [2] refers to how closely the actual dependable system behavior is in line with expectations for that system. *Survivability* [3] seeks to ensure that a system retains dependability properties in the presence of malicious attacks as well as natural failures and accidents (although we have chosen to use this as an attribute of dependable systems: see Section 2). Most such systems are also *critical*, in that their failure may result in loss of human life, injury, significant environmental harm, or great monetary loss. Therefore, special attention needs to be paid to the dependability of such systems [4].

The users of the complex systems such as government and business, as well as the technology enablers including policy makers, engineers, scientists, and regulators have a stake in the successful and productive deployment of dependable systems in any area of endeavor. Therefore, the techniques developed, and the lessons learned during the course of engineering and use of complex systems cut across disciplines of computer & communications, manufacturing, construction, transportation, etc. This cross-pollination of ideas and translational development of knowledge are essential in the collective progress of state of the art of dependable engineering. This also helps minimize actual costs of progress without repeating painful lessons learned in a specific discipline because of unforeseen faults and catastrophic failures. Lessons that are learned in one area of dependability and reliability are often applicable in other areas, with a slight change of vocabulary and application of appropriate context. Whether small- or large scale, such systems require multifaceted approaches that balance the issues of efficiency, cost-effectiveness, regard for national laws, robustness, accountability, stability, and interoperability [5].

In the subsequent sections discuss different terms employed in the dependability communities and review basics of dependable technologies. We present examples of dependability in actual systems from several domains. Often special insights are provided when production systems fail in an unexpected manner, and we include examples of lessons gleaned in the aftermath of such failures. Where appropriate, we place special emphasis on the security aspects as a component of dependable systems. We observe that beyond the raw processing power, bandwidth capacity, strength of materials, etc., systems can and do fail. The lessons point to challenges posed by interactions among the complex system components and the intractable nature of calculating all outcomes, thus making *dependable system* a relative term. Risks are minimized by proper use of various protocols and realistic and conservative expectation of risks for faults and failures. The contention is that engineering and maintenance of dependable systems require incorporating multifaceted objectives before they are certified to be sufficiently robust to form the viable basis of critical systems infrastructure.

2.   What Are Dependable Systems?

Dependable systems are desirable since they are "trustworthy," as discussed in the security communities and reliable engineering communities. Dependable systems are typically characterized by the the following attributes:

- *Reliability:* the system behaves as expected, with very few errors.
- *Availability:* the system and services are mostly available, with very little or no down time.
- *Safety:* the systems do not pose unacceptable risks to the environment or the health of users.
- *Confidentiality:* data and other information should not be divulged without intent and authorization.
- *Survivability:* The system services should be robust enough to withstand accidents and attacks.
- *Integrity:* System data should not be modified without intent and authorization.
- *Maintainability:* Maintenance of system hardware and services should not be difficult or excessively expensive.

These attributes have some overlap among themselves. For example, just like security, it is a weakest link phenomenon, in that the strength of the whole is determined by the weakest link in the chain. Thus, for a product or system to be considered dependable, it should posses all the aforementioned attributes. Conversely, a system is *not* dependable in proportion to the degree of lack of these dependability attributes. In most cases, dependability is also not a binary phenomenon (present or absent) but based on gradations and acceptable thresholds. These thresholds are specific to infrastructures such as electronic, electromechanical, and quantum, as well as applications, such as communications, process control, and data processing.

Among the dependability attributes, some need to be emphasized over others in specific system applications. For example, in banking transactions, accuracy is crucial, and if accuracy cannot be guaranteed, the transaction must be aborted and rolled back. In contrast, sensors controlling a deep sea oil rig may be large in number, and the base station utilizes all the signals, including signals from malfunctioning sensors and a composite picture is constructed from all available data. Hundred percent accuracy can be sacrificed if sufficient degrees of availability, survivability, and maintainability are achieved within a budget threshold. Similarly, intelligence communications demand security and privacy but might not be that concerned with delays of the order of seconds or minutes.

One of the keys for dependable systems is that they should be empirically verifiable in terms of their dependability. That means that fashionable or trendy methodologies that may be very popular need to be objectively assessed on the basis of their true effectiveness. One of the measures for dependability is the number of *faults*. Faults are errors in design or implementation that cause *failures*. A *failure* is deemed to have occurred if any of the functional specifications of the system are not met.

Failures can range from minor to catastrophic, depending upon the impact of failure on the system and the immediate environment. Minor failures are referred to as *errors*. The underlying faults may thus be prioritized, based on their potential impact. Lack of dependability means that the system is undependable due to shortcoming in one or more of the dependability attributes, caused by faults in the system and potential cause of system failure.

Faults can manifest themselves during the operation of a system. Such faults are known as active. Otherwise, the faults may be present and possibly manifest themselves in the future. Such faults are referred to as dormant, and the purpose of the testing phase in systems engineering is to discover as many dormant and active faults as possible before deployment and general use of the tested system.

3. Classical Approaches to Engineering Dependable Systems

Dependable systems must have a minimal number of failures that are caused by faults. Therefore, attention needs to be paid to minimizing the faults in a system and countering possible faults to ameliorate the negative impact of dormant faults. This involves prevention, detection, and removal of faults during the design, construction, and testing phases. After deployment, fault treatment during execution (also referred to as *fault tolerance*) and continuing proactive fault monitoring and removal from systems are also necessary.

Early period of computer era used nondigital components and engineers were deeply concerned about dependability, as detailed in [6]. Fault tolerance research was a staple in computer and communications systems studies, and IEEE had reliability, availability, and serviceability were akin to the aforementioned dependability attributes. Safety, security, and survivability were not named explicitly, since the penetration of computers in complex systems was still in its infancy, and thus these were more peripheral concerns.

Over time, the utilization of complex computer systems has moved from sophisticated engineers and scientists to the current much larger base of nonspecialist end users. Another change that has occurred over these decades is that application domain has significantly widened, growing out of the controlled environments of research labs into almost all facets of business. This expansion exposed the systems to much wider variety of environmental factors, including temperature, EM interference, dust and other contaminants, moisture, noise, and so forth. The changed nature of utilization of current and future systems necessitates a much higher degree of in-built intelligence within the systems service interfaces in order to effectively deal with the full variety of heterogeneous peers and environments encountered.

The pervasiveness of complex systems means that more and more applications require dependable processing, distribution, storage, and delivery. Many of these objectives are interrelated, such as security depends on integrity and confidentiality. Another observation is that tools are distinct from objectives, and a single tool would typically be utilized in the realization of multiple objectives. For example, good software engineering practices are essential for building software systems [7]. Although good SE practices go a long way in enabling dependability objectives, they are not sufficient by themselves in the construction and maintenance of dependable systems. We examine key issues and concerns that need to be considered in the deployment of dependable infrastructures and policies for complex systems.

3.1 Enabling Technologies for Dependable Systems

We are witnessing a period of computer and communications history when advances in technology coupled with advances in algorithms, software, and hardware have made an exiting array of services that were never before practical on a large scale. The scale and complexity of these systems pose daunting engineering challenges and require utilization of sophisticated techniques and best practices during design, development, and operation. Besides normal dependable operation, these large systems must also be able to resist deliberate sabotage by the introduction of malicious faults or direct attack from the external environment.

In order to build and maintain dependable systems, faults need to be combated all stages with the following activities:

- fault avoidance and prevention: this is done during design and construction phases;
- fault tolerance and recovery: this happens when the system is operational and in use;
- fault removal and repair: this is part of ongoing maintenance during the lifetime of the system;

An essential supporting activity is to statistically estimate the number, type, severity, and impact of faults. This allows the developers and maintainers of the systems to prioritize the repair of faults with limited budget and personnel. Fault estimation also allows dependability risk assessment for a system. These risk estimates have a measurable basis and can form the basis of quantitative risk assessment that can be divulged to managers, stakeholders, and users. Finally, fault frequency information in a given system is useful when developing future systems with similar specifications.

3.2   Fault Avoidance and Prevention

Ingredients of this include good practices in the building of systems. The start is with through and unambiguous requirements gathering from users and stakeholders. After that, compatible specifications are derived from the requirements. The specifications are realized as subsystems through component engineering, that is, using relatively small components to build larger systems. Each partial system is based on part of the specification, and all components together must cover the specifications in their entirety. The smaller components must be dependable, since they form the building bricks for the final systems. Faults may be introduced through unforeseen interactions among components. Therefore, integration testing should be performed after components have been put together to form bigger components. Testing of compatibility with specifications all stages should be performed. This will require testing of components as soon as they are ready, and regression testing after components is combined. For example, if C is constructed by combining A and B, then (i) A and B should be tested independently; (ii) C, formed from A and B should be tested independently; (iii) functionalities within A and B should be tested again after integration into C (regression testing).

3.3   Fault Tolerance and Recovery

Except for the simplest of systems, faults cannot be eliminated entirely. There is a possibility of undetected faults. There could be faults that are not fixed deliberately due to the prohibitive costs of their removal. Fault tolerance and recovery are required in order to deal with system errors that manifest due to such faults. Errors may occur and stay undetected until they propagate to the system interface or impact a visible system function. In order to facilitate early detection of errors, a system could be taken offline and scanned for latent errors in early stages. Corrective action could then be means to avoid the manifestation of errors or failures in later stages in the system.

Another aspect of fault tolerance is the recovery of the system *after* an error has occurred. The minimal level of action is the full disclosure of the nature and severity of the error to all the peer systems and the stakeholders. Such disclosure is essential to allow stakeholders to assess risks caused by the newly manifested error and make optimal decisions in regard to what corrective action needs to taken in terms of development, patching, change of policies, etc. If the error impacts the service interface, the users should also be apprised of the error in an expeditious manner. Delay in their timely updating generates doubts about the integrity of the organization in charge of creating the system, undermine confidence, and may thus cause loss of large portions of the user base. This is precisely what happened in the case of Intel

Pentium bug as Intel delayed the acknowledgment of the full extent of the fault in the Pentium chip discovered by their customers [8]. Potential damage done to customer confidence is estimated to have cost Intel about half a billion dollars.

In terms of actual recovery from an error, if the error causes any changes in data beyond acceptable specifications, the state of the system is required to be restored to a saved point before the occurrence of the error. This is referred to as *rolling back* the state of the system to one of the previous stable points in time for the system (a *checkpoint*). An example of rollback is when a database transaction is canceled in presence of an error. The transaction may consist of multiple computational steps. If any step fails to complete, or if the transaction is aborted by an outside agent such as the user or the server, then all completed steps in the partial transaction need to be rolled back. This requires that the system maintains enough meta information about the system state that allows it to undo the effects the steps that have completed.

The specific errors can be ignored when the changes they cause within the system state fall within the acceptable noise threshold specifications of the system. This requires care, and the actual course of action in the aftermath should fully incorporate the feedback from the system users. This is best for long-term stability of a system, since even innocuous faults can escalate into failures, and even critical failures within documented expectations are more acceptable to users and conducive to building assurance in the actual capabilities of the system.

In still others, a specific course of action needs to be followed when an error occurs. This is referred to as the *exception handling* procedure. Exception handlers need to be incorporated in the design of systems. The description of exception handlers should be included in the design phase of a system. In terms of implementation priorities, errors deemed to have the highest probabilities and the most impact are the most serious, and definitely should be have detailed risk plans and exception handlers.

Once incorporated in the system, these exception handlers could invoke actions to compensate for the error, provide alternate data, hardware, or functionality to move forward, disable affected functionalities (causing service outage) to prevent damage, avoid erroneous results, or for the sake of safety. The exception handlers could also raise external alarms for alerting human operators, or for consumption by peer systems. In extreme cases, the service outages could also cascade into total system shutdown. A recent example that illustrates many of these fault recovery ideas is the shutdown of Fukushima nuclear reactors after partial or total meltdowns of the cores of at least three reactors due to damage caused by an earthquake and tsunami. The active fault revelation prodded the project managers (in this case the government) to shut down at least two more reactors vulnerable to seismic activity. Intermediate fault treatment consisting of cooling the cores by addition of water failed and alternate course of action was taken. Explosions caused weakening of the containment infrastructure and the foundations. This could lead to structural collapse and fallout of large amounts of radiation into the environment. Catastrophic failure of one system will typically produce a range of preventative reactions in other similar systems. As a safety measure, other system managers could decide to close down their systems until further review and risk assessment. In this case, the failures of Japanese projects prompted Germany to close seven nuclear plants, with the remaining slated for closing during 2011. Through review, but not immediate closure, of similar systems, design as well as real-time monitoring protocols to assess probable risks is being performed for many sites in China, the EU, etc. Yet another approach has been the relative lack of action in the short term, such as delay by owners in upgrading fire protection systems of the Indian Point reactor complex in the USA that is deemed to to be in close proximity of very large population centers [9]. Such a course of action is not recommended but depicts realties of friction between business interests, regulation, and policy making for public good.

One challenge is that offline scanning of dependable systems requires downtime, and this may not be acceptable in many real-time and business systems. Continuous monitoring of system for faults while the system is in use (online monitoring) can address the problem of downtime, but only partially so. In addition, some faults require that the system be offline. Continuous monitoring utilizes resources such as CPU time and communications bandwidth and therefore can impact the performance of the system and be a very expensive resource sink. In order to make optimal cost-benefit decisions about the type and frequency of fault monitoring, it needs to be clear what levels of degradation in performance as well as outage of the system are acceptable for a given systems. Based on those values of acceptable costs, the optimal strategy is to use offline monitoring for fault detection that is too resource intensive or requires that the system be offline before treating the faults. All other faults are treated through continuous monitoring of the system.

3.4   Fault Removal and Repair

Fault removal and repair take place during design and construction of a system, as well as during the production phase. Sufficient time and budget should be allocated for thorough testing of all system components. Testing involves checking of compatibility of the system functions against the specifications of the system that detail the expected functionality. This is also referred to as *validation* of the system. The most insidious errors occur because system specifications are incorrect or incomplete. Under such circumstances, the system is built according to specifications, and therefore testing limited to validation of the system does not indicate any errors. Errors only show up when the system is live and when the components are integrated into other components, or worse, errors are discovered when the system is in production phase, with typically greater losses. Fault removal then involves corrective maintenance through discovery of whether the failure is in specification, design, construction, or testing. Depending on the results, if errors or omissions are discovered in the specification or design documents, those documents should be revised to correct those errors, followed by revised engineering and regressive testing. In complex systems, potential errors are large in number and testing and fixing all possible paths is not tractable.

One technique under such circumstances is the controlled introduction of faults in the systems, known as *fault injection*. The system is then stress tested with live data but before production to indicate the behavior of various exception handlers, as well as the overall stability of the system in probabilistic terms. The results are especially useful in predicting the behavior of the system when unexpected errors manifest and to determine overall failure risk for the system. Managers may thus make informed decisions to determine if a system is dependable enough in terms of stability, safety, and security for live production use.

In contrast to fault tolerance via inbuilt mechanisms such as thresholds, alarms, exception handlers, and internal exchange of execution paths and activation of alternate components, *fault removal and repair* involve interaction with agents outside the system. Besides self-repair and recovery, such fault removal is an essential component of *maintenance* of dependable systems and is referred to as *preventative maintenance*. Vendors continue to improve and refine a system already in production in order to discover latent faults and possible improvements and enhancements. Based on the results of the improvements, the vendors release mods such as patches, repair components, or procedures to be applied to production systems to correct faults. Critical mods require urgent application to avert potential failures. Less critical mods could be applied periodically, such as every day, or every quarter, etc., applied as part of regular preventive maintenance and might be packaged with minor feature enhancements. All changes are preserved in logs that allow for process improvement in the future, such as project black books in companies such as Boeing, or postmortem reports compiled by the development team after the completion of a project. Systematic oversights and errors that are repeated in several components or multiple systems designed and built in the same organization can also be discovered and corrected through this methodology. Some systems may be unique enough that failures warrant a closer look by engineering review by an independent body. Such was the case of the space shuttle *Challenger* failure when a panel led by former Secretary of State William P. Rogers and included the late Prof. Richard Feynman was constituted to discover the reasons for the failure for the failure of the space shuttle [10], and it was determined that NASA failed to discover technical flaws as well as administrative problems [11]. The Appendix by Feynman states engineering design problems that clearly apply to software engineering practices, such as:

The Space Shuttle Main Engine was handled in a different manner, top down, we might say. The engine was designed and put together all at once with relatively little detailed preliminary study of the material and components. Then when troubles are found in the bearings, turbine blades, coolant pipes, etc., it is more expensive and difficult to discover the causes and make changes.

This emphasizes the importance of through unit testing of all software components before integration testing takes place. Quite often, deadline slippage and change of scope of projects become causes to scuttle testing phases and reduce the dependability of the systems. This also relates to the management culture, as also observed in the report: *To be sure, there have been recent suggestions by management to curtail such elaborate and expensive tests as being unnecessary at this late date in Shuttle history.*

4. Security Assurance in Dependable Systems

As discussed in Section 2, the following objectives are required in the engineering of dependable systems: reliability, availability, safety, confidentiality, survivability, integrity, and maintainability. A subset of these, along with other essential attributes, comprises the *security* of the system:

- confidentiality: keeping secret the communication between the sender and the receiver, as well as the stored content, and other information;
- integrity: ensuring that data are not modified accidentally or maliciously;
- authentication: verifying the identity of the principals in communications;
- nonrepudiation: inability of the principals to disown earlier communications;
- availability: ensuring that system services are operational and usable whenever the principals require to use them, including survivability in the presence of malicious attacks.

Security is considered paramount from many customer perspectives where survivability, safety, or maintainability are not the foremost concerns. For example, this is true for client-end of the cloud services (Section 5) because the clients have implicit confidence and high assurance about availability, reliability, survivability, etc., based on the personal experience & user expectations, as well as the reputation and track record of the cloud service provider as compared with other vendors with similar service offerings (relative performance). Examples of such user applications include online email, entertainment services, and much of online advertising. In such instances, users' major concerns about the system dependability are captured by the attributes of security mentioned above. Therefore in such systems, the focus of dependability boils down to strong security. Since all dependable systems incorporate at least some attributes of security, we shall discuss implementation issues related to security of computer and communications systems in the following sections. At the software level, security objectives other than availability can be implemented through the use of cryptographic security protocols. Survivability is subsumed by the more general concept of availability, the difference being that survivability is in face of malicious attack and may degrade system to a subset of core functionalities. Given these cryptographic functions, it should be relatively simple to achieve all of the following dependability objectives, at least in theory.

4.1   Technologies for Secure Dependable Systems

For the security objective, at a very basic level, the technology of cryptography utilizes a *key* to allow the transformation of input data into unintelligible material that cannot efficiently be deciphered to obtain the original data without using the key. Thus if the key can be kept confidential, the encrypted data are deemed to be secure from revealed or divulged to parties without access to the original key.

The available cryptography techniques may be broadly divided into secret-key cryptography and public-key cryptography. In secret-key cryptography, a secret (or key) is shared between the sender and the receiver. This shared secret is used to process the data at each end of the communication. Without possession of the secret, it should be computationally infeasible to encrypt or decrypt data. In public-key cryptography, a key for user x consists of a pair, *(public(x),private(x))*. For the purpose of encryption, the owner of the key uses private, whereas all others use *public(x)*. In addition, it should be computationally infeasible to discover *private (x)* given only the value of *public(x)*. With a slight modification, the above system can also be used to provide unforgeable digital signatures [12].

As part of dependability, many applications in business and communications demand *confidentiality* of messages that are exchanged between the systems. Confidentiality is also a key attribute of dependable systems as defined by researchers such as [5,13]. For example, business customers involved in online shopping using credit cards do not wish to divulge their credit card numbers to third parties. Similarly, content of emails needs to stay secure during transport through routers. Cryptography solves the problem of transporting such communication over public channels, that is, channels that may be monitored by a third party in order to observe what data travel over it. There is a tradeoff between level of security and the efficiency of specific encryption protocols, and desired level of dependability can determine the selection of a protocol. Thus after DES was broken, US government has stipulated the use of AES in all sensitive installations and systems.

Another dependability attribute, *data integrity*, guarantees the accuracy of data being stored or exchanged among systems. Verifiable accuracy of data is a requirement of many dependable systems. Data may be corrupted due to many reasons: through physical phenomenon such as radiation, heat, light, magnetic or electric induction, and vibrations; through erroneous or unexpected system interactions due to weaknesses in the protocols; or deliberately corruption of data by malicious agents. Integrity is particularly relevant in terms of financial transactions, quantitative data, textual data, and critical data such as that used for management and feedback of real-time embedded systems in transportation and industrial control. Some applications may require other dependability attributes but tolerate loss of integrity to some extent. For example, reduction of resolution or addition of noise in audio or video data will compromise integrity but may still be acceptable to a certain extent. An efficient means of measuring data integrity is through the use of *cryptographic hashes*. A "fingerprint" of the source data file is generated and packaged along with the source. The recipient can generate the fingerprint of the received file and tally with the enclosed fingerprint to detect if there has been any modification of the source [14]. Many vendors publish software or patches along with hashes to prevent unauthorized modification of their published files.

Authentication of the source is essential in order to avoid impersonation attacks, where a malicious intruder masquerades as a genuine principal. In today's highly connected world, it would be desirable to have two-way mutual authentication, that is, both the source and the destination authenticate each other before full communication can be established between them.

Nonrepudiation is essential to prevent a principal from denying a previous commitment with another principal. Thus in the case of a dispute, a third party, such a judge in a court of law, should be able to ascertain and affirm the identities of concerned parties in the context of a given transaction.

Secure, authenticated communication in different domains of business or government often requires all of the above attributes. For example, secure and verifiable public transactions (such voting in a national referendum) using public-key infrastructure (PKI) will require a dependable system with all of the above transaction attributes. To ensure confidentiality, each principal could vote after encrypting the vote with the voter's private key. For the purposes of verification, each particular vote could be readily verified by using the respective voter's public key. This process could be repeated as many times as necessary by different entities.

On the other hand, a large number of votes could be divided up into batches of much smaller jobs, and these jobs could be processed in parallel. In this manner, a community can potentially accelerate the vote counting process to any desirable speed. We see that we have integrity, since tampering the voting information will effective destroy it; nonrepudiation, since only the concerned voter knows the private key; and verifiability, since anyone can use the public key and verify a particular vote. As far as confidentiality is concerned, it is a policy issue. If needed, confidentiality could be incorporated by either using secret-key encryption or by not publishing public keys except to the concerned parties, such as election commissions and judges. Further elaboration may be found in standard texts such as [14].

4.2 Infrastructure for Secure Dependable Systems

Security attributes are implemented using underlying technologies of cryptography and associated security protocols. The proliferation of weak cryptography was abetted in large part by restrictive export controls of the US government. This had major international impact since an overwhelming proportion of internationally traded software is produced by a handful of well-known US firms and based on US stipulated standards such as DES.

For almost three decades, weak protocols have been the main-stay of conventional cryptography, and probably bulk of hitherto secret information has encrypted with them. For example, DES was developed and standardized by the NSA along the lines of an IBM proposal and uses a 56-bit key. There have been a strong concerns regarding DES. One is that the NSA may have deliberately left a trapdoor in the standard that would allow it decipher encrypted data with relative ease. The relevant authorities deny such a design loophole, but unease about DES somehow persisted. The other and probably more practical concern was that a key length of 56-bits is not sufficient for the current adversaries computational prowess. Thus anyone who is well-funded (such as many governments and corporations) may be able to listen in to DES-encrypted communication. For example, distributed.net and EFF responded to an RSA Inc. challenge designed to emphasize the need for newer protocols by breaking a DES key in under 24h. Users and designers of dependable systems should therefore make allowances for the fact that data that are secure today could conceivably be public in a few decades due to advances in technology.

Besides advances in technology, secure systems could also be compromised due to weakness in the protocols or their specific implementation. Quantum communications are provably secure based on the laws of physics. However, a specific implementation was broken. Researchers showed through experiment that detectors in commercially available quantum communication systems could be controlled using remote sources of photons and thus tracelessly acquire the full secret key [15]. Such incidents underscore the need for continuous review and remediation of systems to keep them dependable.

Adversaries can be ingenious in defeating the security of a system, and we continue to see frequent examples of this phenomenon. It is surprising how many systems' dependability has been compromised through simple techniques such as snooping the electromagnetic spectrum to capture keys, or discovering calculations within a smart card through reverse engineering. An excellent primer of related engineering issues and examples, where the author provides numerous examples of compromised systems in the domains of traffic, banking, utility metering, computer hardware, biometrics, etc., and suggests a mix of technological and management strategies to make information security more dependable in diverse systems is provided in [16].

Dependable systems researchers need to develop integrated architectures, algorithms, and protocols to that incorporate security requirements in the design, and not as an afterthought. This requires the development starting from comprehensive study of possible security threats, and the techniques available to combat those threats. Thus, security engineering professionals should be indispensable in the building of requirements, design, and construction of the protocols in dependable systems [17].

In addition, there are a few other usable international standards available that fit the bill of strong crypto, such as IDEA, etc., that have been well documented [18]. In some of there standards, there are a myriad of problems such as patent protection, efficiency of execution, etc. These may be the determining factors in deciding the specific strong cryptography technology to use in a specific dependable system.

5. Dependability in the Cloud

An increasingly significant amount of data processing, transactions, and communications are taking place online through service vendors such as Google, Facebook, Amazon, and Microsoft [19]. Data storage and application service processing are centered at the vendor servers (i.e., *the cloud*), and the end users are provided through lightweight clients. The clients are connected to the vendor cloud through communication services. There are many reasons for increasing popularity of the cloud computing paradigm since it allows users to use essentially limitless resources without major commitment to hardware and software and scale up their consumption on a pay as you go model. In addition, concerns about updating hardware and software are greatly reduced due to delegation to the cloud. Similar model was used in high-performance computing consortia, but it is only recently that cloud computing has been embraced by larger numbers of consumers and businesses. These communication services form the Achilles heal of cloud computing, because of issues of inefficiencies of moving large amounts of data as well as information security issues. Besides low-bandwidth services such as email, social networking, photo, and video sharing, cloud computing has started making inroads into more data intensive applications such as enterprise resource planning (ERP), despite difficulties in the areas of security, interoperability, adapting ERP business processes to specific organizations [20].

Although everything that we discussed about dependable conventional systems apply equally to cloud-based systems, cloud services are characterized by requirements of enormous scale in terms of large user base and demand for 24×7 operation of services, putting special demand on the attribute of *availability* of dependable systems. In addition, the daisy chaining of many systems in the cloud paradigm can impact failure probabilities, since failure of one system amounts to failure of all the systems in the chain.

Actual failure modes in the cloud have been studied, such as [19], and provide guidance of avenues for effort to decrease failure rates and thus increase dependability. A number of open issues are related to the dependability of the cloud systems [21].

5.1   Scale and Complexity in the Internet

Most cloud systems use the Internet as the essential underlying infrastructure, and therefore dependability of the Internet is an additional component in determining the overall dependability of the cloud-based services. The Internet is very big, containing some 37,000 autonomous systems (ASes) and 355,000 blocks of addresses. Because it is so huge, a large-scale external event such as a major natural disaster will have a minimal, localized effect on the Internet. However, if even a small part of the Internet goes down, it will have a direct effect on a large number of people and steep reduction in the overall dependability of the systems tied to it. Therefore, it is very often the case that reliability and performance bottleneck is between the cloud servers and the end user, that is, in the Internet.

There are many issues to consider when thinking about the dependability of the Internet as part of the cloud service. The complexity of the Internet results from its huge size and the number of interconnections between ASes. The problem is compounded by other factors. Modeling the interconnection system is hard because we only have partial views of it. Another factor is that the interconnection system depends on other complex and interdependent systems. The interconnection ecosystem is also self-organizing and highly decentralized. It is also dynamic and constantly changing, and the patterns of use are also constantly evolving. Finally, the Internet is always increasing in size, and as a result, all of its related components grow with it, that is, the number of ASes, the number of routes, the number of interconnections, the volume of traffic, etc. All of these factors make dependability in the cloud difficult to define and measure.

The recommended course of action for cloud services is to have sufficient redundancy in software, hardware, and communications for failover processing in case of critical faults. Designers should also avoid single points of failure by having distributed control for all services. It is also recommended to introduce changes such as new hardware, software, or protocols gradually, for example, in a machine, then in a system, then in several Ases, and then the entire Internet. Because of the contagious nature of the Internet, there need to be effective quarantine policies and mechanisms in place when faults in any portion of the Internet are detected [22].

5.2   Survivability of Systems in the Cloud

Survivability is the ability of a system to adapt and recover from a serious failure, or more generally the ability to retain service functionality in the face of threats. This could be related to small local events—such as equipment failures, and reconfigure itself essentially automatically and over a time scale of seconds to minutes. Survivability could relate to major events, such as a large natural disaster or a capable attack, on a time scale of hours to days or even longer. Another important part of survivability is robustness. While survivability is to do with coping with the impact of events, robustness is to do with reducing the impact in the first place. Assigning probabilities to potential dangers is difficult because of uncertainty. In addition, there are no effective measures to actually assess the performance of the Internet [23]. Because of these and other issues, dependability is based on statistical measures of historical outages, faults, and failures.

At every level of the interconnection system in the Internet, there is little global information available, and what is available is incomplete and of unknown accuracy. Specifically, there are no maps of physical connections, traffic, and interconnections between ASes. There are a number of reasons for this lack of information. One is the physical complexity of the network fibers around the world, which change from time to time as well. Another reason is that probes have limited paths and will only reveal something about the path between two points in the Internet at the time of the probe. A security threat also exists, because if the physical aspect of the Internet is mapped, it could be potentially dangerous material in the hands of certain individuals and groups. Some groups have a commercial incentive for encouraging Internet anonymity and not having the networks mapped out. Another reason is that networks lack motivation to gather such information because it does not seem to serve them directly while being costly. Finally, there are no metrics for a network as a whole, and stakeholders must look closely at the idiosyncrasies of the specific subsystems in use [22].

6.   Further Considerations for Secure Dependable Systems

For the past decade, a lot of research has taken place in developing tools and techniques for secure dependable systems. In the security arena, these efforts have been highlighted with the development of such standards as Rijndael, IDEA, etc.

Strong cryptography provides an essential ingredient of privacy and security in the emerging IT infrastructures. Technologies for strong cryptography are also readily available. However, as is true in the maturing of most new technologies, technical feasibility of a product or service is but one part of the wider picture. In the case of incorporation of strong cryptography in dependable systems, there are a variety of issues that are needed to complete the picture. These include infrastructure development, security policies, and appropriate use of technology. These dimensions need to be incorporated in consumer education and cost-benefit analyses of the dependable systems. We elaborate below on each of these dimensions related to viable provision of security services in dependable systems.

6.1   Infrastructure Support for Secure Dependable Systems

Dependable systems communication is one of the more voracious consumers of available data bandwidth. Sometimes the communication overhead could be as high as 3000%. In addition, IT planners need to ensure widespread access to security services, including a robust, diverse, and secure PKI. In some applications, such as secure online voting, one can anticipate millions of encrypted transactions from an extremely wide geographic area, and with stringent timing requirements. This means that adequate infrastructure facilities are required for the provision of practical and sustainable security-enhanced goods and services [24]. Large amount of communication bandwidth should be provided among all centers of cryptographic data exchange. Clusters of public workstations fully equipped with pertinent software and hardware need to be available for people until at least the PCs become as common as the radio and the television. This will allow access to security services to virtually everyone, including those on the other side of the "digital divide."

There is large potential for rapid growth of e-business, and as such, encryption of communication needs to become widely prevalent rather than an exception. There are also things that, on first sight, may seem outside the purview of policy makers and IT administrators of non-IT-savvy countries. However, informed and intelligent choices in many instances are required to avoid security debacles [25]. Operating systems need to incorporate and support current open security standards. Application-level software needs to pay particular attention to robustness in the face of malicious attackers. Dependence on products from a single company should be avoided, and consumers should be empowered with choices. Products not conforming to open international standards should be avoided but tolerated to an extent.

6.2   Privacy of Information in Secure Dependable Systems

A major policy dichotomy is how to balance between users' right to privacy and anonymity on one hand, and the need and desire to have a maximum amount of information on the part of various law enforcement agencies. System developers may also wish to access information for statistical purposes or differential report generation. Policy making bodies will need to balance sometimes conflicting goals of business interests, efficiency, public good, national laws, and civil liberties. For example, there may be a requirement that all cryptographic keys be deposited securely with (or even generated by) a third party before they are used for encryption. This only delegates the original problem to another level, that is, to the level of trust of users in the selected third party.

In either case, there is a detrimental effect on the users' confidence in the privacy of their content, and adoption of selected applications proliferation and deployment of such systems by users' e-business and e-government. Another challenge for transnational system vendors is that a country's dependable computing and communications infrastructure in the business and service sectors may not be compatible with international peers. Under such circumstances, dependability definitions and thresholds need to be adjusted and potential growth in certain service sectors may suffer [26,27].

On the flip side, situations that demand transparency or accountability require that unconditional privacy or anonymity be tempered with key-recovery or key-disclosure mechanisms. These mechanisms should be well documented, consistent, applied with proper safe-guards (such as search warrants from law enforcement agencies). All the concerned parties should be clearly aware of the defined scopes, rights, and responsibilities. This also points to a need for competent, fair, and stable conflict resolution environment for all the concerned parties, including those inside the system [28].

In short, regulation should be well thought out, carefully measured, and follow the minimalist credo. Finding the optimal balance between consumer freedom and governmental oversight will require careful calculation of risks and benefits. Over-regulation can easily kill the growth potential of the IT sector.

6.3   Implementation Issues for Secure Dependable Systems

Sometimes current technology has full potential to provide an envisaged security service. However, the way a particular service is implemented and deployed may well compromise its security value by introducing dangerous vulnerabilities [29].

This is not an easily addressed problem, as experts in software engineering and theory of computation will attest. However, preventive measures can be employed to ameliorate the problems. These measures include formal protocol testing and verification methodologies; sound design methodologies; extensive prototype testing; and adopting the open systems paradigm.

Unlike consumer transactions themselves, protocols and specific implementations must be placed under the microscope of rigorous scrutiny in order to assess potential weaknesses, scalability, robustness, etc. Bulk of this must be done before the implementations are deployed. Any flaws that are discovered in the production phase should be expeditiously communicated to all the concerned parties, along with recommended course of action to combat the flaws or minimize potential damage [13].

7. Future Directions for Dependable Systems

Classical systems are continuing to evolve in many aspects. Transactions are increasing in scope and complexity, specific operations are being performed faster, and the average number of operations per transaction is on the rise. Several hardware and software technologies have come to prominence. Increasingly dependable communication technologies have enabled cloud computing based on server farms. Along with untethered wireless access, we are living through a paradigm shift in computing tasks away from restraints of the machine on the desk, with its power and space requirements, and limitations of up to date software and hardware resources [21].

As dependability increases, cloud technologies are permeating beyond early adopters such as consumers in education and entertainment to industrial control, medicine, and government. Many areas of concern in cloud computing are open research and search is on to find solutions that address those concerns, assure the user base about viability and dependability, and thus maintain the momentum cloud computing [20]. These areas include data center design, computer security within the cloud and communication systems, new programming languages to enable broadest participation of technology users, mobile computation and reliability, and user interfaces to tackle the challenges of increasingly diverse end users [30].

Another promising direction for dependable computing is the distribution and delegation of hard computing jobs for processing to a large number of end user systems and utilizing their unused CPU cycles, cache, and communication bandwidth resources. This has sometimes been referred to as *public computing* and poses new challenges in security and privacy. In particular, most data pass over systems of broadband communications over public channels, introducing intermediate systems that may be independent of the source point, and additional performance, security, and reliability challenges. However, this model of dependable computing has been successfully used in domains where security is less of concern, such as scientific research in *SETI*, DNA folding, prime number search, etc. [31]. Obvious benefits of public computing include enormous resource base, scalability, and efficient resource utilization. Solutions need to address major open questions related to fair resource billing, optimal division of large tasks, distribution, and recombining the results within the public resource base. In order to extend usage in all domains, researchers are trying to device methods to process information without compromising anonymity [32]. With the proper tools and infrastructure in place, public computing may in the future challenge the dominance of the privately owned cloud, with the benefits of higher assurance of continued services and greater transparency about what happens to consumer data.

Among specific technologies, quantum phenomenon-based communications show some promise, especially in the domain of secure key distribution, known as *quantum key distribution* (QKD). Quantum security protocols apply to transmission of polarized light quanta and have been shown to be feasible over noisy channels where photons may be lost during the transmission. Information is encoded in qubits sent into the channel, consisting of discrete photons along with the state described in the protocol. Although theoretical foundations have been laid out for some time [33], practical implementations are still not widespread and prone to implementation protocol failures. There have been successful QKD implementation, and increases in the reliability and efficiency of secure point to point communications, with data exchange rates of 1 Mbps over a point-to-point QKD link of 20 km, and such rates can certainly be useful in QKD in geographically limited dependable systems. Before quantum security goes mainstream in large production systems, further investigations and possible breakthroughs are needed to improve efficiency, reliability, and to study the impact of side channel attacks and scaling to build secure PKIs, public certification of QKD systems, and the interplay of classical security with quantum security [34].

There has been an exponential increase in the interdependence and interaction of geographically and logically disparate system components. Future systems will therefore need well-defined criteria for translational dependability for transient transactions that reside fleetingly in a subsystem. Lessons learned from decades of data networking and telecommunications research that has resulted in mature implementations in *quality of service* and reliability measures and methods for hand-off mechanisms [35] may be translated to dependable systems.

Given that some faults in any complex systems are inevitable, the roles of checkpointing, rollback, and recovery are critical in the dependable systems of the future. Rollback and recovery present challenges due to speed and scale in practical implementations in petaflop capable systems constructed out of thousands or millions of nodes, and fault recovery processes may demand additional portion of the system resource pie [36], and future investigations will determine the impact on resource usage of parent systems.

In relation to data networks, there has been incremental improvement over the past several decades in the speed and reliability of components related to switching. Information packets traveling over digital networks share many characteristics with transportation networks consisting of roads and vehicles. Although similar in many ways, there are distinct differences including costs of replication (very low cost in data networks, very hard in transportation networks), speed (many orders of magnitude faster in data networks), size (internode distances are similar, but transfer entities are orders of magnitude smaller in data networks), and complexity. Modern routers have designs that incorporate these differences to a large extent, but implicitly model transportation networks. During the past decade, a new approach for switching of network packets has been under investigation that breaks away from the transportation model in a fundamental way [37,38]. At a very basic level, instead of forwarding information, evidences about that information are forwarded toward the final destinations. A subset of all available clues about that information is used to construct the original information. These methodologies are built upon techniques from data compression and information theory as applied to data streams in real time. Network coding promises higher efficiencies because several bits can be combined into one bit at congestion points (the routers). These techniques can also introduce greater dependability since multiple subsets of clues can be used to reconstruct the original information. Thus, if some clues are lost due to component failures, power outages, or congestion, other existing clues may help to reconstruct the original information and prevent its loss. One of the challenges in network coding approaches is the lack of proper hardware support and algorithmic implementations in the current switching network. This may change as efficiencies and reliability that are demonstrated in prototype ASes.

8. Conclusion and Recommendations

Dependable systems engineering practices must be incorporated at all stages of systems life cycle: planning, specification, development, deployment, maintainable, and postproduction. In addition, the engineering process must be supported with clear and realistic policies that deal with risk assessment for system failure, expectations of users, and understanding of limitations of technology.

Many tools have evolved for use in the construction and maintenance of dependable systems, including automated specification and test generators, fault injectors, and fault profilers. These tools are essential but not sufficient to build, deploy, and use dependable systems. For example, strong crypto is but one ingredient in a robust security service menu and by itself is not sufficient as the basis of a viable security infrastructure. Policy makers and researchers need to address other issues before practical deployable solutions are found. These issues include a strong and interoperable PKI; a robust conflict resolution mechanism; transparency and accountability in the deployment of communication, hardware, and software primitives; etc.

A few relevant issues that are beyond our scope of this chapter but should be mentioned include physical security; stability and some level of continuity in terms of national security policies; international interoperability; prioritization of dependability in terms of budgeting and manpower; and dissemination of general and technical knowledge related to the limitations, potential, and utilization of the afore-mentioned technologies to all stakeholders. Like any other engineering solutions, it is difficult or impossible to bulletproof the systems against all possible risks and determined adversaries: there will probably be unexpected interactions and lapses of logic in design, and faults will manifest in complex systems, including those built from dependable components. This is where each designers and users will have to make choices after weighing the potential benefits of probabilistically dependable systems against potential costs and potential risks.

Furthermore, universal metrics to measure risks and failure rates of systems need to be developed. Users in critical applications will often avoid using systems where risk benefit ratios are unclear or questionable. Quantifiable risks and tangible measures of dependability of complex systems will allow stakeholders to utilize systems with high assurance of actual risks of failure.

Improved communication between users and system architects can prevent many costly system failures. Progress in improving communication between stakeholders and developers is being made through domain specific languages (or DSLs). DSLs allow fewer misunderstandings through shared vocabulary and removing ambiguity, thus adding value to the system development process by reducing implementation errors [39].

An area that can be helped along by regulatory bodies and professional societies is the encouragement of the gathering and publishing of data related to software failures [40]. Such data about software failures can then over time accumulate in sufficient amounts and be used to develop evidence about empirical dependability of software and software-based systems. This will bring software systems development more in line with practices in engineering dependable systems in other disciplines such as construction, manufacturing, and pharmaceutical industries. As of today, there are no agencies that deal with requirements and compilation of software failure data.

Finally, it is essential that all stakeholders have up to date technical and policy information about the availability, limitations, capabilities, idiosyncrasies, as well as risks of catastrophic failure within the system of all components and services related with dependable systems. Armed with this knowledge, scientific and business communities at large will be willing to adopt and fully benefit from these systems. Sharing will be greatly helped by creating mechanisms for expedient publishing of pertinent information about dependability, risks, and liabilities in a transparent manner. Vendors, developers, and maintainers will be willing to contribute to transparent sharing of information as they realize its collective benefits in the long run. Free and transparent flow of information will also lead to policies related to dependable systems that are efficient and most conducive to human welfare in the long run.

ACKNOWLEDGMENT

This research is supported in part by the National Science Foundation (NSF) under the XSEDE grant award #CCR120001, NSF award #1137732, and NSF award #1126251.

REFERENCES

[1] J. Gray, D.P. Siewiorek, High-availability computer systems, Computer 24 (9) (1991) 39–48.

[2] W. Hasselbring, R. Reussner, Toward trustworthy software systems, Computer 39 (4) (2006) 91–92.

[3] R.J. Ellison, D.A. Fisher, R.C. Linger, H.F. Lipson, T.A. Longstaff, N.R. Mead, Survivability: protecting your critical systems, Internet Comput. IEEE 3 (6) (1999) 55–63.

[4] S.K. Shukla, J.P. Talpin, Guest editors' introduction: special section on science of design for safety critical systems, IEEE Trans. Comput. 60 (8) (2011) 1057–1058.

[5] A. Avizienis, J.C. Laprie, B. Randell, Fundamental concepts of dependability, Technical Report Series University of Newcastle upon Tyne Computing Science 1145 (010028) (2001) 7–12.

[6] M.Y. Hsiao, W.C. Carter, J.W. Thomas, W.R. Stringfellow, Reliability, availability, and serviceability of IBM computer systems: a quarter century of progress, IBM J. Res. Dev. 25 (5) (1981) 453–468.

[7] Y. Yusuf, A. Gunasekaran, M.S. Abthorpe, Enterprise information systems project implementation: a case study of ERP in Rolls-Royce, Int. J. Prod. Econ. 87 (3) (2004) 251–266.

[8] L. Hoffman, In search of dependable design, Commun. ACM 51 (7) (2008) 14–16.

[9] A. Piore, Planning for the black swan, Sci. Am. Mag. 304 (6) (2011) 48–53.

[10] R.P. Feynman, Personal observations on the reliability of the shuttle, Report of the Presidential Commission on the Space Shuttle Challenger Accident 2 (1986) 1–5.

[11] D. Vaughan, Autonomy, interdependence, and social control: NASA and the space shuttle challenger, Adm. Sci. Q. 35 (2) (1990) 225–257.

[12] C. Kaufman, R. Perlman, M. Speciner, Network Security: Private Communication in a Public World, Prentice Hall Press, Upper Saddle River, NJ, USA, 2002.

[13] B. Christianson, B. Crispo, J.A. Malcolm, M. Roe, in: Security Protocols: 14th International Workshop, Cambridge, UK, March 27–29, 2006, Revised Selected Papers, Springer-Verlag, 2009. Published online at: www.enisa.europa.eu/act/res/other-areas/inter-x.

[14] A.J. Menezes, P.C. Van Oorschot, S.A. Vanstone, Handbook of Applied Cryptography, CRC Press, Boca Raton, 1997.

[15] L. Lydersen, C. Wiechers, C. Wittmann, D. Elser, J. Skaar, V. Makarov, Hacking commercial quantum cryptography systems by tailored bright illumination, Nat. Photonics 4 (10) (2010) 686–689.

[16] R.J. Anderson, Security Engineering: A Guide to Building Dependable Distributed Systems, Wiley Publishing, New York, 2008.

[17] L. Gong, P. Syverson, Fail-stop protocols: an approach to designing secure protocols, Dependable Computing for Critical Applications 5, 1995 Citeseer.

[18] P. Junod, M. Macchetti, Revisiting the IDEA Philosophy, in: O. Dunkelman (Ed.), Fast Software Encryption, Springer, Heidelberg, 2009, pp. 277–295.

[19] D. Oppenheimer, A. Ganapathi, D.A. Patterson, Why do Internet services fail, and what can be done about it? Proceedings of the 4th conference on USENIX Symposium on Internet Technologies and Systems-Volume 4, 2003, pp. 1–15 USENIX Association.

[20] P. Hofmann, D. Woods, Cloud computing: the limits of public clouds for business applications, IEEE Internet Comput. 14 (2010) 90–93.

[21] M. Armbrust, A. Fox, R. Griffith, A.D. Joseph, R.H. Katz, A. Konwinski, G. Lee, D.A. Patterson, A. Rabkin, I. Stoica, et al., Above the clouds: a Berkeley view of cloud computing, 2009 EECS Department, University of California, Berkeley, Tech. Rep. UCB/EECS-2009-28.

[22] T. Leighton, Improving performance on the internet, Queue 6 (6) (2008) 20–29.

[23] I. Abbadi, Toward trustworthy clouds internet scale critical infrastructure, Information Security Practice and Experience (2011) 71–82.

[24] T.W. Madron, Network Security in the '90s: Issues and Solutions for Managers, 1992 No.: ISBN 0-471-54777-8, p. 302.

[25] J.P.G. Sterbenz, D. Hutchison, E.K. Çetinkaya, A. Jabbar, J.P. Rohrer, M. Schöller, P. Smith, Resilience and survivability in communication networks: strategies, principles, and survey of disciplines, Comput. Network. 54 (8) (2010) 1245–1265.

[26] J. Zittrain, B. Edelman, Internet filtering in China, IEEE Internet Comput. 7 (2) (2003) 70–77.

[27] C. Thompson, Google's China problem (and China's Google problem), The New York Times Magazine 2006 23.

[28] D.J. Weitzner, H. Abelson, T. Berners-Lee, J. Feigenbaum, J. Hendler, G.J. Sussman, Information accountability, Commun. ACM 51 (6) (2008) 82–87.

[29] C. Hall, R. Clayton, R. Anderson, E. Ouzounis, Inter-X: Resilience of the Internet Interconnection Ecosystem, European Network and Information Security Agency (ENISA), 2011.

[30] J.R. Larus, The cloud will change everything, Proceedings of the sixteenth international conference on Architectural support for programming languages and operating systems, 2011, pp. 1–2 ACM.

[31] D.P. Anderson, Public computing: reconnecting people to science, Conference on Shared Knowledge and the Web, 2003, pp. 17–19.

[32] V. Sassone, S. Hamadou, M. Yang, Trust in anonymity networks, in: P. Gastin, F. Laroussinie (Eds.), CONCUR 2010—Concurrency Theory, 2011, pp. 48–70.

[33] P.W. Shor, J. Preskill, Simple proof of security of the bb84 quantum key distribution protocol, Phys. Rev. Lett. 85 (2) (2000) 441–444.

[34] R. Alléaume, N. Lütkenhaus, R. Renner, P. Grangier, T. Debuisschert, G. Ribordy, N. Gisin, P. Painchault, T. Pornin, L. Slavail, et al., Quantum key distribution and cryptography: a survey, Schloss Dagstuhl-Leibniz-Zentrum fr Informatik, Dagstuhl Seminar Proceedings. 09311—Classical and Quantum Information Assurance Foundations and Practice, 2010.

[35] R.H. Jan, Design of reliable networks, Comput. Operations Res. 20 (1) (1993) 25–34.

[36] E.N. Elnozahy, J.S. Plank, Checkpointing for peta-scale systems: a look into the future of practical rollback-recovery, IEEE Trans. Dependable Secure Comput. 1 (2) (2004) 97–108.

[37] R. Ahlswede, N. Cai, S.Y.R. Li, R.W. Yeung, Network information flow, IEEE Trans. Inform. Theory 46 (4) (2000) 1204–1216.

[38] S. Jaggi, M. Langberg, S. Katti, T. Ho, D. Katabi, M. Médard, M. Effros, Resilient network coding in the presence of byzantine adversaries, IEEE Trans. Inf. Theory 54 (6) (2008) 2596–2603.

[39] D. Ghosh, Dsl for the uninitiated, Commun. ACM 54 (7) (2011) 44–50.

[40] D. Jackson, A direct path to dependable software, Commun. ACM 52 (4) (2009) 78–88.

ABOUT THE AUTHOR

Raymond A. Paul serves in command and control (C2) Policy and conducts research concerning network enabled command and control service oriented systems engineering development in the Department of Defense. His current research focus is on high assurance systems engineering, software engineering, C2 networks, dynamic adaptive decision making, and trustworthy sensor networks. Paul holds a doctorate in Software Engineering and is an active Fellow of the IEEE Computer Society and Professional member of the ACM.

M. Farrukh Khan is an Assistant Professor in the Department of Computer Science at Texas Southern University. His current research interests include secure e-commerce, scientific data curating, high-performance computer systems, and computer literacy for the under-priviledged students. Khan holds a PhD in Computer Science from Purdue University, and a BS from California Institute of Technology.

Author Index

Subject Index

177

Contents of Volumes in This Series

Printed and bound by CPI Group (UK) Ltd, Croydon, CR0 4YY

03/10/2024

01040410-0019